American Birkebeiner

slumberland
BIRKIE
Ski. Run. Bike. Live!
BIRKIE
3
12424
slumberland
FURNITU

AMERICAN BIRKEBEINER

The Nation's Greatest Ski Marathon

JEROME P. POLING

WISCONSIN HISTORICAL SOCIETY PRESS

A portion of the proceeds from sales of this book will go to the American Birkebeiner Ski Foundation.

Published by the Wisconsin Historical Society Press
Publishers since 1855

The Wisconsin Historical Society helps people connect to the past by collecting, preserving, and sharing stories. Founded in 1846, the Society is one of the nation's finest historical institutions. *Join the Wisconsin Historical Society:* wisconsinhistory.org/membership

Publication of this book was made possible in part by a grant from the Alice Smith fellowship fund.

Front cover image courtesy of the Norwegian American Historical Association; photos on pages ii and vi courtesy of the American Birkebeiner Ski Foundation.

Printed in Canada
Cover designed by Mayfly book design
Text design and typesetting by Percolator Graphic Design

29 28 27 26 25   1 2 3 4 5

Library of Congress Cataloging-in-Publication Data available.

♾ The paper used in this publication meets the minimum requirements of the American National Standard for Information Sciences—Permanence of Paper for Printed Library Materials, ANSI Z39.48-1992.

To the skiers and supporters of the
American Birkebeiner, past, present, and future.

> **“The Birkebeiner is about community, about a gathering of like souls for a day of celebration—not a celebration of the speed of skiing, but of the wholeness of the sport. The Birkebeiner is a celebration of what we are and who we are. There are some who might say that skiing the race makes them better than those who don’t. That is not true. What is true is that skiing the race makes us better than we would have been had we not skied it.”**

—MITCH MODE

longtime Birkebeiner entrant and 1978 citizen champion

CONTENTS

slumberland
BIRKIE
Ski. Run. Bike. Live!
2
12343
2023 American Birkebeiner

PREFACE

AFTER PASSING FIFTY YEARS, the American Birkebeiner, much like its skiers at fifty or more kilometers, deserves a big medal. In the early 1970s, Tony Wise and his team created an unprecedented tour de force in the sparsely populated North Woods of Wisconsin. Today, the American Birkebeiner Ski Foundation and the communities of Hayward and Cable have taken up the baton. True to Wise's vision, the Birkebeiner has grown into one of the best, and best-run, ski marathons in the world.

People like me, citizen skiers, have been among the biggest benefactors. I was introduced to the Birkebeiner as a young writer in 1982, the first year that skiers glided down Main Street. Impressed with the electric energy and color on that gray day, I published a two-page spread in the newspaper where I was sports editor. Weeks later, I received a letter of thanks from a stranger, Tony Wise. Four years later, another skier and I briefly met the famously loquacious Wise as he shoveled snow outside his Hayward home and talked animatedly about getting back the race that no longer was his. That was the year I trudged through my first ski race, the Kortelopet, the Birkebeiner's half-marathon counterpart. It was my longest ski ever, and I couldn't imagine skiing twice as far. Now a Birchlegger—a veteran of more than twenty Birkebeiners—I have attended nearly forty races as either a reporter or skier or sometimes both on the same day. The challenge of the Birkebeiner has inspired me and thousands like me to push ourselves year-round to achieve a demanding goal.

Along the way, I began collecting fascinating stories about the race and its skiers—far more than would fit on the sports pages of the newspaper. Eventually these stories became the impetus for a book, which came together as the race's golden anniversary approached and after several years of dedicated research and writing. I conducted dozens of interviews and studied archival material from the Birkebeiner Foundation and the Wisconsin Historical Society's Anthony Wise Collection. My goal was to produce a narrative strong enough to capture the attention of casual skiers and non-skiers, while offering

Facing page: A skier heads down the International Bridge during the 2023 American Birkebeiner. AMERICAN BIRKEBEINER SKI FOUNDATION ARCHIVES, PHOTO BY CHRIS JUHN

insight that leaves even veteran skiers with a greater appreciation for how the Birkebeiner was born and has evolved. Six of the book's ten chapters cover this history through the decades—the groundbreaking first race, exponential early advances, major challenges and changes, thrilling finishes, important and dynamic people, and waves of post-2000 change and growth. Leading off are two chapters about the carnival-like spectacle of a modern race day and an in-depth look at the life of the legendary Wise pre-1973. Interspersed are chapters about the iconic Birkebeiner Trail and that singular phenomenon known as Birkie Fever. Narrowing down the tens of thousands of great photos to the one hundred fifty or so that appear here was its own challenge.

Though Tom Kelly's *Birkie Fever* offers an invaluable review of the race's first ten years, this is the first book to capture the definitive five-decade-plus history of the American Birkebeiner. It's my hope that *American Birkebeiner: The Nation's Greatest Ski Marathon* represents a medal of honor for this widely revered international event and provides important context for the race's standing in the history of the sport.

I also hope that fifty years is but the first wave of a much longer and even more successful race history. What might American Birkebeiner 100 or 300 look like? I hope we can get there. Let it snow, and keep on skiing.

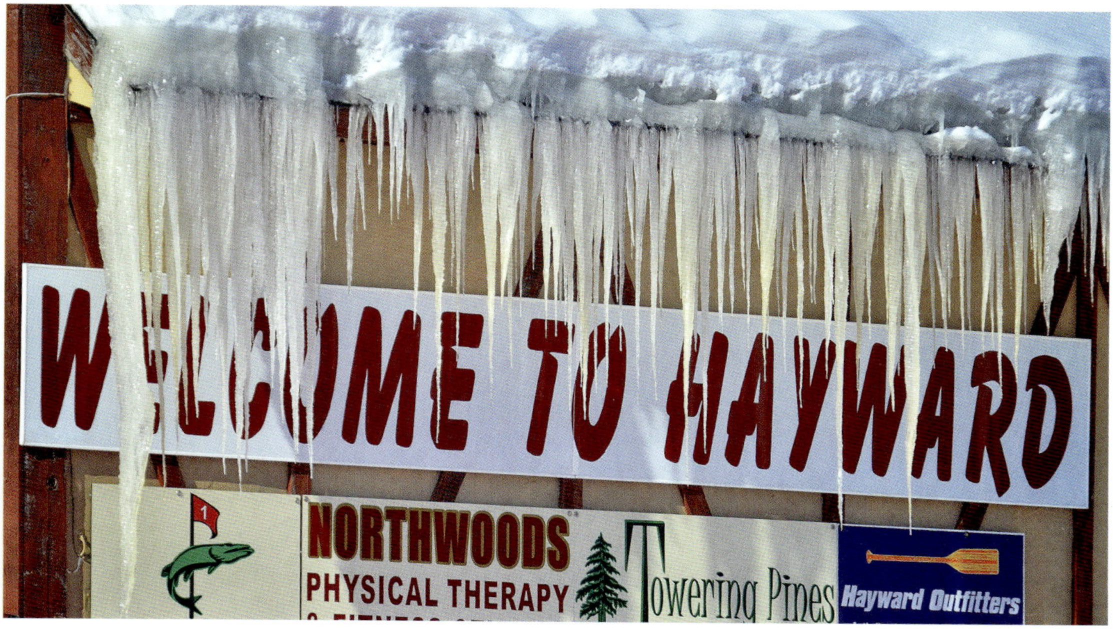

Snow, cold, ice, and a celebration of winter in Wisconsin are staples of the American Birkebeiner experience.
AMERICAN BIRKEBEINER SKI FOUNDATION ARCHIVES

American Birkebeiner starting line, 2022
AMERICAN BIRKEBEINER SKI FOUNDATION ARCHIVES, PHOTO BY BOB PEARL

ONE

VELCOMMEN TO THE BIRKIE!

IN FAR NORTHWESTERN WISCONSIN, the small city of Hayward occupies about three and a half square miles near the Namekagon River. It's "up north," as folks say, a land far from the cities and farms to the south, where rolling plains have given way to mere clusters of people betwixt forests and freshwater lakes. At slightly more than halfway from the equator to the North Pole, and on the fringe of the Lake Superior snowbelt, Hayward averages nearly five feet of snow each winter. Green grass doesn't return until the loons do. Go a little farther north, and the streams and rivers flow north.

On a typical February morning, the temperature in Hayward is well below freezing, the nearby lakes have twenty or more inches of clear, hard ice—enough to support villages of anglers—and the snow is snowshoe-worthy deep. But when late February arrives, this quiet North Woods outpost transforms into a winter sports mecca.

For one week each February, legions of people from almost every state and twenty or more nations descend upon Hayward for a cross-country marathon called the American Birkebeiner. In cross-country, skiers go down *and* up the hills (and, of course, over flat and rolling land)—unlike downhill, or alpine, skiing with its mechanized assist via chairlifts. This small city of twenty-five hundred people rolls out a snow-white carpet for more than thirteen thousand skiers in ten events over four days and for their twenty-five thousand or more supporters.

At the beginning of the week, workers bolt together fifteen wooden sections to create the temporary yet iconic International Bridge over Highway 63 in downtown Hayward. With its high arch and flags, it resembles a drawbridge to a Medieval castle. After crossing Lake Hayward, skiers will cross the bridge and begin the several-block homestretch to the finish line. With the bridge in place, the Birkebeiner is officially on.

Crews have dumped more than eighty truckloads of snow, turning Main Street into a busy ski trail. Skiing begins on Wednesday, with the Open Track Birkebeiner and Open Track Kortelopet—noncompetitive tours rather than races. On Thursday, in the Barkie Birkie Skijor, skiers are pulled by their energetic dogs. In the Sons of Norway Barnebirkie, one thousand or more rosy-cheeked children, ages three to thirteen, glide toward hot chocolate, cookies, a medal, and a hug. Hundreds more compete in the Junior Birkie race as coaches and parents cheer them on. At dusk, six-person Giant Ski teams—wearing huge wooden skis the length of a bass-fishing boat—try to coordinate their strides in the funkiest race of the week. The night ends with food and live music at the Birkie Bash kickoff.

Giant Ski teams prepare to compete on Hayward's Main Street.
AMERICAN BIRKEBEINER SKI FOUNDATION ARCHIVES

Kortelopet skiers on the trail, 2014
AMERICAN BIRKEBEINER SKI FOUNDATION ARCHIVES, PHOTO BY MARK MILFORD

By 9 a.m. on Friday, festivities are in full swing. Hayward is bustling with the Worldloppet breakfast for foreign skiers, the adaptive ParaBirkie, and the Birkie Expo and race bib pickup at the high school. City schools are shut down, like something from a Scandinavian fairy tale. No school! Go ski!

North of town, skiers in Lycra pile into steamy yellow school buses and travel up Highway 63 to the blink-and-you-miss-it town of Seeley, then turn east on Highway OO. They're headed for the start of the 29-kilometer Kortelopet in the heavily forested Seeley Hills. Before noon, Kortelopet winners will be skiing up Hayward's Main Street to the finish. The Prince Haakon 15-kilometeter race, also finishing downtown, begins after lunch. The Birkebeiner, Kortelopet, and Prince Haakon are all held on the main trail.

Throughout the day, anticipation continues to grow for Saturday's big event—a 50-kilometer skate ski and 53-kilometer classic ski race along the famed Birkebeiner Trail. It's North America's largest ski marathon—and one of the largest ski marathons in the world.

THE AMERICAN BIRKEBEINER began in Hayward in 1973, on a frozen lake inlet in town. Founder Tony Wise looked on as thirty-five cross-country skiers split for Telemark Lodge, the alpine (or downhill) ski operation that Wise operated twenty miles north in Cable, Wisconsin. Few people in Hayward noticed. At the time, relatively few people around the state or country knew much about cross-country skiing; the concept of crossing a snowy landscape under one's own power for enjoyment was, for practical purposes, foreign. How the sport and event have grown! Today, the American Birkebeiner Ski Foundation, which hosts the event, prepares year-round and spends about $1 million on race week alone.

Hospitality is old hat for Hayward. The region has been a tourist haven since the early 1900s, with its pristine lakes, resorts, private cabins, fishing, hunting, and fall colors. A winter tourism season began to thrive in the mid-twentieth century, sparked by Wise's alpine skiing operation and the invention of the snowmobile. Then Wise created the Birkebeiner. From its humble beginnings in 1973, the race quickly grew into a Super Bowl of Nordic skiing. As many a governor has proclaimed: It's Birkebeiner Week in Wisconsin.

Race week has many layers. Hotels, motels, and rental cabins are filled for up to fifty miles around. Locals offer spare bedrooms to visitors, sparking many long-distance and international friendships. Skiers who can't find lodging (known as "flying economy" in Birkebeiner lingo) roll out their sleeping bags and camp on the floor of a designated church or school, an all-comers Nordic hostel.

Merchants prepare for their own Birkebeiner challenge. From Hayward to Seeley to Cable, restaurants, bars, grocery stores, and coffee shops hire extra staff to handle the big week. Steps from the racecourse, Angler's serves bratwurst, chili, and beverages on its packed outdoor patio. At Hayward's Firehouse Bakery and Deli, racks are filled and refilled. Local ski shops are full of skiers buying wax, clothing, and equipment. St. Joseph's Catholic Church, near the finish line, prepares to feed five hundred or more at its annual prerace spaghetti dinner. It all amounts to a big "Welcome—or *velcommen*—to Hayward!" The Birkebeiner is an economic avalanche for the region.

AFTER THREE DAYS of preliminary events, it's Saturday—and everyone is on the move. The foundation staff, volunteers, medical teams, and law enforcement personnel get ready for the rush of activity. A government command center opens, and chatter begins on officials' state emergency management radios. Skiers of all levels have paid entry fees of $200 or more, and each will spend perhaps $1,000 during race week on food, accommodations, equipment, and travel. They are counting on a positive experience. They want to feel weary but wonderful, the elixir of cross-country skiing and finishing the Birkebeiner.

Race day begins with bright lights in dark woods—headlights from the red-and-black PistenBully groomers, which have caterpillar tracks like army tanks. Kurt Proctor, the foundation's chief groomer, and his five-person team start on Friday and work for twenty-four hours straight. They smooth out the thirty-plus-mile highway of snow with two grooming machines up north, one around midtrail, and two on the southern half. If it's snowing, they wait as long as possible to set up the course. They firm up the start, various bridges along the course, and the trail across Lake Hayward built just for the race. The lake has been its own race week project. "You can spend days building the course across the lake, plowing up snow from over by the shoreline," Proctor says.[1] That's if the ice is safe for that year's race. In all, Proctor and his team are responsible for keeping about 62 miles—100 kilometers—groomed during the week, including the trails and start areas for the various races.

Among the earliest risers on race morning are subsets of race workers and skiers—the bus drivers and forerunners. Forty-plus drivers are at Hurricane Busing by 4 a.m. doing safety checks. Over Friday and Saturday—the two main race days—drivers will cover ten thousand miles transporting sixteen thousand skiers and spectators. A dozen or more forerunners, young to older, fit and experienced, are the first skiers on the trail, as early as 4 a.m. They will go either halfway or the full distance and finish before most entrants even get to the start. Carrying their own food and drink, forerunners press any new snow into the striding tracks, break trail on the skate deck (the combed trail used by skate skiers), and remove newly fallen tree limbs and branches (using cell phones to call for help with something big). Their bobbing headlamps and chatter are harbingers of the masses to come. "You get to ski the trail on the best possible grooming conditions," says Eric Maki, a forerunner for three years before volunteering to organize the group. "Skiing through the sunrise is a great thing to experience."[2]

By about 5 a.m., volunteer crews begin to arrive at the start area. Down the trail corridor, lights of the food station cabins blink on one by one. Skiers will depend on more than two thousand non-skiers to make sure the day goes well.[3]

AFTER EATING a carbohydrate-heavy breakfast, skiers and their supporters pile into buses and cars and stream toward the Birkie Ridge parking lot north of Seeley and another lot in Cable, backing up along Highway 63 for several miles in both directions. A traffic jam in sparsely populated northern Wisconsin on a Saturday morning is a rare sight—but not on Birkebeiner weekend. It's also the rub of race day: most skiers will spend about as much time getting to and waiting for the start as they'll spend skiing the marathon. To ease the tension, some tune to local radio station WOJB, which provides live race coverage throughout the day. Skiers in later waves will hear the starting gun on the radio while still in their cars.

By 6:30 a.m., buses begin to rumble up Telemark Road, and the first Birkebeiner hopefuls emerge with skis, poles, and dreams of Main Street. The start area is tucked into the snow-covered forest beyond the former Telemark Lodge. As dawn breaks, the scene is the opposite of the race itself: people are going every which way, a winter beehive of activity. Skiers loosen up on a practice loop; wait in line at rows of portable toilets, some of three hundred ordered for race day; or head inside the Great Hall, a heated all-purpose building that has turned into a standing-room-only locker room, where skiers can get ready and wait for their turn at the start line. Thousands of pairs of skis and poles—by Fischer, Madshus, Salomon, Rossignol, Yoko—lean against the building or are speared into snowbanks. On this morning, skiers are family, and they trust that their expensive gear will stay just where they left it.

In some ways, the scene resembles a military deployment. Bayfield County sheriff's deputies, whose duties include security and traffic control, circle up to discuss issues. The cost of race-day law enforcement support: $150,000. First responders prepare to drive four medical evacuation snowmobiles onto the course—it's hilly, curvy, fast, crowded, and tree-lined; accidents and emergencies happen. A few people stay warm around a start-area bonfire, wood smoke curling into the hazy dawn. Some classic skiers smooth out tacky kick wax midski to help them alternately push and glide. A drone capturing video footage buzzes over the start line. Volunteers direct skiers to the starting gate. The temperature may be single digits, but somehow it doesn't feel cold.

Facing page: Grooming the trail in preparation for the 2014 race
AMERICAN BIRKEBEINER SKI FOUNDATION ARCHIVES, PHOTO BY DARLENE PROIS

Skiers mingle around a firepit in the start area before the 2023 race.
AMERICAN BIRKEBEINER SKI FOUNDATION ARCHIVES, PHOTO BY BOB PEARL

Running to the starting line, 2023
AMERICAN BIRKEBEINER SKI FOUNDATION ARCHIVES, PHOTO BY CHRIS JUHN

The honor of starting first typically goes to the more than forty historically elite skiers who have done at least thirty-five Birkebeiners. It's called the Spirit of 35 wave, an homage to the number who entered the first race. Another special starting group a little later is Wave 70 for skiers ages seventy and older—more than two hundred of them who are living, skiing proof that cross-country is a lifelong sport.

Skiers will start the race in groups, or waves, according to skill level and experience. The elite wave is made up of professional and top amateur skiers who finished in the top two hundred men and top sixty-five women in the previous year's skate race, or the top one hundred men and top forty women in the previous year's classic race. Others qualify for the elite wave by earning points in a sanctioned FIS—International Ski and Snowboard Federation—event. FIS skiers receive a preferred, or seeded, starting position at the front of the wave. They are the super-elites, the thoroughbreds at the gate.

Elite skiers face extra scrutiny. Their skis must be checked into a holding area at the start, where volunteers mark them with the skier's bib number and a special stamp. Their skis are spot-checked for fluorinated wax, which has been banned at the Birkebeiner and in US Ski and Snowboard Association events since 2020. These wax products, commonly called "flouros," enhance speed by repelling water and dirt and were long a staple among avid skiers. But they also contain polyfluoroalkyl substances, the artificial "forever chemical" also known as PFAS. Most skis will have some "flouros" from past waxing—but if test results show a high percentage of fluorinated wax, the skier is disqualified.[4]

Elite skiers can't retrieve their skis until they head to the start line, by way of a separate path. They must finish the race with their marked skis to prove they didn't pull a switch and gain an unfair advantage.

THE LOW WINTER SUN peeks over the tree line, and suddenly it's race time. After the Spirit of 35 wave start, elite skate skiers shift anxiously, final instructions are announced, and the countdown is on. Cheering rises, the start gun bangs, a banner lifts, and off they go, first the elite women, then a wave of elite men, bursting from the gates in rapid-fire double pole, crunching pole tips into the snow like pistons to push forward. They do this for a required one hundred yards in parallel tracks to minimize crashes. Then, as the skate track begins, they rise, as if emerging from a cocoon, and spread their limbs, shifting gracefully into V2 skating technique—one perfectly timed double-pole push each time a now slightly lateral ski hits the snow—for maximum speed and efficiency. And they're flying, going about twenty miles per hour. The race to Hayward, where they'll hit speeds of thirty-five miles per hour or more on the downhills, is on. Out front, a snowmobile mounted with camera gear films the leaders. The action is described kilometer by kilometer by two announcers on WOJB.

Elite skiers go in style, each one outfitted with up to $4,000 worth of gear and clothing. Their skis, about six feet long depending on skier weight, are high-tech, cambered, flexed "boards" one and three-quarters inches wide and one and a quarter inches high, tapering to one-sixteenth of an inch thick at the shovel (the front end) and one-eighth of an inch at the tail. The raised core of the skis could be supported by foam or by thin wood panels with honeycomb-like walls, covered in layers of carbon fiber, fiberglass, and polyethylene, and finished with colorful graphic overlays. Total weight: about two pounds per ski, spread out so they feel even lighter. They likely come from a factory in northern Europe, the sport's motherland. Skate skiers' ten-ounce carbon poles, almost as tall as the skier, have the swing weight of reeds and feel like nothing in their toned arms. Their carbon shell ski boots—stiff, waterproof, and nine and half inches high, with rail bindings underfoot—are more like alpine ski boots than the old, low-cut, three-pin classic boots. Body-hugging, sweat-wicking, Lycra race suits stretch in every direction. Most non-elite skiers are outfitted with similar, although likely less expensive, gear and clothing; in total, there is maybe $30 million worth of gear and clothing on the trail, or $1 million a mile. How did Norwegian Roald Amundsen and his team cross the Antarctic in 1911 on heavy wooden skis, wearing wool, fur, and sealskin to become the first to reach the South Pole?

The ensuing waves—about twenty of them total for skate and classic, with about five hundred skiers in each—begin to roll out between 8:15 and 10 a.m. The Great Hall slowly empties as skiers march toward the starting pens, hand their postrace clothing bag to a volunteer waiting at a line of delivery trucks, then enter the gate with the rest of their wave. An announcer looks down from the upper deck of a two-story building, where race start timing computers are housed. The announcer keeps the skiers loose, telling them to let out a cheer, asking them, "Are. You. Ready?" He tells them to wish their fellow competitors a good race and be kind to each other out there. It's the moment skiers

Skate skiers do the required double pole in the tracks to start the 2023 race.
AMERICAN BIRKEBEINER SKI FOUNDATION ARCHIVES, PHOTO BY WENDY MILLER

have been waiting for since finishing their long training ski maybe three weeks earlier, since the first snow back in December and sending in their entry fee perhaps ten months ago. And then, off they go.

Viewed from behind, waves of skiers appear to move in unison like flocks of birds, silently disappearing in the muffle of the snow over a rise in the trail. Viewed from the front, they rush in like an ocean wave, a foam of carb-fueled energy, seeking shore more than thirty miles away. They're clad in green, orange, red, blue, purple, black, and other wave-specific bibs, freestyle and classic skiers, elites and beginners, first-year and forty-year skiers, young and old, male and female, the superfit and those who wish they were. They all have stories about how they came to love the sport, and they all will leave with a story from the events of this day. (One year, for example, a skier doing windmills with his arms in the starting pen broke another skier's nose. The afflicted skier completed the race with tissues stuffed into his nostrils.)

A wave of elite skate skiers in the 2005 race, including Chip Tabor (center), who finished in forty-second place. AMERICAN BIRKEBEINER SKI FOUNDATION ARCHIVES, PHOTO BY KELLY RANDOLPH

Elite and early wave skiers attack the trail; others come on more slowly, but their feelings and thoughts are near universal: they're trying to avoid disaster in the traffic jams early on, gauge whether their skis are running fast, and comfortably crest the first few hills to get their legs into gear and avoid lactic acid buildup. Then they settle into the up-down rhythm that defines the Birkebeiner, hoping they ration their energy well enough to finish and finish strong. They ski from food stop to food stop—the first at 7 kilometers and the remaining six stops every 5 to 7 kilometers down the trail—where they catch their breath, down some form of energy, thank a volunteer, and push on.

The kilometer markers click by. Skiers watch for them, especially later on, as they get closer and closer to Hayward. Along the trail, there are crashes, bruised egos, and broken equipment; skiers who don't feel well; skiers who

Facing page: Viewed from above, skiers in the 1995 race appear to be moving in almost complete unison. AMERICAN BIRKEBEINER SKI FOUNDATION ARCHIVES

didn't train enough and drop out; and skiers who are smiling and having the time of their lives, blowing past their wave and into the waves ahead of them. There's some chatter on the course, friends and family who come across one another or ski with each other, and shouts of "on your left" and "skier down!" Someone usually says, "It's all downhill from here!" at the trail's highest elevation point, Fire Tower Hill, about 11 kilometers into the race. Geographically it is the high point, but it's gallows humor because everyone knows the hills of northern Wisconsin just don't go away.

SPECTATORS ON THE TRAIL ARE FEW, a cluster or two near a food stop. One support group at about 4 kilometers into the race, the Power Line Drummers formed by Gary "the Fat Man" Crandall, keeps a beat on garbage can lids and other improvised instruments. A few cow bells ring with chants of "Heia! Heia!" ("go" in Norwegian). If skiers look down an open stretch of trail, they may see the big picture, literally and figuratively, similar to the scene author Bill McKibben described from Norway's Birkebeinerrennet marathon: "It was as crowded as Fifth Avenue at lunch hour. Instead of individual triumph, a kind of collective glory hovered over the tracks." Mostly, though, it's quiet out there, except for skis scraping, a silent sport even among the masses.[5]

When skiers cruise into a food stop—spending a minute or less to refuel and take off—most give little thought as to how tables of fresh bananas, warm water and energy drinks, energy gels with the tabs already cut, and sandwich cookies happen to appear in the middle of the forest. It's a frosty woodland oasis, at first a mirage, made possible by hundreds of volunteers.

Volunteer leaders Jerome and Karen Malmquist, from the Cable area, run the Gravel Pit Road food station, at 30 kilometers for skaters. The Malmquists begin planning soon after the Christmas holidays when they firm up their crew of approximately fifty volunteers. The cumulative effort of running their food station for the open-track event on Wednesday, the Kortelopet on Friday, and the main race on Saturday adds up to more than eighty volunteer shifts and hundreds of hours of effort for just one station.

A few days before each race, food station crew leaders pick up supplies at a 5,400-square-foot warehouse outside of Hayward. The warehouse is stocked with boxes upon boxes containing 24,000 sandwich cookies, 18,700 energy gels, 9,400 energy chews, 5,600 bananas, 2,400 oranges, enough base to make

Top: A young participant in the 2014 Barnebirkie. *Above:* A skier at the 2014 finish line sports the iconic Birkebeiner ice beard. AMERICAN BIRKEBEINER SKI FOUNDATION ARCHIVES, PHOTOS BY DARLENE PROIS

6,000 pounds of soup, and enough powder to make 2,400 gallons of energy drink. Supplies include 100,000 drinking cups, serving equipment, signage, cleaning supplies, and the all-important Aid Station Guide. Food and supplies were sourced soon after the previous year's event, and most items were ordered about five months before the race. The fruit was ordered in late January and trucked to the warehouse earlier in the week.[6]

Food and supplies are preportioned for each food station, and extras of everything are in the warehouse just in case. Foundation officials make sure the heat and on-demand water heaters are working at the seven remote cabins, where volunteers will serve 5,800 gallons of warm water and warm energy drink to skiers to prevent hypothermia. At Gravel Pit Road, the Malmquists hang speaker wires for music—skiers love some tunes to keep them charged up and might even dance a bit if they're feeling good. Oranges, bananas, and energy gel tabs are cut. Fires are started inside (for extra heat) and outside (to keep the volunteers warm and as a place to grill hot dogs). Everything must be done on cue—skiers will be coming down the trail soon.

Each food stop along the trail, like this one in the 2011 race, can have fifty or more volunteers.
AMERICAN BIRKEBEINER SKI FOUNDATION ARCHIVES, PHOTO BY KELLY RANDOLPH

Then, the real work and best part of the day—supporting and encouraging skiers—is at hand. Here they come! At three-fifths of the way into the race, Gravel Pit Road is the third-to-last stop. Skiers arrive thirsty and in need of energy. They've begun to deplete their carbo load and need more to maintain their pace and avoid "bonking"—the endurance sport phenomenon when athletes hit the proverbial wall and suddenly feel weak or faint. More hills are ahead. The food can't be prepared all at once or it will freeze, so there's a constant "just in time" flow of items to the front line. Skiers appreciate a soft energy gel or banana chunk that they can down in a few seconds; their jaws are stiff from the cold.

A LITTLE MORE THAN TWO HOURS after the starting gun, after the last couple of long, twisting climbs that sear weary thighs and shoulders, the lead elite skate skiers emerge from the woods at 45 kilometers, tuck down the west side of Duffy Hill, cross Wheeler Road, and glide onto Lake Hayward. After crossing the lake, they'll ski several blocks to the Main Street–Highway 63 intersection, climb the International Bridge over the highway, and ski the final several blocks to the finish. When they reach the lake, church bells begin to ring on Main Street, heralding the skiers' imminent arrival. The announcement revs up the excited Main Street crowd lining the sidewalks three or four people deep. Necks crane east toward the bridge. The lead skiers, some of the world's best, are coming fast.

Suddenly, one or more skiers appear atop the bridge, driving toward the finish, and the cheering rises. They've averaged fifteen miles per hour across this rugged country but somehow have mustered additional glycogen and competitive fire to ratchet up the pace even more—if it's a race to the finish. They are going top speed now as the crowd brings them home. Then, the winner thrusts arms and poles in victory or, if it's been a sprint to the finish, thrusts a ski tip forward and collapses, totally spent. Soon, the top three finishers for both men and women are off to the podium for photos, a change of clothes, and a news conference, where they look surprisingly fresh as they recount the competition that unfolded. The skate race winners collect $7,500 each, part of $39,000 total prize money, with $1,000 each for the classic race winners. The first American man and woman to finish the skate race receive the Tony Wise award and another $2,500.

On Main Street, the victory party is just getting started as more skiers arrive, two and three, then six or ten, then an hours-long parade of them. They'll keep coming until sunset—some wobbly and worn, others smiling, some playing to the crowd with a 360-spin or twirl of a pole. The cheering is sweet music they have longed all day to hear. Their names, hometowns, and number of race finishes are announced as they cross the finish line. This is the glorious, raucous finish—considered one of the best in all of cross-country skiing—that keeps many professionals and citizen skiers coming back to the Birkebeiner.

After they collect themselves and their medal or pin, take off their skis, and grab a Wisconsin chocolate milk, skiers' next stop is bag pickup. Magically, the bag with their change of clothes—which they handed to a volunteer at the frenzied start—is waiting for them. Even more magically, it's now in a neat row, arranged with military precision by wave and number.[7]

Skiers sit down, slow down, enjoy a warm cup of soup and some bread and fruit, rehydrate, reenergize, and reflect. If they're injured or don't feel well, Hayward Area Memorial Hospital has a medical station. For many, Wisconsin beer and bratwurst are waiting down the street. Then, for some, it's another bus ride back to the parking lot to their vehicle.

The modern-day International Bridge, shown here in 2018, was introduced in 2015 to ease race-related detours and traffic jams. AMERICAN BIRKEBEINER SKI FOUNDATION ARCHIVES, PHOTO BY BOB PEARL

Spectators, using a race app on their phones, can track friends and family by bib number almost to the minute they will reach the Main Street finish. AMERICAN BIRKEBEINER SKI FOUNDATION ARCHIVES, PHOTO BY JOHN RADLOFF

About midafternoon, three skiers who look to be from another era glide into town on traditional wooden skis. They're keeping the race true to its roots by reenacting the rescue of baby Prince Haakon of Norway during a civil war in the year 1206. The skiers represent two Norwegian Birkebeiner warriors, Torstein Skevla and Skjervald Skrukka, and the prince's mother, Inga. The warriors wear birch bark on their lower legs, rustic tops and pants, and Viking helmets and shields; Inga wears a cape and long skirt and carries an infant or doll representing the young prince. They will be the subject of many a photo, which is fine because as historical race ambassadors they're in no hurry—unlike the original warriors.

Before the race is done, parts of it begin to shut down. Crews are closing up shop at the now mostly deserted start area. Food stations begin to fall like dominos from start to finish along the trail as the last skiers pass.

Not all skiers get past the food stops. Some arrive after various cutoff times. Volunteer leader Erik Hansen runs the Mosquito Brook Road food stop, 36 kilometers in. "The worst part of my job is when I have to tell someone they

Each year, skiers apply to the American Birkebeiner Ski Foundation to land the coveted roles of Inga, Torstein Skevla, and Skjervald Skrukka. Pictured here during the 2010 race are Josie Nelson and David Nelson of Medicine Lake, Minnesota, and Grant Nelson of Duluth.
AMERICAN BIRKEBEINER SKI FOUNDATION ARCHIVES, PHOTO BY KELLY RANDOLPH

will not be able to finish," Hansen says. "These individuals have most likely been at it all day, gone way beyond their expectations, and feel they have a right to finish. Some take offense when I deliver the bad news. It has never come to anything other than an exchange of words. More often it is more than a little emotional." Hansen and his crew kindly help dejected skiers get something to eat and drink and get on a bus with other DNFs (did not finish), a sad ending to a once-promising day.

At Gravel Pit Road, the crew will pick up twenty-plus bags of trash, return unused food to the warehouse, and take broken poles and other items to lost and found. Leftover perishable food at the warehouse will be donated to nonprofit groups, Hayward schools, and the Hayward Community Food Shelf.

The majority of skiers walking through downtown know they've overcome a mental and physical challenge. They feel drained but, unlike running a marathon, not overly sore and seem to recover quickly, endorphins flooding their systems. The hills and curves that whizzed by and the feel of gravity-defying, fluid motion will be embedded into their consciousness for days to come, a reflection of the intense concentration that ruled their brains for hours, their psyches for weeks. Finishing the race feels amazing, even for those who have done it forty or more times.

AS NIGHT FALLS, the final skiers head up Main Street to a sparse crowd, a snowmobile following behind them. Officials make sure every skier whose bib was recorded at the start line has been accounted for at the end; no one gets left in the woods on a cold winter night. Some skiers have logged eight hours or more by the time they reach the finish but still are cheered on like champions—maybe they are the real champions, those who somehow gutted it out. City snowplows and dump trucks, lights flashing, are waiting to clear the snow from Main Street and let traffic return. The race command center closes. Volunteers go home, though a few—like baggage pickup race chief Dave Tworek, whose race day is sixteen hours long—stay behind to shovel snow off the edges of the International Bridge so it can be taken down early the next week. Skiers, meanwhile, head for a shower, a nap, and maybe a night out. Live music and plenty of food and beverages will be on hand across the northland, infused with slightly embellished tales from the trail. First-time Birkebeiner finishers will proudly wear their bronze medal.

One person who never experienced finish-line euphoria, but who did receive a medal from the king of Norway, was race founder Tony Wise. He wasn't a skier, although he gave the sport a whirl a few times. Yet, he loved everything about his race, especially the goal-driven people who embraced the sport and flocked to Hayward every year.

As skiers come up Main Street, three decades after Wise's passing, he's still watching. On the side of a brick building at the corner of Main and Second Street, a huge mural depicts important people in Hayward's history. The figures, each fifteen feet tall, are looking west toward the finish line. One of them is Wise. The depiction of Wise, standing in front of his former Telemark Lodge at Cable, is labeled "Visionary—Entrepreneur." This isn't overstated. Wise's race helped change Hayward and Cable and spurred major changes throughout the skiing world.

Who was this native son, and how did he come to create this international event in such an out-of-the-way place? How did he inspire countless others to relish the thought of a good glide *across the country* in northern Wisconsin? And how, a half century later, did the American Birkebeiner become virtually everything Wise dreamed of?

Tony Wise during his high school years. COURTESY OF THE WISE FAMILY

TWO

A MAN FROM HAYWARD

AS A CHILD OF THE 1920S, Anthony "Tony" Wise grew up on big ideas in a small, remote town—Hayward's population at the time was 1,302—set amidst the dark green forests and blue lakes of northwestern Wisconsin.

Wise was born on March 15, 1921, as the region's top industry, logging, was ending. His family lived in a Queen Anne–style house at 124 Kansas Avenue, one block off Hayward's Main Street. Wise was eight and a half years old when the nation entered the Great Depression, but the Roaring Twenties had already inspired him. It was a time when no idea was too big—the era of the first motion picture, the first radios, the great Babe Ruth, and the daring Charles Lindbergh. "I wanted to be the first," Wise later said. "Who ever heard of the second guy to fly the Atlantic?"[1]

The "think big" mindset may have been hereditary. Ancestors on his mother's side were aboard the Mayflower when it landed at Plymouth Rock in 1620, and one, Edward Winslow, became a governor of Plymouth. "That always gave me inspiration," Wise said. "The greatness of America came from the new ideas, from taking big risks."[2]

Wise's paternal grandfather, also named Anthony Wise, was a six-foot-seven lumberman, a Paul Bunyan of his day who reportedly could bend railroad spikes with his bare hands. He moved his family from Lyndon Station, Wisconsin, to the logging country of Birchwood, Wisconsin. In 1907, after the railroad reached nearby Stone Lake, he started the A. Wise Land Company selling residential lakefront lots in cutover country. He opened an office in Hayward in 1916.[3]

When the elder Wise died in 1920, his sons—Lawrence, Scipio, and Clarence (Tony's father)—took over the company. In 1925, the brothers broke ground on the sprawling Northwoods Beach subdivision southeast of Hayward. With 7,700 lakefront lots and thirty miles of roads, Northwoods Beach would dwarf most other developments up north even a century later.

Young Tony admired his parents. He described his dad as an "aggressive, hustling businessman. He was very impressive." His mother, Vera Mitchell Wise, was a former schoolteacher and University of Wisconsin–Madison graduate. She was "such an honest person," Wise later said; she "taught me to do everything first-class, and she gave me a strong compassion for people."[4]

As a teenager in Hayward, Wise became king—Winter Carnival king in 1938. A family photo shows him at the event, next to a girl holding a pair of snowshoes; he's holding a pair of long wooden skis that tower above his head, with snow on his dark clothing as if he had taken a fall. The Winter Carnival, a four-day community event in late February, advertised a "cross-country ski run," ski jumping, something called a "ski slide" (perhaps a mini-alpine run?), and a toboggan chute that ran down Norwegian Hill west of downtown. Other activities included speed skating, figure skating, an ice pageant, a torchlight parade, and a lighted ice castle. An estimated eight thousand people attended the second annual event (it ended after 1939). Was Tony impressed with his community's passion for winter? Did he imagine being king of a winter attraction of his own, one that also brought thousands of people to Hayward?[5]

WISE'S PASSION as a young man was basketball. He played guard for Hayward High School and was one of the team's leading scorers. In his senior season, the team had a winning record and took third place in the Class B regional playoffs. His two free throws with a few seconds remaining clinched a 26–25 win over archrival Spooner in his final high school game.[6]

Tony's dream was to play at Ohio State University for legendary coach Harold Olsen, the former University of Wisconsin basketball star from Sarona, Wisconsin, south of Hayward. Olsen held summer basketball camps in Sarona beginning in 1929, and Tony attended in the mid-1930s, hoping to get noticed.[7]

His plan worked, although a sad twist of fate may have helped Wise's dream come true. When Wise was twelve, his father, who was president of Sawyer County State Bank in addition to being in the family real estate business, died

Tony Wise (right) at the Winter Carnival in 1938. COURTESY OF THE WISE FAMILY

in a car accident. Tony was the oldest of four brothers and had older, twin half-sisters born to his father's first wife, who died in childbirth. He became the man of the house—it was his first calling as a leader, according to his daughter Frances many years later. His mother was the beneficiary of a double indemnity insurance policy, $200,000, which helped support the family after his father's death and likely helped Tony go to far-flung Ohio State.[8]

Wise played for Coach Olsen but sparingly. In his first year, 1938–39, Ohio State lost to the University of Oregon in the inaugural NCAA tournament championship game in Evanston, Illinois. Olsen is credited with helping start the NCAA event—now known as March Madness—as a way to compete with the more prestigious event at the time, the National Invitation Tournament. Tony, who would have a penchant for the big and historic, was there.

As a guard, Tony played for Ohio State in a single game in the 1939–40 season, not at all in 1940–41, and in two games during his senior season. However, he finished in style, scoring ten points in the season finale loss against Indiana University and receiving a letter for the 6–14 Buckeyes. He graduated in June 1942 with a business administration degree and left campus having led the construction of a new house for his fraternity, Sigma Alpha Epsilon, for which he was manager. Already, Tony Wise was leaving his mark.[9]

After graduation, Wise moved to Cambridge, Massachusetts, to attend the MBA program at Harvard University. The United States was ramping up its involvement in World War II, and on June 23, 1942, a week or so after he arrived in Cambridge, Wise enlisted in the Army Reserve's Officer Training Corps. A deferment until April 1943 allowed him to begin his MBA studies, alongside several of his former Ohio State classmates.[10]

By June 1943, the MBA program was suspended because of the war and wouldn't resume until February 1946. In October 1943, Wise entered Officer Candidate School and was commissioned as a second lieutenant in the Fourteenth Armored Division, 125th Armored Engineer Battalion, Company C. His unit spent time at Fort Lee, Virginia, and Camp Campbell, Kentucky, before shipping out from New York on October 14, 1944. Four troop transport vessels (Wise's battalion likely was aboard the SS *James Parker*) and fourteen support freighters arrived in Marseilles, France, on October 29. The division spent 133 days in combat from approximately mid-December 1944 to May 1945.[11]

The Fourteenth Armored Division earned the nickname the Liberators for its role in liberating POW camps in Germany, most famously Stalag VII-A at

Tony (far left) in a German village during World War II, where he served as a platoon leader in the Fourteenth Armored Division. COURTESY OF THE WISE FAMILY

Moosburg in late April 1945. The camp was the largest in Germany, with one hundred and ten thousand prisoners, including thirty thousand Americans who hailed the arrival of their saviors. The 125th and another unit built a bridge that allowed the troops and tanks of the Fourteenth to flow into Moosburg.[12]

The Fourteenth Armored Division liberated other POW camps, including one that Wise recounted in a letter to his mother in April 1945, prior to Stalag VII-A:

> The other day, I think I saw my most spine-tingling sight yet. We went through a town, and as we got about a half-mile past it, we saw a lot of barracks with wire fence around them. All of a sudden the place seemed to burst with humanity. Across the fields came 5,000 Polish, French, Russian, Yugoslavian prisoners. They pummeled our hands. They thanked us, "Merci," and really made you feel you were fighting for something. Returning the salute of these war prisoners gave you a thrill every time you did it.[13]

He concluded the letter with a P.S.: "I got the Silver Star for 'Gallantry in action against the enemy at Steinfeld, Germany on 21 March 1945.'" On March 20 and 21, Wise's Third Platoon of forty men needed to clear a path through an area of Dragon's Teeth, antitank fortifications made of reinforced concrete and rebar, so troops could advance. Wise led a reconnaissance mission with a corporal, crossing open terrain under intense rocket and artillery fire, to reach the Dragon's Teeth. After additional infantry support arrived, Wise and his fellow soldiers breached the Dragon's Teeth with TNT explosives. With a path cleared, Wise then led his men into town. Facing more automatic weapons fire, they eliminated log-wall antitank barriers. The platoon built a bridge across a ten-foot crater, clearing the way for the 125th armored column to pass through fortified Steinfeld by the twenty-second; two engineers and two infantrymen died from enemy fire during the encounter. First Lieutenant and eventually Captain Wise was just one of thirteen in his battalion to receive the Silver Star, the third highest honor for valor in combat.[14]

Wise also received the Bronze Star for heroism. On April 4, 1945, he and two sergeants drove ahead of their unit to check on a vital bridge crossing. They found it was set to be detonated by the Germans. Wise looked up and saw a German guard standing on the bridge. Wise and one of the sergeants quickly pulled the wires, neutralizing the charges. The guard heard them and alerted others, forcing the Americans to speed away under a hail of machine-gun fire. They survived, though one of the bullets hit Wise's helmet and passed out the front. He narrowly escaped death at least twice more during the war, including the time his convoy was passing through a village and a sniper shot and killed the soldier sitting next to him in their jeep.[15]

Germany surrendered in May 1945 and Japan almost four months later, bringing the war to an end. Wise's unit remained in Germany and spent the winter of 1945–46 building bridges and fixing roads in several German towns. One of the towns was Garmisch-Partenkirchen, in the Bavarian Alps, near the country's highest peak, Zugspitze (9,718 feet). The town had hosted the 1936 Winter Olympics—the first Olympics to feature alpine skiing.[16] While in Garmisch-Partenkirchen, Wise encountered the sport for the first time when he accompanied his men to the local ski areas "to keep the guys out of trouble." Wise was hooked. "I couldn't get over how much skiing was done down in the Alps, and I thought it would be a hell of an idea to transform that over to here," he remembered later. "This sport seemed to me to be the perfect solution to the winter economic doldrums back home."[17]

Wise returned to the United States on July 26, 1946, and took a two-month leave in Hayward before returning to Harvard for his final semester. He hadn't thrived academically at Harvard before the war; but upon his return his grades improved, and he graduated with his MBA in early February 1947. Years later he called the military the best "entrepreneurial education" of his life. "I had a feeling of being superior to other men when I came home," he said. "It gives you a great feeling of strength to know you've been through one of the toughest ordeals in the world."[18]

BACK AT SCHOOL, Wise began laying the groundwork for an alpine ski resort in Wisconsin. First, he needed to learn more about how such places worked. On weekends during his final winter at Harvard, he drove to New England's ski resorts—chief among them Stowe, Vermont—and soaked up what he could about their operations.

In December 1946, at home in Hayward for Christmas break, Wise searched for a hill big enough for downhill skiing. He looked at Norwegian Hill west of downtown, where the Winter Carnival had been held, but it wasn't big enough. As a last resort near the end of his break, Wise visited the forest ranger station in Hayward, where he met Scandinavian Punce Johnson, a towering woodsman rumored to be a Bunyanesque "eight ax handles tall," who told Wise to check out the big hill outside of Cable.[19]

Wise drove the twenty miles to Cable, found the wooded hill, and snowshoed up. He learned that the hill was owned by a farmer and local school janitor named Walter Kliszcz. Wise inquired about buying the land, but Kliszcz didn't respond.

After graduation, Wise didn't head to corporate America or Wall Street like many of his Harvard classmates. Instead, Wise and a military buddy left Boston for a winding road trip through New England, Canada, and Michigan's Upper Peninsula to see more ski operations. That buddy was Lieutenant Hobart B. "Mac" Hewett, a platoon leader like Wise. After the war, Hewett, a Virginia native, had returned to Carnegie Institute of Technology (now Carnegie Mellon University) in Pittsburgh to finish his engineering degree.

By March 1947, Wise and Hewett landed in Hayward, determined to open a ski hill of their own. "When I went to college, I never had any idea that I wouldn't come back to Hayward," Wise said in 1979. "I was going to put that baby on the map."[20] At first, Wise worked in the family business, Wise Brothers Land Company, and Hewett worked at a local lumber company while they developed their idea.

Wise was still intrigued by the hill near Cable, so he went to see Kliszcz, the owner, sometime in March of 1947. Kliszcz, who had told his kids, "That mountain is all mine," was skeptical that Wise actually wanted to create a downhill ski resort there. Kliszcz had heard rumors that the hill contained a mother lode of gold, silver, and copper. Traces of silver had been discovered in the Namekagon River during the region's logging era, and locals had long suspected that the big hill nearby—a kame, or type of hill created by glacial rubble ten thousand years earlier—was the source.

Wise recalled their meeting many years later:

> It was the funniest deal. Kliszcz asked me what I was going to do with that hill, and when I told him [I wanted to] make a ski hill out of it, he thought I was giving him the old fake-a-roo. After sarcastically asking me to show him this "ski hill" of mine, I walked him through the knee-deep March snow all the way up the hill twice—explaining to him in great detail where all the trails would go. By that time, we were on a first-name basis, and I said, "Well, Walter, are you going to sell it to me or not?"

Finally, Kliszcz was convinced that Wise was serious about his plans. Kliszcz directed Wise to stand on one side of a big birch tree and write down his offer, while Kliszcz stood on the other side and wrote down his asking price. "I had written down $500, and he wrote down $1,000," Tony said, "so we settled for $750."[21]

The price was for 120 acres—three 40-acre tracts. Using the same rate of $250 per 40 acres, Wise and Hewett bought three more tracts from neighboring property owners (including the Frels brothers of Cable), thereby officially launching the Telemark Company. Wise would keep buying land, eventually owning 1,700 acres at the site.

Wise and Hewett went in fifty-fifty as owners, each investing $5,000 plus a $15,000 GI loan. Wise was president and Hewett secretary-treasurer. Like his grandfather, father, and uncles, young Tony was in business. It was the first of five companies he would create in Cable and Hayward. Kliszcz, meanwhile, lived on Highway M near the ski hill turnoff. He eventually became a Telemark employee, dutifully chasing down people who tried to sneak in without paying and hauling them to Wise to let him determine if they would be allowed to stay.[22]

Part of the hill already had been logged to support war efforts, but by May 1947, more land was cleared for the initial run, called Morgedal, and a beginner slope. By September, Wise and Hewett had hired Oliver Olson, of Cable, to build a forty-eight-by-thirty-foot chalet. Wise formed the Telemark Ski Club in October to help build interest in the sport. By November, three downhill runs were bulldozed and finished, and the chalet was ready for customers.[23]

In the meantime, Wise and Hewett announced their grand plans to the public. On July 31, 1947, an open letter from the Telemark Company titled, "To Citizens of the Hayward-Cable Recreation Area," appeared in the local newspaper, heralding the duo's intention to use skiing to boost the local economy. Snow, one of Wisconsin's most abundant, if ephemeral, natural resources, could be Hayward's and Cable's winter equivalent of its lakes, Wise and Hewett proclaimed—a different kind of gold mined from the big hill:

> We have about given up the idea of changing the weather from snowy blasts to balmy breezes during the months of December through March. Instead, we plan to go in partnership with Old Man Winter and see if we can create a "second" tourist season during that period. One needs only to look at the resort areas in New England to realize that private enterprise coupled with cooperative community can really turn a "dull season" into one of high business activity and real outdoors fun.[24]

Wise had done his research. He estimated that in the US, "winter sports as a commercial enterprise" was only about a decade old. Snow, tow ropes—"the American skier abhors having to climb hills," he once said—and nearby population centers were key to alpine ski resort success.[25]

Lodging and transportation were part of the equation, too. Wise and Hewett lined up fourteen hotels and summer resorts to open for the winter to handle the expected influx of visitors. Skiers could drive to Telemark, of course, but they also could take the Chicago & Northwestern Railroad and Soo Line. Trains stopped one hundred miles to the south in Eau Claire and in nearby Spooner and Stanberry, and bus lines or cabs would take skiers the rest of the way. Eventually charter buses from as far as Chicago and Minneapolis were filled with people looking for winter fun ($1.50 for a day, or $21 for a three-day package of skiing, lessons, lodging, and meals). Wise had everything covered, including ski rentals (which made it easier for curious newcomers to try out the sport), and it all was the result of his exhaustive Northeast research.[26]

Initial Telemark advertising included a blue-and-white brochure announcing the chance to "Ski Mount Telemark in the Northern Highlands of Wisconsin," with a sketch of the chalet nestled into the hills. At the top of the brochure was a shield featuring a single Norwegian warrior on skis, an adaptation of an image of two warriors on skis that Wise had seen on an information booklet about Norway. Wise didn't understand the historical significance of that image at the time, but he would come to embrace it some twenty-five years later.[27]

Choosing the Telemark name was part suggestion, part family history, and part marketing. Wise's roommate at Harvard was from Norway and suggested Telemark, famous around the world as the birthplace of modern skiing. The decision went deeper than that, though. Wise's paternal grandmother Gjertina was born in Rendal in southern Norway's Telemark region, where the Telemark landing in ski jumping had been invented. Wise's ancestry was about one-quarter Norwegian and the rest English, Prussian, and Luxembourger.[28]

The 1947 pamphlet heralding the arrival of a new downhill skiing attraction
AMERICAN BIRKEBEINER SKI FOUNDATION ARCHIVES

The brochure also advertised a Norwegian ski school, with one-hour lessons that cost one dollar. The instructor was "Skimeister" Ola Stormoen, a former ski racer from Rjukan, Norway, hired by Wise to help authenticate the Norwegian experience (the chalet also served lefse). Eventually, Wise would name one of the alpine runs after Stormoen. (Stormoen appeared as a German skier in the 1948 film *The Battle for Heavy Water*, about Operation Telemark, the successful Norwegian resistance to stop Germany's efforts to develop an atomic bomb. A US version of the film starring Kirk Douglas came out in 1965, titled *The Heroes of Telemark*. Wise co-opted that title a decade later when he began calling his Birkebeiner champions the Heroes of Telemark.)[29]

Wise likely was aware of a famous cross-country ski marathon held in Norway every year since 1932 called the Birkebeinerrennet (pronounced "birk-ah-BI-ner-ren-et"). It could be why his 1947 brochure touted the presence of "Complete Downhill and Cross Country Facilities." Cross-country? At least two news publications at the time reported that Telemark would have eight miles of cross-country trails, one of them saying "for the langlaufer of the clan," using the traditional German term for cross-country skier. Furthermore, the reports said the downhill runs and trails were designed by Kristofer Berg, a noted Norwegian alpine skier.[30] Berg had competed across Europe and took part in his country's Nazi resistance during World War II. Then, in February of 1946, Berg "was the picture of grace" when he won the US Eastern Amateur Ski Association's slalom and downhill titles at Mount Mansfield near Stowe, Vermont.[31] Did Wise happen to meet Berg in Stowe on one of his fact-finding visits? Or at Harvard, where Berg also was a student? Was Berg the roommate who suggested that Wise use the Telemark name? Wise, at least publicly, didn't say.

Assisting in the ski hill and trail designs were Ruth-Marie Stewart, the US Eastern alpine ski champion who would ski in the 1948 Olympics, and Pierre Jalbert, the Canadian alpine champion and 1948 Olympic team captain. Jalbert went on to star in the TV series *Combat!* and work as a sound editor, including on *The Godfather* and the *Shogun* miniseries, earning an Emmy nomination.[32]

Wise's intention may have been to provide cross-country trails and complete a Norwegian winter wonderland vision in Wisconsin, but either the Nordic skiing idea quickly was mothballed or there was little local interest in the sport, which certainly was true nationally at the time. Even without cross-country, Wise and Hewett had an out-of-the-box big idea for the Hayward-Cable area. Skiing wasn't completely new to the state or region—elsewhere, Wisconsin had fifteen other ski hills with rope tows (ropes on a mechanical pulley that skiers grabbed for a ride to the top of the hill), and Minnesota had three. Many of those hills reported having cross-country trails, ski jumps, and other winter sports facilities for tobogganing, skating, and more.[33] None of those operations, however, were powered by the energy of Tony Wise.

When Telemark opened on Saturday, December 13, 1947, seven hundred people arrived, some just to witness northwestern Wisconsin history. It was big news in an area where tourism otherwise shut down between Labor Day and Memorial Day. The modest hill, with a 351-foot vertical drop, had three runs, the longest 2,600 feet, with a bunny hill and two rope tows. Three days before opening, four thousand feet of rope was delivered. Hewett rigged surplus army jeep engines to power the rope tows, which didn't always work well. "We didn't know what the hell we were doing really," Wise said.[34] An estimated 2,400 to 4,000 skiers hit the slopes that winter. The Harvard MBA graduate had proved that his market research was spot on, his business plan worked, and he could close the deal with his marketing skills. And maybe more importantly,

An early photograph of the Mount Telemark chalet. A sign close to the building reads, "Ski School meeting place." AMERICAN BIRKEBEINER SKI FOUNDATION ARCHIVES, PREVIOUSLY PUBLISHED IN *TELEMARK MEMORIES*

his hunch was right: some Upper Midwesterners actually liked snow and winter and would travel and pay to enjoy it, if promised a good time.[35]

Wise opened Telemark when he was twenty-six years old. For Wise, this was only the beginning. "He was above all an ideas man," his daughter Janie Wise said. One of those ideas involved other ski hills. At the same time they were getting Telemark off the ground, Wise and Hewett also helped start Mont du Lac—both as part owners and Wise as the first manager—which opened in 1948 near Superior, Wisconsin, about seventy miles northwest of Hayward. Wise wasn't fond of the hill and left the business after a year. Later, he was interested in expanding his business but lost a bid to manage Rib Mountain at Wausau to the south.[36]

IN 1952, WISE AND MARY SHEILA MALINE, an English teacher from Superior, were married and went to Niagara Falls on their honeymoon.[37] Meanwhile, Wise's ideas kept coming. He expanded the company in 1954 by opening a summer attraction east of downtown Hayward on Highway B called Historyland, which attempted to re-create two eras in regional history. An Ojibwe village with wigwams and medicine lodges was built, staffed, and maintained by members of the Lac Courte Oreilles Band of Lake Superior Ojibwe, whose reservation was four miles south of Hayward. They offered biweekly summer powwows and daily live demonstrations, during which visitors could watch how the Anishinaabe tanned hides and made birchbark canoes, reed mats, and maple syrup. "You'll be amazed to learn about the people who occupied Wisconsin before the whiteman [*sic*]," a brochure stated. Nearby, the North Wisconsin Lumber Company's logging camp was re-created with veteran lumberjacks demonstrating their skills, along with a logging museum. The popular Cook Shanty served up a $3 buffet, with red-checkered tablecloths and a giant red-handled ax hanging from the log beams. One thousand customers once ate an entire ton of prime rib in a day, and local high school students working as waiters often financed their college educations on the tips.[38]

Historyland quickly became an Upper Midwest summer tourist draw, including an attraction called Old Hayward. Over several years it grew to include the Clark House, a restaurant and bar offering free peanuts and live entertainment (originally the Hayward Hotel and used for housing lumberjacks, the building was trucked to Historyland for $10,000); the *Namekagon Queen* excursion boat on Lake Hayward (brought in from Wisconsin Dells for $15,000); seven railroad cars; the old city train depot; and more to create the impression of a frontier town. Wise patterned it after Jackson, Wyoming, which in 1954 held the Junior National Alpine Ski Championships and eventually became a ski center in the West.[39]

In August 1960, next to Historyland, Wise started another major venture, the World's Championship Log Rolling event, eventually called the World Lumberjack Championships. He didn't create the event from scratch—he had Telemark general manager Jerome "Jerry" Berard bid $1,500 to buy the Log Rolling World Championships from Escanaba, Michigan. Wise saw potential for expanding on the logging demonstrations at Historyland, and the addition truly was part of the city's history, rooted in the days of the logging boom: Wise had seen log rolling and chopping in town as a kid in the 1930s.[40]

The new venture, part of the city's Lumberjack Days, featured athletes from around the world competing in the international roleo—the term for a log-rolling competition, coined in the 1920s as a mashup between "roll" and "rodeo." Wise expanded the event beyond log rolling to include sawing, chopping, axe-throwing, and pole-climbing competitions, at the suggestion of employee Clayton Farnsworth. Wise spent $200,000 on the inaugural event, featuring a lumberjack stuntman dancing the Charleston and standing on his head atop an eighty-foot pole. Attendance was low, but Wise wasn't deterred.[41]

The World Lumberjack Championships eventually drew up to ten thousand spectators annually, attention from *Life* magazine, and television coverage by ABC's new hit show, *Wide World of Sports*, which began airing in 1962. Wise had put Hayward on the map at age forty-one. Bob Treland, who would become one of Wise's most trusted employees and helped start the Birkebeiner, recalled seeing his hometown Hayward on television once while in Houston, Texas. The events took place then, as they still did in 2024, at the Lumberjack Bowl, a four-thousand-seat stadium Wise built surrounding the town's old mill pond.[42]

AS TELEMARK GREW throughout the 1950s and 1960s, Wise became a master at promoting it. Wise and Telemark were featured in national ski publications, the *New York Times* and other major newspapers, and national magazines. A 1962 *Chicago's American* article featured classic Wise, explaining how the hills had "pampered snow" that was groomed and tilled with a "magic carpet" chain device until it was powdery soft. *Ski Magazine* called Telemark one of the "Ten Most Loved Ski Areas" in the nation and claimed the resort's Christiana run was one of twenty favorites among US skiers. A reporter for *Sports Illustrated* was amazed that a place like Wisconsin, "with hardly a topographical lump worth mentioning," could draw tens of thousands of skiers, especially since Telemark only had half-mile or shorter downhill runs.[43]

The Telemark Company incorporated in 1955, with Wise and Hewett each receiving 50 percent of the stock. Hewett had been a silent partner after the first years, becoming an engineer with tractor and jeep maker Minneapolis Moline and then Honeywell in the Twin Cities. He remained half owner until 1978, when he sold his portion to Wise for $175,000 or more, although Wise said he was able to pay Hewett only about 10 percent of it at the time.[44]

Even as Wise pursued other ventures, he continued investing in his original enterprise. He added a second floor to the ski chalet in 1955, including a lounge with a wall of windows facing the ski hill and a balcony decorated in colorful Norwegian rosemaling where a Dixieland band would play. By the late 1950s, the ski hill featured ten rope tows and three T-bar chair lifts. The T-bars were installed in 1957 with the help of Hewett and Telemark employee

An undated promotional postcard for the Mount Telemark chalet, after its expansion
WHI IMAGE ID 84755

"Forklift" Fred Vortanz, who, at six-foot-three, could hoist them to the connectors on his shoulders. People began flocking to the hill not only for skiing but purely for socializing as well—it was the place to be and be seen up north in the winter—in part because Wise had secured a local liquor license for Telemark, becoming one of the first (if not the first) Midwest ski hills to have one. (The license was granted in 1955; however, Wise's mother was anti-liquor, so he didn't use the license until after her death several years later.)[45]

Another renovation in 1962 resulted in three restaurants on three floors—the popular Rathskeller on the ground floor, the Fjord Room on the second floor, and the American Room cafeteria on top. Up to fifteen hundred skiers visited each weekend, keeping the 140-person, red-uniformed staff hopping. The *après-ski*—the "after ski" social activity—included live music at two venues, one of them the Lovin' Roomful dance club. Guests enjoyed infrared heated decks with redwood tables where they could lounge in the midday winter sun in a sweater. Wise even hired a musician to play the accordion as he skied the slopes. "They came to Telemark not because it was the best ski area but because it was the most fun," said daughter Frances Wise.[46]

During the winter of 1960–61, Wise faced an unexpected challenge. The usually reliable Wisconsin snow hardly fell that year, and Telemark was able to open for just one day of the season. With the help of Wisconsin Governor Gaylord Nelson, who later founded Earth Day, and US Senator William Proxmire, a fiscally conservative Democrat, Wise secured a $180,000 federal loan from the Small Business Administration—one of the first to a ski resort—to purchase snowmaking equipment. To help build support for the loan, Wise organized a citizen letter-writing campaign at the National Guard armory. The SBA saw the value: area businesses lost an estimated $1 million when Telemark was shut down that winter.[47]

When the money came in, seven miles of pipe were laid and three wells dug at a cost of $210,000. It was believed to be the largest snowmaking operation in the country—Wise billed it as the largest, even, in the world—and that included Vail and Aspen. The ability to make snow helped Telemark remain competitive, not only with the larger ski resorts out west, but regionally as well, where the sport was becoming increasingly popular. More than 150 ski hills operated in the region by the early 1960s—up from fifteen when Telemark opened—and many hills closer to urban centers were beginning to cut into the need for a weekend trip to Telemark. The first chairlift for skiers, taking them

A snow gun, part of Wise's new snowmaking equipment, using compressed air and water mist to simulate the natural formation of snow. AMERICAN BIRKEBEINER SKI FOUNDATION ARCHIVES, PREVIOUSLY PUBLISHED IN *TELEMARK MEMORIES*

to the top of Valhalla, was installed at Telemark in 1964, one of the first in the Midwest.[48]

Around 1965, Wise expanded his appeal to skiers and tourists by bringing in big-name musicians (and some of his personal favorites) to perform at the nearby Old Hayward Big Top music venue. Among them were Duke Ellington, Woody Herman, Louis Armstrong, the Buckinghams, the Detroit Wheels, and Jimmy Dorsey. "Skiers go where the action is," Wise explained to the *Milwaukee Sentinel*. The famous rock band Buffalo Springfield, featuring Neil Young and Stephen Stills, performed on July 29, 1967, in a show so widely publicized that even heartthrob Davy Jones and the rest of the Monkees were in the audience. The Monkees had flown into Duluth, Minnesota, and had taken a bus to Hayward just to watch Buffalo Springfield, as they explained to a surprised and screaming crowd.[49]

Meanwhile, more and more skiers kept going down Telemark's hills. On Saturday, January 2, 1965, 2,206 skiers passed through the gate to set a one-day record. Nearby hotels and motels were regularly full. Telemark set a seasonal record in 1965–66 with more than sixty thousand skiers over about four months. Wise celebrated by blasting dynamite in the hills. Telemark, officially, was a success.[50]

WISE WAS A CIVIC-MINDED BUSINESSMAN. He sat on the Hayward City Council and was elected mayor of Hayward twice, serving from 1953 to 1957. His lobbying and military connections brought a National Guard armory to Hayward that originally was slated to go to nearby Ashland. From 1949 to 1952, Wise commanded Company B of the Wisconsin National Guard's 724th Engineer Battalion; the company won numerous state awards and a national award from the Thirty-Second "Red Arrow" Infantry Division. (Wise retired from the Guard in 1965 with the rank of lieutenant colonel after his wife, Sheila, told him that with all his ventures and their six children, enough was enough.)[51]

Beyond Hayward, Wise helped lobby for regional highway improvements—such as the four-lane expansion of US Highway 53 from Eau Claire to Superior—which he considered good for the region and for his businesses. He also lobbied for the National Wild and Scenic Rivers Act, leading a canoe excursion in 1966 with then–US Senator Gaylord Nelson along the Namekagon River to raise awareness for the legislation, which passed two years later. He founded the Sawyer County Historical Society in 1957, served two terms on the State Historical Society of Wisconsin Board of Curators, and co-led an excavation of a site where fur trader Michel Cadotte may have wintered in northern Wisconsin in 1764.[52]

By the time he turned fifty in 1971, Wise already had accomplished much, but he was in the midst of hatching the two biggest—some might say grandiose—ideas of his life. Who would build a mammoth lodge and residential development in the middle of a forest? Who would start a cross-country ski race that required people to cover thirty miles through hilly terrain at a time when the sport itself was obscure? Who would do those things almost simultaneously? (In the midst of this, in true Tony Wise fashion, he also was looking into creating an antique train excursion line from Hayward to Bayfield.) "It never occurred to him that things wouldn't work," Frances Wise said. "He had this indomitable spirit. He was a driven guy with ideas going through his head at all times. Some of them were really terrible ideas, but he had a lot of great ones."[53]

A lodge and housing development had been in the back of Wise's mind since as early as 1963. Though the chalet offered restaurants and entertainment space, the ski hill's only lodging was provided by the American Youth Hostel. Most overnight visitors—and a lot of potential revenue—went elsewhere. Meanwhile, ski resorts in Colorado had begun offering condominium units for sale, as part of a full-service "ski village" concept. This proved to Wise that people would buy second homes for recreation even if they weren't on the water.

Wise's initial hotel concept was a twenty-story cylindrical glass tower piercing the sky at the top of the ski hill—"shoot for the moon," he would say. It would have two hundred rooms and a rotating restaurant on the top four floors and would be surrounded by a Norwegian-themed village. He wanted it to be the region's first modern building and first high-class resort, predicting the recreation industry would become "bigger than steel." By 1965 he'd hired an artist to draw up a rendering of the hotel. The plans were slow in developing, however, and by 1967, Wise still bemoaned that Telemark could have had more skiers during the holiday season except that all area hotel rooms were booked.[54]

Over time, his glass tower hotel idea morphed into something more realistic but still grand, a hotel at the base of the ski hill to be called Telemark Lodge. It would be the centerpiece of a sixteen-hundred-acre Norwegian-style development called Telemark Villages, promoted as a "second-home" and "environmental recreation community."[55]

Wise developed his master plan with environmental sustainability in mind, and with help from the University of Wisconsin Department of Landscape Architecture. Telemark Villages would be, as Wise described, "the first recreational community in mid-America to create a homesite where the streams, valleys, ridges, bogs and wetlands are linked together in a total environmental plan." Gaylord Nelson called it "environmentally, the most thoroughly planned recreational community in America." Wise was influenced by his good friend Martin Hanson, a noted Wisconsin environmentalist and eventual member of the Wisconsin Conservation Hall of Fame. Like Hanson, Wise believed in protecting the land as "the basis of all wealth and happiness."[56]

Wise hired Fred Goold, a landscape architect educated at UW–Madison, to design Telemark Villages, with a goal of eventually housing two thousand people—ten times the population of nearby Cable. The project began to take shape in the late 1960s, starting with sixty-two individual homesites at Village Kame and Nordmor Ski Village. Construction on Valhalla townhouses began in 1970, and the first 28 out of a planned 225 units sold in six months. Dave Carley (a former Wisconsin gubernatorial candidate) and brother Jim Carley, both executives of Inland Steel in Madison, put up $1 million to finance the townhouses and supported lodge planning. A village center with twelve shops and stores between the lodge and residences was planned but never developed.[57]

Construction on Telemark Lodge began with a groundbreaking ceremony on August 27, 1971, which included special guests Gaylord Nelson and Governor Patrick Lucey. Wise called the development "a 24-year dream."[58]

Telemark Lodge was big—a $6 million, two-hundred-thousand-square foot, two-hundred-room hotel. Prebuilt units from Shelter Homes in St. Paul were shipped to the site and stacked like logs to create two wings on either side of a central hub. The hotel was designed by Herb Fritz Jr., an apprentice under Frank Lloyd Wright from 1938 to 1941, whose father, Herb Fritz Sr., was a draftsman at Wright's Taliesin in Spring Green, Wisconsin. Architect Charlie Radloff of Minnesota handled the detailing and selecting of materials, like cedar

Telemark Lodge, pictured here in 1977, with the downhill slopes in the background and a growing cross-country trail system in the woods. AMERICAN BIRKEBEINER SKI FOUNDATION ARCHIVES

boards. The canopy-like hub had low lines, a graceful bow to the landscape that blended site and structure.[59] Still, it stood out. "When visitors came around that last turn in the road," Wise later recalled, "I wanted them to say, 'Wow!' And they did!"[60]

US Olympic alpine gold medalist Billy Kidd attended the grand opening. Although Kidd famously referred to the hotel as the only ski lodge larger than its ski hill, he also called it one of the most beautiful lodges he'd ever seen. He complimented it as a great place for ski racers to train because of the hard-packed conditions and opportunity for quick, repeated training runs, including at night. "It's an exceptionally well-designed, modern, full-season resort complex," Kidd said.[61]

Rooms were sold on a fifty-two-year lease, $25,000 for a single unit and $50,000 for a suite. The rooms sold out, returning roughly the full cost of lodge construction. When not occupied by the leaseholders, the rooms were rented, initially for $44.50 a night. The owners were to receive 20 percent of the revenue. Wise said it was the first condo hotel in the region, an "amazing real estate idea" he borrowed from a hotel in Florida.[62]

Telemark Lodge impressed from the inside, too, with massive, exposed wooden beams, some eighty feet long; the creak of real wood on the open main staircase; the fifty-five-foot-high "world's largest" fireplace (which cost $45,000 and was made with 155 tons of native stone) in the cavernous entryway; plus several bars and restaurants, a theater, sauna, retail shops, meeting rooms for conventions and conferences, and indoor and outdoor pools. The main dining room served gourmet meals; the sous chef for a time was a young Emeril Lagasse.

Wise, who regularly read *Billboard* magazine, brought famous musicians to Telemark, and there were house bands, so the party never seemed to stop on the weekends. People danced on the tables, and when they fell off, they didn't hit the floor because it was standing-room only. The fun included a legendary New Year's Eve party and plenty of acclaimed entertainers year-round—Jerry Lee Lewis, Ronnie Milsap, Chubby Checker, Buddy Rich, Count Basie, Ricky Nelson, Maynard Ferguson, Duke Ellington, Luther Allison, Bonnie Raitt, Tommy James, and more. Rising country singer Louise Mandrell performed every night during 1978 Birkebeiner week.

Outside, visitors could ski in the winter and play golf in the summer—first on a nine-hole, then an eighteen-hole scenic course designed by Art Johnson of

Madison and set amid the surrounding forest of birch, spruce, pine, and hemlock—or use one of the four tennis courts, go horseback riding, or go trout fishing. The Cable Union Airport, a 3,700-foot cement airstrip, had plane parking 200 feet from the lodge's front door. Telemark was a place for everyone, including the jet set.

The lodge had one major drawback when winter ended: no lakefront property, forcing Wise to market heavily in the summer and bring in customers with concerts, conventions, and special events. The tourism industry in northern Wisconsin from spring to fall had always been built around water, about one thousand lakes (more than the number of farms) in Sawyer and Bayfield Counties alone. But while the narrow Namekagon River flowed past Telemark and prime recreational lakes were nearby, no lakefront was in sight.

WISE'S RESPECT FOR THE ENVIRONMENT was intertwined with his support for the region's Native peoples. The ski hill is a sacred and historic place to the Ojibwe. They named the hill Kawabaming, or "place to look out from."[63]

Wise was one of the first non-Native employers in the region to hire Native workers. Dozens of Ojibwe tribal members from the nearby Lac Courte Oreilles (LCO) reservation worked nearly full time at both Historyland and Telemark, at one point comprising up to one hundred of Telemark's four hundred employees. They often called Wise "Ogima," or "big boss." He made efforts to learn the Ojibwe language and arranged travel and lodging so they could attend powwows around the Midwest.[64] "The main thing I remember about [Tony] is his kinship, his closeness to Native Americans," John "Little Bird" Anderson, an LCO tribal chairman and elder, said more than a decade after Wise had died. Anderson and Wise had been friends since the 1950s, when Wise hired him to perform at powwows.[65]

For many Thanksgivings, Wise opened Historyland's Cook Shanty and hosted a free banquet for Native employees and residents. Throughout the year, any Native person could eat at the Cook Shanty for free when in need. And each year, Telemark employee Fred Vortanz ordered a semitruck full of beef sections for the restaurant's all-you-can-eat prime rib special, saving the ribs for the local July 4 powwows.[66]

Tony invited the Lac Courte Oreilles tribe to use the Cook Shanty for wakes whenever a tribal member passed away. Some are buried nearby at a Native

American cemetery that Wise founded and his general manager, Jerry Berard, created. The graves are topped with wooden spirit houses, two-foot-high structures with a peaked roof and escape path for the spirit. The cemetery is in a grove of pines, at the end of a dirt road. It has no sign, although informally some call it the Historyland Cemetery. LCO member Ernie St. Germaine, a former Wise employee, knows it as bakiiya bashkigan jiibayak, or Hayward spirit land.[67]

Local Native children skied for free at Telemark. If they spotted Wise's big, green Buick sedan on Main Street, they would pile in and he'd take as many as he could to Telemark, with children sitting on top of each other along with Wise's own children. Or he would drive around and pick up children from the LCO reservation on his daily trip to Cable.[68]

St. Germaine—whose mother was Lac Courte Oreilles and whose father was Lac du Flambeau (an Ojibwe band with a reservation about two hours east of Hayward)—was a teenager when he started dancing in the Tuesday and Thursday powwows at Historyland. He began working at the Cook Shanty, then on the *Namekagon Queen*, and eventually at the lodge as a Nordic ski instructor. St. Germaine was a skilled athlete, which Wise quickly noticed. "Don't ever let money be the cause of you not reaching your goals," Wise once told him. St. Germaine didn't have much money as he was growing up, but often he would find that something he needed had been paid for; he knew it was thanks to Tony. St. Germaine's parents divorced when he was young, and he didn't become close to his father until high school. "Tony is the number one mentor in my life," St. Germaine reflected later. "In our culture, elders are important. We call them uncles. Tony was Uncle Tony. I didn't want to call him Dad, but he knew."[69]

TONY AND SHEILA, WHO DIVORCED IN 1987, had five daughters and a son. They had separated six years earlier, but because of financial complexities they lived in the same house on separate floors. Tony's seventh child, daughter Angeline Cloud, was born to Vivian Cloud, a member of Lac Courte Oreilles with whom Tony had a somewhat open affair in the late 1970s and early 1980s. The Wise siblings acknowledged their half-sister as part of their family.[70] Angeline and her dad "were extremely close," she said. "I saw him every day of my life. We did a lot of fun things together. He embraced the Native American culture and my other siblings as his own. He was just an amazing man."[71]

Five of Wise's children (left to right): Frances, Janie, Elizabeth, Winslow, and Mary, outside the Telemark chalet. AMERICAN BIRKEBEINER SKI FOUNDATION ARCHIVES, PREVIOUSLY PUBLISHED IN *TELEMARK MEMORIES*

To his children, Tony seemed larger than life. He once drove the family to a summer picnic atop the ski hill, then he slalomed down in the Buick at breakneck speed with Sheila and the kids screaming. Another time, he was stopped for speeding between Hayward and Cable while doing 110 miles per hour, but he was playing jazz music so loud that at first he didn't hear the sirens. His personality matched the way he drove—"like a madman," daughter Janie said, but she "adored him and dogged his heels. I couldn't get enough." He was generous, affectionate, funny, and energetic—a real-life Tony the Tiger—but as a boss, he could be highly demanding and "mercurial because he was so passionate about what he did," Janie said. Longtime assistant Jeanette Vortanz recalled that if Tony asked you a question, you had to know the answer or it could "set him off."[72]

Wise could be incredibly soft-hearted—he'd wave goodbye to his children from the window until he could no longer see them. "He really missed his dad when he died. It made him an emotional guy," Janie said. He didn't like flowers, so when he was hospitalized in Ashland in 1969 with his first heart attack, Jeanette Vortanz brought him a bouquet of tree leaves in peak fall color and he loved it. When Vortanz's mother died, Wise bought her a horse that she'd been wanting. It was a gift so generous and thoughtful that Vortanz was touched more than forty years later. "I could still cry thinking about that," she said. "There was not a thing in the world he wouldn't do for you."[73]

Wise was an open book, with his talents, charms, passions, and flaws on display for all to see. The men in his World War II platoon swore by him as a leader, his daughter Frances learned at a reunion. He loved bringing people together, watching his customers dance the night away in the Rathskeller or playing matchmaker with his employees, and always acted like a kid at his own birthday celebrations.

Wise was flawed by hubris, however, and his business empire crashed in the 1980s, much like the stock market had done when he was eight and a half years old. Until then, Tony Wise was a sight to see. His train was moving full speed, and either you jumped on board or you were left behind. In some ways, that's how the American Birkebeiner, the largest cross-country ski race in North America, began on February 24, 1973, at the frozen Lumberjack Bowl in Hayward.

Tony Wise, with Berit Mordre-Lammedal, 1977 women's winner (left), and Alison Owen-Spencer, runner-up. AMERICAN BIRKEBEINER SKI FOUNDATION ARCHIVES

Skiers on the Birkebeiner's original course had to contend with gravel, railroad tracks, snowmobile traffic, and other nuisances.
AMERICAN BIRKEBEINER SKI FOUNDATION ARCHIVES

Three

1973
THE AMERICAN BIRKEBEINER IS BORN

THE BRAND-NEW TELEMARK LODGE opened on Tuesday, January 9, 1973, with a six-day celebration coinciding with the ski attraction's twenty-fifth anniversary. The slopes, restaurants, and bars were full. Alpine skiing was king of the hill at Telemark and across the country.

During celebration week, few people paid attention to the nascent sport of cross-country skiing. A special anniversary edition of Tony Wise's house newspaper, the *North Wisconsin News*, all but ignored Telemark's 15 kilometers of new, tracked ski trails right outside the door, and his next big idea scheduled to happen the following month: a ski race *across the countryside* instead of *down the hill*. Not that it would have mattered much. Virtually no one in the region was a cross-country skier. Wise even remarked at the time that if he gave someone a pair of cross-country skis, they probably would give them back. However, Wise did coordinate a cross-country outing at the grand opening for a large group of invited media. Led by trail designer Sven Wiik and ski instructor Erik Ersson, reporters saw Wise's new cross-country trails but largely failed to mention them—or the upcoming cross-country race—in their glowing reviews of the lodge.[1]

Why was Wise expanding into cross-country skiing? Why did he think a race—an extreme one at that—had any chance of succeeding? Few people at the Telemark celebration might have guessed that the winter of 1972–73 would be best remembered for something other than the new lodge, and something few of them had even heard of: the Birkebeiner cross-country ski marathon. What a tiresome, solitary-sounding event, compared to the chic social scene Wise had created around his alpine lodge.

Prior to 1970, Nordic skiing lacked cachet in the US, even though it was a way of life in northern Europe, where it had been used as a means of transportation and by hunters for at least eight thousand years. Skis found in northern Russia date to about 6000 BCE; by 1200 CE, Norwegians so efficiently used skis while hunting elk that laws were passed to protect the animals. In the United States, cross-country skiing dates to around 1850 with the influx of Scandinavian immigrants; but for more than a century it was the least popular form of skiing, trailing far behind ski jumping and, later, downhill.[2]

Cross-country races and trails were slow to develop across the US in the twentieth century, especially before the advent of mechanical grooming. The nation's first cross-country championship was held in 1907 in Ashland, Wisconsin, though early races drew small fields, eight to twelve skiers or none at all. Cross-country skiing in the US was mostly concentrated in the Northeast, which supplied most of the nation's Olympic skiers beginning in 1924, when men's Nordic skiing became an Olympic sport (women were added in 1952). The Northeast also had some of the first trail systems and citizen races in the country beginning in the 1920s. By comparison, the Central US Ski Association's Cross Country Committee noted in 1939 the "general lack of interest in this form of skiing in the Midwest."[3]

After World War II, alpine skiing in the US took off, further burying cross-country. Soldiers (like Tony Wise) had seen the popularity of the sport in Europe and returned with engineering know-how, including many who (unlike Wise) had served in the war as skiing soldiers. Veterans from the army's white-clad skiing Tenth Mountain Division returned home and started sixty alpine ski resorts across the northern US, giving the sport a major boost; five army veterans skied in the 1948 Olympics. Alpine skiing had drawbacks, however, including expensive equipment, clothing, and lift tickets; travel required to reach mostly remote ski hills; a learning curve; and long lift lines.[4]

Social upheaval in the 1960s helped lay the groundwork that would bring cross-country skiing into vogue. In 1962, Rachel Carson's seminal book *Silent Spring* brought widespread public attention to the harms of pollution and helped to popularize the nation's burgeoning environmental movement. In *Ski Magazine*'s annual survey in 1965, skiers' favorite aspect of cross-country was being close to nature. The antiestablishment, counterculture movement, fueled by musicians like Bob Dylan, was taking hold. Skiing independently through the woods in a wool sweater suddenly sounded groovy. The sport could be enjoyed virtually anywhere there was snow, by anyone, with minimal investment. "Cross-country skiing is in tune with everything Americans want now," Wise said in 1975. "It's a reasonably economical recreational pastime that provides the added bonuses of physical fitness and a return to nature."[5] The environmental appeal of cross-country aligned with Wise's support of the federal Wild and Scenic Rivers Act in the mid-1960s and his efforts to reduce environmental impacts when planning Telemark Lodge.

Becoming more physically fit suddenly was popular, too. In 1960, President-elect John F. Kennedy wrote an article in *Sports Illustrated* titled "The Soft American," in which he encouraged the Marines to reinstate the fifty-mile hike and announced the start of a national physical fitness program. By the time the Birkebeiner began in 1973, sixty million adult Americans—more than a quarter of the country—had taken up a sport for exercise and, for the first time, more bicycles were being sold than automobiles. Foot races had begun to proliferate, and the nation had a new running hero, Frank Shorter, who sped through the streets of Munich, Germany, in September 1972 to win Olympic gold.[6]

By the mid-1960s, signs began to suggest a surge in cross-country's popularity. In 1964, ex-Olympian and Dartmouth College skier John Caldwell's *The Cross-Country Ski Book* was a national hit. In February 1965, *Skiing* magazine published a special issue on ski touring, a common term at the time for recreational cross-country, noting that in "the past couple of years, a strange thing has been happening. Ski touring, the sport of old-timers, the sport of purists, the sport of he-men, has seen an enormous revival of interest . . . largely because of this universal appeal the sport has." Some of the earliest citizen-style Nordic races and tours in the US emerged in the 1960s and early 1970s in Vermont, Minnesota, Colorado, Idaho, California, and Alaska.[7]

The North Star Ski Touring Club in Minneapolis–St. Paul exemplified this growth in the sport. Formed in 1967 with nineteen members, the club grew to four hundred members in four years. In February 1971, the club held its first VJC race and tour (VJC stood for the villages it went through—Victoria, Jonathan, and Chaska, in that order), as nearly three hundred skiers traveled 15 kilometers through weedy, snow-covered fields with no set tracks. In 1972, VJC race entrants tripled, to 873.[8]

Word about cross-country's new popularity spread. Wise's general manager at the time, Jerry Berard, heard from a friend in the Twin Cities that cross-country ski sales there were taking off. Berard shared that news with Wise, adding, "Tony, maybe we should look into this." One day early in March 1972, Wise approached two friends who had cross-country experience, George Hovland of Duluth, Minnesota, and Rick Scott of Superior, Wisconsin. In the coffee lounge of the old alpine chalet, with the new lodge under construction next

Jerry Berard in an undated photograph taken at Telemark, where he was general manager and late-1970s race director. COURTESY OF JERRY AND JOAN BERARD

door, Wise asked Hovland and Scott if they could do a little research for him about cross-country's rising popularity.[9]

Hovland was the 1943 Minnesota high school cross-country and slalom ski champion, then made the US cross-country ski team for the 1952 Olympics in Oslo, Norway. After serving in World War II, Hovland started a ski shop in Duluth, and he and Wise helped start the Mont du Lac downhill operation near Superior. Hovland also was a sales rep and once lost a shipment of ski boots from Italy when the *Andrea Doria* sank off the coast of Nantucket in 1956. In the early 1970s, he was helping to start the Spirit Mountain downhill and cross-country system in Duluth (with longer downhill runs than Telemark), which opened in 1974.[10]

Scott, originally from Eau Claire, had been an alpine instructor at Telemark before enrolling in the University of Minnesota's dental school; now, he was working part-time as an instructor at Minnesota's Lutsen Mountains ski area (started in 1948 by Tenth Mountain Division veteran George Nelson Jr.). Scott had learned to love cross-country and ski jumping as a kid on the Third Ward hills of Eau Claire and later skied backcountry. In Minnesota's Boundary Waters Canoe Area, he was part of a group that retraced explorer Alexander Mackenzie's late 1700s route. In Alaska, he skied village to village in Yukon bush country while working as a dentist for his Vietnam War deferment. Scott, Hovland, and a third friend named Jon Stephenson once skied from the Canadian border to Duluth in two and a half days, covering about 140 miles along the North Shore of Lake Superior.

Later that March, Hovland and Scott talked with ski importers at a national ski show in Las Vegas. They gathered some "pretty astounding" facts about "the number of pair of cross-country skis being sold," Scott recalled later, and passed that information on to Wise. "That just added fuel to the fire," Scott said. "Tony took it from there and decided to get into cross-country. Basically, Tony saw this was a way to attract people to a great sport for the area."[11]

The Nordic ski numbers *were* astounding. The number of cross-country skis sold in the US had grown from 30,000 pairs in 1967 to 150,000 in 1972 (sales would hit 350,000 in 1973). The sport's popularity had officially reached far beyond the Northeast. Bob Woodward, who later worked at Telemark as a Nordic instructor, personally sold up to five hundred pairs of cross-country skis in a single winter in the early 1970s at a shop in Berkeley, California, as ski camps in the nearby mountains overflowed. With large numbers of residents in Minnesota, Michigan, and Wisconsin of Scandinavian heritage, combined with plenty of snow and great terrain, the sport finally was on track to take off in the Upper Midwest, too.[12]

Equipment changes were helping to drive even more people to the sport, as the old, heavy hickory skis were replaced with lighter, more colorful fiberglass skis from Fischer, Karhu, Kneissl, Landsem, Epoke, Toko, and other Scandinavian manufacturers (fiberglass became the ski material of choice after dominating the 1974 World Championships in Sweden). Sleek aluminum poles soon replaced bamboo. Skis with fish-scale and mohair strips in the kick zones helped skiers inexperienced with waxing get kick. And the price was right—a package of new skis, boots, poles, and bindings cost $80 to $125 in 1974, although future Olympian Kevin Brochman of Minnesota remembers paying just $21 at Target for his first combination set two years later.[13]

Cross-country ski centers with groomed trails began to emerge by the late 1960s. Although almost nonexistent in northern Wisconsin and only slightly more common in nearby population centers like the Twin Cities, they were established in winter tourism areas elsewhere in the northern quarter of the country. Boyne Highlands and Boyne Mountain in Michigan each boasted a tracked 50-kilometer trail. New England had several; the Trapp Family Lodge in Stowe, Vermont, hosted twenty-five thousand cross-country skiers on its fifty miles of trails during the winter of 1971–72. Jackson, New Hampshire, had a seventy-five-mile system, and Waterville Valley, New Hampshire, had thirty-five miles. In the West, well-developed trail systems could be found in Vail and Ashcroft in Colorado; Big Sky in Montana; Mount Bachelor in Bend, Oregon; and in several areas around Mammoth Lakes, California. A chain of eight touring centers was operated by North American Nordic, with locations in several eastern states.[14]

WISE KNEW HE NEEDED to ride the Nordic wave, and he would have little to no competition in the Midwest. Adding cross-country trails—twenty-five years after it was part of his original plan at Telemark—was a business decision. Western resorts, with their superior alpine runs, had begun to proliferate and offer package deals with flights. The number of alpine skiers at Telemark peaked at seventy thousand during the winter of 1973–74 and then gradually declined. Northern Wisconsin, however, was well suited for cross-country, with its reliable snow cover, undulating terrain, forests to help hold the snow, and the right altitude for an aerobic sport. Wise called it the "natural sport" for the region.[15]

"When I teach somebody to ski downhill, all I'm doing is creating customers for Aspen and Vail," Wise told *Skiing* magazine in 1979. "When I teach someone to cross-country, I'm creating customers for myself. . . . I want to make Telemark the center for cross-country skiing in North America."[16]

Wise took his first step into cross-country in spring 1972. After considering what Hovland and Scott had found, Wise sent general manager Jerry Berard, ski area manager Jim Bauer, and Telemark planner Fred Goold to Colorado to look at cross-country ski operations there and find a trail designer. The three men went to Aspen and then to Steamboat Springs, where they saw Sven Wiik's Mount Werner Touring Center—*Ski Magazine* called it first-class—and the Scandinavian Lodge that Wiik opened in 1969 with his wife and daughter.

The three Telemark ambassadors were impressed with Wiik's trail operation and met him at a Denver hotel. Wiik, the son of a tailor, was born in 1921 in Sollefteă, Sweden, and taught skiing at a Swedish resort. He nearly made the 1948 Swedish Olympic track team as a pole vaulter and did make it in gymnastics, which was a demonstration sport that year. Wiik emigrated to the US in 1949 and quickly became a pioneer of Nordic skiing, eventually coaching three US ski teams in international competitions, including as head coach of the 1960 Olympic team. For nineteen years he coached the Western State College ski team in Gunnison, Colorado; a dozen of his protégés made the Olympics or other international competitions. He also wrote a book on ski touring. "As soon as I started talking with Sven, I knew he was the man, so I hired him to come and set up cross-country skiing at Telemark," Berard said. Bauer agreed: "Sven was really, really respected in cross-country circles."[17]

The March trip resulted in a September announcement: Wiik, who was temporarily working on location in Wisconsin, was designing 1-, 5-, and 10-kilometer cross-country ski trails in the woods near the new Telemark Lodge and would be directing, through an assistant, the Sven Wiik Ski Touring School at Telemark. They weren't his only designs beyond Steamboat Springs. Around the same time, he also created 32 kilometers of trails at Ashcroft, Colorado, and 20 kilometers at the Whitecap Mountains resort in northeastern Wisconsin.[18]

Day after day for about three weeks, Wiik walked through the woods around Telemark with Jim Bauer on his heels. They used topographical maps to guide their way and orange ribbons to mark trees for removal, with Wiik drawing on memories of Sweden's Vasaloppet course for inspiration. Wiik, five-foot-seven, was fifty-one and Bauer in his thirties, but Bauer said he could hardly keep up with the barrel-chested Wiik who "went through the woods like a madman." The trail designs cost Wise $1,600 a kilometer, or about $25,000.[19]

As Wiik designed Telemark's trails in the late summer and early fall of 1972, he encouraged Wise to create a symbolic race to help bring attention to the new ski touring center. Wiik was staying at the lodge, and Wise typically arrived midafternoon, so they began having dinner and talking in the evenings. Wiik "told Tony, 'You must have a race,'" recalled Berard, who often

Sven Wiik, former Olympic coach and a key figure in the Birkebeiner's history, talks with Frances Wise at the chalet after the 1974 race. AMERICAN BIRKEBEINER SKI FOUNDATION ARCHIVES

was present for these conversations. In fact, Wiik "is the one who insisted on it," Berard said. "That, I think, is really the soul of how the Birkie got started." Wise agreed with Wiik's reasoning. "We were getting into the cross-country business and needed a promotional event that could tell the world we were committed and going to go first-class."[20]

Wiik's assertion concurred with what local resident Carl Hanson had been telling Wise for many years. Hanson, originally from Mora, Sweden, had emigrated to the US in the early 1920s. He was an avid fan of Sweden's popular Vasaloppet, a 90-kilometer cross-country ski race that had begun in 1922 with 119 skiers and now attracted thousands. Each year, Hanson reported the Vasaloppet results to Wise—along with his belief that such a race could be held in Hayward, too.[21]

The Norwegian theme for the race was a late development. Norwegian Ola Stormoen, Telemark's original alpine ski instructor (after whom Wise had named an alpine run), had returned for Telemark's twenty-fifth anniversary and talked with Wise about the highly successful Norwegian Birkebeinerrennet, where skiers raced from the village of Rena to the city of Lillehammer to commemorate Prince Haakon's rescue in 1206. Stormoen sent Wise a book on the race. As luck would have it, Wise realized, the distance between Rena and Lillehammer was about the same as the distance between Hayward and Cable. Wise also noticed the book contained an image of the famous Norwegian painting he'd seen before, of the Birkebeiner warriors skiing Norway's baby Prince Haakon to safety (the word *Birkebeiner* refers to the warriors' birch bark leggings). Twenty-five years earlier Wise had sketched one of the warriors to use as his Telemark alpine logo. Now, he finally understood the history behind the painting—it was about *cross-country* skiing.[22]

An early promotional sticker bearing Telemark's logo. AMERICAN BIRKEBEINER SKI FOUNDATION ARCHIVES

Wise's big idea was gelling. He had a general race route in mind—Hayward to Cable—and a theme that fit beautifully with his Norwegian-style Telemark Lodge and village: he would create an American version of the famous

Norwegian race. (However, unlike the planners of the much shorter—and short-lived—Birkebeiner held in Bemidji, Minnesota, Wise did not seek permission from Norway to use the Birkebeiner name; he said later that some officials in Norway initially were upset by his brashness.)[23]

Wise's plans dovetailed with the history of Hayward and Wisconsin. Norwegian immigrants had helped found the city and the surrounding Sawyer County, both established in 1883, when they arrived to work in the booming logging industry. (Hayward was named after lumber baron Anthony Judson Hayward, who founded the Big Mill sawmill, the eventual site of Wise's Lumberjack Bowl.) Many Scandinavians chose to emigrate at the time because of a depressed economy in northern Europe, particularly in Norway. By 1900, Wisconsin was home to 25 percent of the nation's Norwegian immigrants, and in Hayward, at least one Lutheran church offered services in Norwegian as late as the 1940s.[24] At Christmas, as Berard later recalled, "the whole town smelled like lutefisk. Hayward was very much a Norwegian town."[25]

The most important factor in the birth of the American Birkebeiner was the man who had put much of his life into commodifying northern Wisconsin snow. Wise had rooms to fill at his $6 million lodge. He no longer could depend on alpine skiers alone to fill them, with the sport's resort centers shifting West. Going big was the ticket—a ski marathon from one city to another, an adventure honoring the Norwegian legend, something in the spirit of the intrepid explorers, fur traders, and lumberjacks of the North Woods and the big thinkers of the 1920s. Wiik was 100 percent behind him. "With all the enthusiasm Tony had," Wiik said, "there was no limit to what could be done."[26]

And so, the Telemark Birkebeiner, renamed the American Birkebeiner in 1974, was born. It would become Tony Wise's greatest legacy and have a lasting impact on his beloved hometown and region. At first, "many people thought it was another crazy idea of Tony's," said executive assistant Jeanette Vortanz. Wise's daughter Janie, a young teenager at the time, didn't think this new idea was anything monumental or out of the ordinary, at least not in their household. "Everything my dad did was big," Janie said, "so this wasn't anything new. He was doing another event. He was all about putting his hometown on the map."[27]

Wise saw himself as a latter-day Earl "Curly" Lambeau, who helped found the Green Bay Packers in 1919 and, in 1921, the year Wise was born, landed an American Professional Football Association franchise. Thanks to Lambeau, little Green Bay went big. "You had to use the Green Bay technique," Wise said, "if you were going to be from a small town and do a big thing. That was always my philosophy."[28]

At the time, going big was the only thing that set the American Birkebeiner apart from other races that had emerged. Was the American Birkebeiner the first ski marathon—at least 42 kilometers, or 26.2 miles—in the United States? In the modern age of the sport, post-1960, it appears to be. While other events as long or longer may have happened sporadically, records suggest the Birkebeiner was the first ski marathon in the country held as an open race (without entrants needing to qualify) and as a sustained, annual event. One race that preceded the Birkebeiner was the Rabbit Ears near Steamboat Springs, Colorado, which began in 1972 at 32 kilometers and was 37 kilometers in 1973 (Wiik was a cofounder of the Rabbit Ears at the time he was encouraging Wise to start his own race). Also held in 1973 were the 30-kilometer Boulder Mountain Tour in Ketchum, Idaho, and the 20-kilometer Frisco Gold Rush in Frisco, Colorado. However, pre-1960, a 68-kilometer race from Fort Klamath to Crater Lake—almost a marathon and a half—was held in Oregon from 1927 to 1938, and the 42-kilometer Donner Trail Memorial Ski Marathon existed from the late 1940s to the early 1950s from Donner Summit to Emigrant Gap Lodge near Truckee, California.[29]

The Birkebeiner itself proclaimed in 1977 to be the longest ski race in the US since its inception, and others agreed. "There was nothing else of that mass scale or scope [at the time]," said famed skier Bill Koch, whose performance in the 1976 Olympics would help further popularize the sport. Olympic coach Marty Hall called the Birkebeiner "the grandaddy of ski marathons in the US." In addition to likely being the first ski marathon in the nation, the Birkebeiner was one of the first—if not *the* first—Nordic ski race of any length in Wisconsin that became an annual event. As John Kotar, one of the Birkebeiner's founding skiers, explained, "The first year we were so excited about it because there were no such races around."[30]

THE TELEMARK BIRKEBEINER was scheduled for Saturday, February 24, 1973—which would prove to be a watershed year for Nordic skiing in the Upper Midwest. In the span of a month, two other major events were being planned. The first, from January 28 to February 4, was the US Ski Association (USSA) National Nordic championships, cross-country and Nordic combined, held at

Hyland Lake Park Reserve trails in Bloomington, Minnesota. Promising young skiers Bill Koch, Tim Caldwell, and Martha Rockwell were among those who competed. The inaugural Mora Vasaloppet, in Mora, Minnesota, was being planned for Sunday, February 25—the day after the Telemark Birkebeiner—and would draw ninety-six skiers. Mora wasn't a marathon that year, at 30 kilometers, but eventually would become one with a 58-kilometer option.

Birkebeiner officials were aware of the Mora race, just one hundred miles west, being held the same weekend. In fact, Wise employee Bob Treland gave Mora officials permission to cross a small section of land he owned there. The two races dickered over the timing of their events, though ultimately neither one agreed to switch weekends.[31]

Once Telemark Lodge was up and running in early 1973, Wise switched gears and ordered several staff to plan the race—including a shorter event for women and juniors—within roughly a month. The expedited timeline was typical Tony Wise. According to Jim Bauer, who worked at Telemark from 1953 to 1979, Wise often said, "The difficult, we do today. The impossible may take a couple of days." Treland recalls telling Wise at the time, "We'll run the race. You make it famous."[32]

In keeping with his top-down, military-style management, Wise had little to no direct involvement in organizing the race logistics. Treland was tapped to be the first race director, with other Telemark employees lending a hand, such as publicity director Fred Morgan, a former downhill ski instructor there. Treland, who was manager at Historyland in the summer and worked at Telemark in the winter, first needed to figure out how skiers would get from the starting line in Hayward to the finish line at the lodge, which was no small task given that there were no ski trails in the region other than the new ones at Telemark. Figuring out such a route may have been impossible in a metropolitan area, but in remote Sawyer and Bayfield Counties it was within reason given the few paved roads that split the forest lands.

Treland turned to his brother-in-law, Ward Williamson, who at age twenty was one of Hayward's first residents to own a snowmobile and had been up to Cable many times on his sled on the forest fire lanes. (Williamson's dad and Tony Wise had been in the National Guard together, and Ward Williamson had done some work at Telemark.) Over about a week, Williamson and Treland, on two snowmobiles, mapped a race route; the shorter race was set to cover the second half of the full route.[33]

Telemark Lodge, near the height of its popularity in the late 1970s. AMERICAN BIRKEBEINER SKI FOUNDATION PAPERS. NORWEGIAN AMERICAN HISTORICAL ASSOCIATION, NORTHFIELD, MINNESOTA

"We ran up there and looked over topographical maps and tried to connect all these dots," Williamson said. "It all pretty much fell into place." The trail they devised started at the Lumberjack Bowl just east of downtown, crossed Lake Hayward, and then followed a funky linkage of railroad bed ditches, fire lanes, and logging roads, which were used by snowmobilers in the days before designated snowmobile trails. Each time the trail transitioned from one road to another, Williamson and Treland tied red and blue crepe paper to trees as blazes to guide the skiers. Wiik reviewed the course on a snowmobile but generally had little to do with plotting the initial trail; in hindsight, organizers and skiers alike agreed the cobbled-together course got the job done but was far less than ideal.[34]

Fred Morgan's efforts to spread the word included sending information to ski shops around the region and a news release to media. A handwritten poster advertised the "Telemark Birkebeiner X-C 45K Men's Race, Hayward to

Telemark Lodge," for ages twenty and older, and promised "Trophies, Party, Challenge, Fun." Also, there would be a shorter 20K race for women and juniors, from Seeley to Telemark. Entry fees for the long race were $7 in advance and $9 the day of the race, and $5 for the short race. In addition, the poster advertised the First Telemark Invitational for USSA cross-country racers and juniors on Sunday, February 25—however, the poster did not include the date of the Birkebeiner itself, February 24, likely an accidental oversight given how quickly the race was put together.

How did the Birkebeiner end up being held the last Saturday in February—a slot it has maintained throughout its history? Berard said the weekend was chosen because it came after the Presidents' Day holiday weekend, traditionally the third weekend of February (it was observed Monday, February 19, in 1973). After that holiday, the alpine skiing crowd always declined at Telemark, providing an opening for staff to stage the Birkebeiner. Wise and his team decided to start the race at the Lumberjack Bowl because it offered seating for spectators and the nearby Lumberjack Bowl Pancake House—a wood-plank cabin Wise purchased and moved from tribal land in the town of New Post in about 1957—was available for registration. Telemark, at the finish line, made a great place for an awards ceremony and for skiers to unwind.[35]

Entries did not pour in. Oddly, two of the ski newspapers at the time, *Ski Week* and *Central Skiland*, promoted Sunday's invitational but didn't mention the Birkebeiner. Neither did ski writers from around the region who attended and reported on the Telemark Lodge grand opening. Wise resorted to calling friends to cajole them into skiing the race.

By the morning of the race, only thirty-five skiers had signed up for the long event, along with nineteen for the women's and juniors' event and just forty for the invitational the next day. Wise was disappointed but, with characteristic bravado, didn't let on.[36] Realistically, how could he or anyone else expect that first Birkebeiner to be a hit? Cross-country skiing was a new religion in a region of ice fishing, snowmobiling, and downhill skiing. Wise had work to do.

BEFORE DAWN ON FEBRUARY 24, Ward Williamson mounted his Ski-Doo snowmobile and headed out of the Lumberjack Bowl. This was track setting at its most basic: Ward used a water-ski tow rope to pull his cousin Robin Williamson, age twenty-one (whose friend Ernie St. Germaine was in the race) and

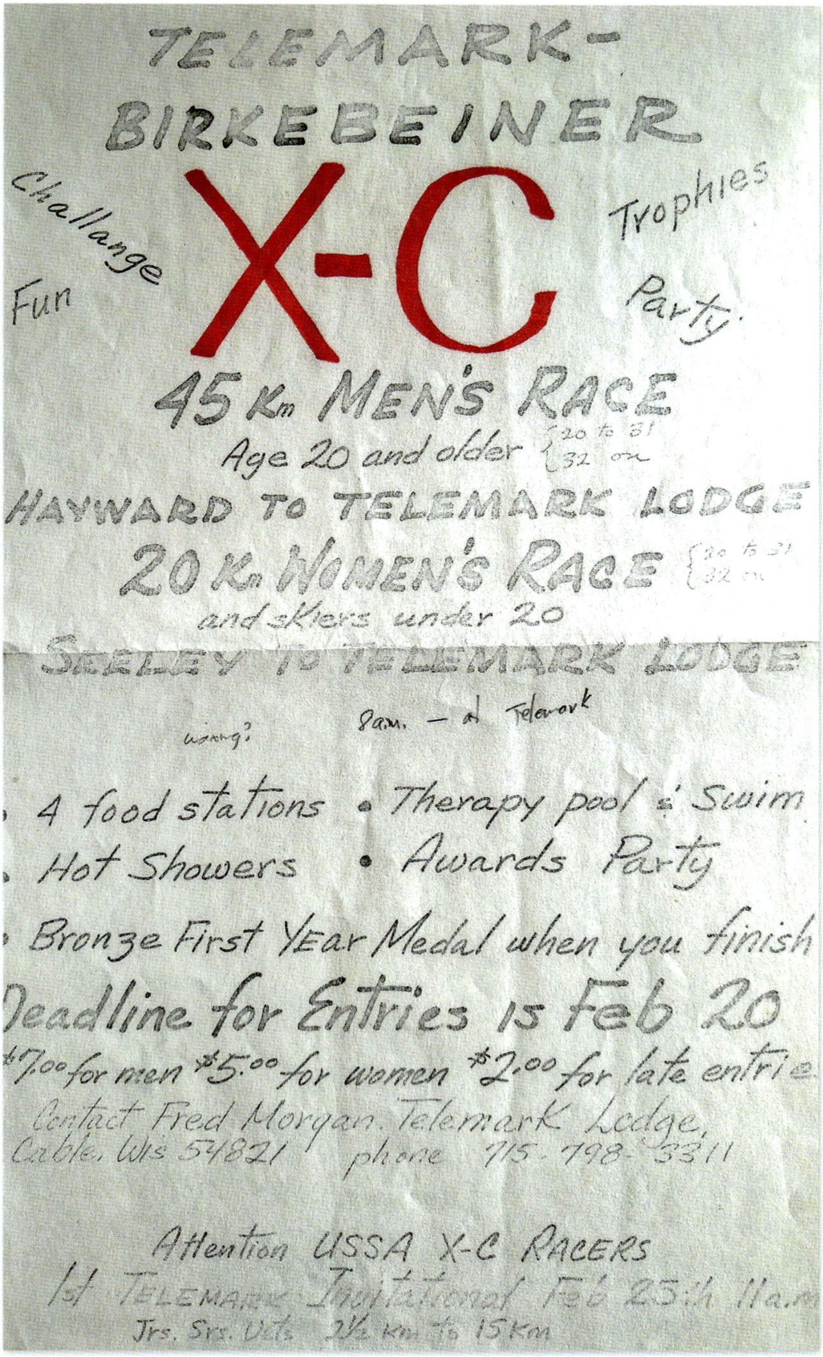

Handwritten poster announcing the 1973 Birkebeiner. COURTESY OF DUNCAN MCLEAN

her fifteen-year-old friend, Steve Maznio, a student at Drummond High School whose family owned the popular Metro's Ski Inn near Telemark. Both Robin and Steve had worked at Telemark as ski instructors. "Tony was looking for a couple of suckers to freeze their asses off for thirty miles," Maznio recalled with a laugh, adding that they volunteered for the job—without pay.[37]

Robin and Steve wore alpine boots and skis. Side by side they went, all the way to Telemark for more than four hours behind Ward, their body weight pressing two sets of parallel tracks into the snow, one ostensibly for passing. "There was a track, but it wasn't very good," Treland admitted. "We were a very crude operation. We didn't know a lot about this." They weren't the only ones. Trail grooming mostly didn't exist at that time, except for in high-level races—and even then, the tracks were set by forerunners after teams of workers had broken through the snowpack. Mechanical grooming began to appear in some places by the mid-1960s, with homemade, boxlike devices pulled by snowmobiles to press in one set of tracks.[38]

As dawn broke, the pace picked up at the Lumberjack Bowl. The temperature hovered around ten degrees Fahrenheit, with an expected high of twenty-two. Light snow had fallen, adding to the base of seventeen inches. Treland and his small team set up race headquarters at the pancake house; a "Start" banner was dragged across the pond and strung up; coffee and donuts were prepped to hand out; a school bus transported skiers from Telemark Lodge to the start; and family, friends, and other spectators began to arrive.

Most skiers registered that morning. Then it was time for final preparations. Some skiers waxed with klister, pine tar, and hard waxes with the hope that their kick would hold up for the long haul, but many were novices and took any advice they could get from the skiers who looked more knowledgeable.

One of those more knowledgeable skiers almost missed the race. Thirty-three-year-old John Kotar drove down from Duluth to Telemark Lodge that morning, thinking the race started there. The bus had already left, so Kotar asked for directions at the front desk, quickly drove to Hayward, and found the start area with twenty minutes to spare. He paid, waxed, and jumped in line.

As a teenager, Kotar had emigrated with his family from Yugoslavia to Milwaukee. He had skied downhill and backcountry in the mountains of Yugoslavia and was disappointed to find the relatively flat land of Wisconsin. As an adult, he settled in Duluth and regularly skied the 10-kilometer trail north of town made by friend and local legend Charlie Banks. But he had never skied anything

The 1973 starting line consisted of thirty-five skiers, thirty-four of whom made it to Telemark.
AMERICAN BIRKEBEINER SKI FOUNDATION ARCHIVES

as long as the Birkebeiner. "Most of us really had no idea what to expect in a 50-kilometer race," Kotar said.[39]

Finally, with the temperature up to fifteen degrees, it was time. A crowd of maybe one hundred people stood in a line outside the pancake house; except for a photographer, no one was in the Lumberjack Bowl stands on the other side of the pond. Treland used a megaphone to give some final instructions at the start line. Then, at 9 a.m., Carl Hanson pulled the string on a twelve-inch race cannon on loan from Minneapolis skier Rufus Jefferson, and the first wave of American Birkebeiner history was underway.[40]

The thirty-five skiers wore an assortment of clothing and gear—knee-length wool knickers, jeans, ski suits, sweaters, coats, flannel shirts, fanny packs stuffed with extra wax and snacks, and, in at least one case, a large back-pack—as they headed out onto the white lake shrouded in gray. They glided toward the black, bare woods and the warmth of the big lodge many miles distant. Jim Bauer was skeptical of the event's future as he watched the skiers disappear. "I don't know if this race will ever go," he thought to himself.[41]

For almost every skier, the race was a trek into the unknown—the course, the race length, and to some degree the sport itself were new. The race was billed as 45 kilometers, but the course that race officials eventually settled on was 48, and a snowmobile odometer measured it at 50. Most of it was hilly and thickly wooded. After Lake Hayward, the course crossed Wheeler Road, went down old Airport Road west of the airport landing strips to the new Airport Road, then up a private road and along a railroad right-of-way to Phipps Tavern, making up about the first 12 kilometers. Then it followed Phipps Fire Lane (east of and generally parallel to the modern race trail) to Highway OO, roughly the halfway point. From there, it snaked down a fire lane called Seeley Fire Tower Road. Closer to Telemark, the course wound along a series of roads—Randysek, McNaught, Telemark, Nordmor, Christiana—until it reached the top of a hill. There, skiers would be able to see the big lodge below, which must have looked like a mirage after hours of seeing almost nothing but trees.[42]

The first Birkebeiner set the tone for the many Birkebeiners to follow—the main event was, in effect, two races: one of speed for the skilled competitors, and one of endurance and personal challenge for pretty much everyone else. In 1973, the tested skiers were few, and they separated quickly from the field. Chief among them was thirty-five-year-old Erik Samuel Ersson. Ersson was born in Högland, Sweden; his parents were farmers and his dad also worked as a logger. In the village of Åsele, Sweden, Ersson had worked as a ski instructor and competed in races, including Sweden's 90-kilometer Vasaloppet in 1966. When Telemark was looking for a director for its fledgling Nordic center, the Swedish ski association recommended Ersson for the job. En route to Telemark a few months before the Birkebeiner, Ersson spent two weeks in Steamboat Springs, Colorado, learning more instruction techniques from fellow Swede Sven Wiik. Then, in late November 1972, Ersson arrived in Cable. He went by his middle name, Sam, but Wise preferred to call him by his first name, Erik, because he thought it sounded more Scandinavian.[43]

Ersson was impressed with Telemark and its alpine operation, but the Nordic shop lacked both skis to rent and customers to rent them. He spent many of his first days on the job skiing, prompting the alpiners to ask what the heck he was doing. He soon ordered more skis and a trail-grooming sled and began helping Treland and others with race planning. Ersson also provided advice on the Swedish-inspired blueberry soup that would be served at the race's food stops.[44]

Soon after the start cannon went off, Ersson was skiing by himself after quickly pulling ahead of his only real competition, Wiik, while still on the lake. Ersson was such a talented skier that Wiik believed he would have won even if other experienced competitors had shown up.[45]

When Ersson crossed the finish line—at the end of a chute made of plastic fencing near the alpine chalet—he was cheered by the handful of people who had gathered there, including some of his new friends and lodge coworkers like Treland, Morgan, and Jeanette Vortanz. His time was 2:48 (two hours, forty-eight minutes)—twenty-seven minutes ahead of Wiik, the runner-up. It's possible Ersson could have finished even faster but "held back so that he wouldn't blow out the competition totally," said his daughter, Lovisa Ersson. "He has never been a person that wanted to be superior to others. He was a humble man." Two more skiers—Kenyon King, of St. Paul, who outdueled Nils Meland, of Oshkosh, Wisconsin—were another eighteen minutes back. Frances Wise placed a laurel wreath around Ersson's neck after he crossed the finish line, the start of a race tradition. The Birkebeiner in the New World had its first champion, a skier from the Old World.[46]

Carl Hanson (left), Fred Morgan (center), and Erik Ersson, during race preparations at the Lumberjack Bowl, where the 1973 Birkebeiner began. AMERICAN BIRKEBEINER SKI FOUNDATION ARCHIVES

Food and aid stations were placed along the course at roughly 15, 30, and 45 kilometers. Telemark bartender Bob McClelland oversaw the provisions, while Sawyer County Sheriff Don Primley led the emergency medical technician crews. The menu included pastries, oranges, and the blueberry soup made by Telemark chef Bill Hotze. The soup was Carl Hanson's idea; he had grown up with it in Sweden, where it was traditionally served at the Vasaloppet.[47]

Was there water at the food stops? Treland doesn't recall that there was; instead, planners assumed the blueberry soup would be the main source of hydration. However, the soup was quite thick and sweet, and skiers had to resort to eating snow to help wash it down. Rumor had it that some food stops ran out of soup. "We certainly didn't know what to make of this 'blueberry soup' idea that was so hyped up among the racers," said Kotar. "We truly believed that the blueberry soup had to contain some magic substance that made it possible for ordinary humans to ski such unbelievable distances."[48]

With just three food stops—for comparison, the modern race has seven—skiers quickly became dehydrated and hungry. When Kotar caught up to Wayne Lindskoog, a skier from Edina, Minnesota, the two men sat down and shared some Mars candy bars that Lindskoog had packed. When they reached the third stop, Kotar stuffed down several donuts and pastries—but then he heard music and realized they were a short distance from the finish line.

Kotar was using wooden Landsem cross-country skis he bought at the Continental ski shop in Duluth. He hadn't bought new bindings or boots, though, instead sticking with his cable mountaineering bindings that held his "massive" mountaineering boots; he unclipped the heel so it could lift and give him kick. ("I couldn't for the life of me see myself skiing in those small cross-country boots," he said.) He also wore mountaineering clothing: a heavy, wool sweater and corduroy knee-length pants with reinforced knees. The gear had served him well when he climbed Rainier, St. Helen's, Shasta, Olympia, Hood, and other major peaks of the Northwest in the early 1970s while attending graduate school in Seattle.

Kotar had heard about the race through his Duluth ski network and entered because he was an experienced skier and had run marathons. "It was a very good, crazy challenge, something only Olympians can do, and it measured up to be," Kotar said. "What the hell do I have to lose? I was doing that sort of thing all the time."

The race felt like a solitary challenge from the start, the furthest thing from the Birkebeiners that were to come. "I remember seeing Sven Wiik taking off and skiing right behind him," Kotar said. "I followed him for a bit and then he was gone. After the lake, it was just me. That was the funniest thing; in front or behind you couldn't see anyone."[49] Complicating matters was the fact that the course would abruptly change directions, and many skiers, with their eyes on the fickle tracks or lack thereof, missed the ribbon blazes and got lost. It happened twice to Kotar. Once, he saw skiers coming toward him and realized they also were lost and were coming back, so he turned around and followed them. "I was never sure I was in the right place," he said. "We pretty much skied hoping we were on the right track and not hopelessly lost. None of us knew how you ski 50K. The thrill of the victory was just to get there." Kotar hit the finish line in 4:53 and Lindskoog a minute behind.[50]

Finishing in 5:21 was Tom "the Polish Prince" Polaski of Bayfield, Wisconsin. A regular downhill skier at Telemark, Polaski had tried the Nordic trails the day before the race using alpine skis, but realized they wouldn't work. The race was his first time on cross-country skis, which was true or nearly true for many other entrants. After finishing, Polaski went to the Rathskellar to refresh, did some downhill skiing, had dinner and danced at nearby Metro's, and went to bed early.[51]

Ernie St. Germaine entered the race as a favor to Lyman Williamson, the father of his friend, Robin, who was on her way to Telemark as a pull-behind track setter. Lyman Williamson had wanted to enter, but his wife, Edna, thought at age fifty-seven he was too old. St. Germaine was intrigued when Williamson said alpine was only "half-skiing." St. Germaine had been a baseball player and had downhill skied at Telemark, but, like Polaski, he had never been on cross-country skis. A week or so before the race, he got a quick lesson in Lyman Williamson's 150-yard-long driveway, and then took his skis out to a snowmobile trail for another half hour of training. "Heck," he thought, "this will be easy."

The morning of the race, St. Germaine was set to go. But he'd neglected to confirm one detail: the length of the race itself. As skiers lined up on the pond and the countdown began, he heard Williamson yell, "See you at Telemark!" St. Germaine couldn't believe it—he had no idea they were going to be skiing that far. He had expected to do a lap or two around the lake and return. He felt exhausted by the time they crossed the lake, and his jeans already were getting sweaty.[52]

St. Germaine had challenged his childhood friend Dave "Davey Boy" Landgraf to enter, too. They'd grown up together in the Northwoods Beach area east of Hayward, playing baseball and running from their homes through the woods to a designated meeting spot to see who could get there first. Landgraf's parents owned a cranberry marsh. Now living in Minneapolis, Landgraf was working on a master's degree in physical education and was about to begin his career as a phys ed teacher. Landgraf, in turn, challenged his roommate, Jim Backus. Landgraf and Backus trained on rental skis in the parking lot of the old Metropolitan Stadium in Bloomington, Minnesota, the only place they could find snow. They climbed a few snowplow hills and figured they had the hang of it. A vehicle pulled up alongside them and the driver asked what in the world they were doing. It was Harry "Bud" Grant, head coach of the Minnesota Vikings and a native of Superior, Wisconsin.

On the course, Landgraf didn't see either of his friends or anyone else much, but he did see a convoy of snowmobiles and had to "dive into the brush to avoid being run over." Landgraf believed he was lost more than once. A few hours into the race, he was out of energy and crawling up the hills on his hands and knees, when at last he heard the sound of chairlifts at Telemark. He began to close in on another skier—it was St. Germaine, also crawling up a hill.[53]

St. Germaine and Landgraf collided at the bottom of a hill that required a turn. Tangled up, they soon heard a loud voice imploring them in a thick Norwegian accent to "get the hell out of the vay." Landgraf instantly recognized the speaker as Karl Andresen, Landgraf's former political science professor at the University of Wisconsin–Eau Claire. St. Germaine recalled how "Karl skied down easily, laid a neat parallel turn, and went on. Nordic skiing was already his way of life. We got up and followed. And of course, as we flew down to the finish line in front of the chalet, we crashed again because that was the only way we knew how to stop."[54]

Lyman Williamson was at the finish line, waiting to hug his weary protégé, St. Germaine, and find his track-setting daughter, Robin. "Now, my boy," he told St. Germaine, "you're truly a Birkebeiner." St. Germaine and Landgraf headed for the chalet and tried to recover. "It was the most miserable athletic event I'd ever been involved in," Landgraf said. "I made a vow right then that I would never be talked into any other kind of ridiculous escapade by Ernie

Dave Landgraf, pictured here during the 1975 race, struggled to finish the first race along with his good friend, Ernie St. Germaine. AMERICAN BIRKEBEINER SKI FOUNDATION ARCHIVES

St. Germaine." St. Germaine wasn't much better off. "We finished," he said, "but I couldn't walk for three days."[55]

At age forty-nine, Karl Andresen was one of the oldest entrants. He had never skied that far either, but when the five-foot-seven, 125-pound dynamo heard about the race, he didn't think twice. Skiing was in his blood, as were soccer, ski jumping, and ice skating. A native of Oslo, Norway, Andresen was raised by his single mother, Nanna Helgesen, until he was five years old, when she contracted tuberculosis and he was sent to an orphanage thirty miles away in Drammen, Norway. He witnessed the Germans invade his homeland in April 1940, when he was sixteen. Schoolchildren were let out early to harvest potatoes for the Germans, but the rebellious ones like Andresen would stomp them into the mud instead.

Andresen finished the Birkebeiner in 4:12, after skiing alone for long stretches of the race. "I had no idea if I was on the right track or on my way to Canada," he said—until he caught up to and passed the two skiers near the finish line who were less than half his age. Out on the second half of the trail that day were two of Andresen's sons, William, twelve, and Robert, two days shy of fourteen, who took fourth and fifth, respectively, in the junior race.[56]

Dave Landgraf's roommate, Jim Backus, had no better experience than his friend. He broke a pole along the way and replaced it with a tree branch. Throughout the race, which Backus called "surreal," he experienced myriad emotions "ranging from loneliness to euphoria." Coming down a Telemark downhill run to the finish, Backus also literally crashed across the finish line, in just under five hours. After some celebrating, he spent the night on a couch in the lobby of the lodge.[57]

Rick Scott, who had helped provide Wise with information about the growing popularity of the sport, heard about the race through a ski shop and signed up on a whim. Partway through the race, Scott realized his kick wax was giving out, possibly because snowmobilers destroyed some of the track and exposed gravel under the snow. "I was very happy about finishing," Scott said later. "The last part of the way, all I could think of was, 'When is this race going to end?' "

Forty-five-year-old John Holmquist, a runner and member of the North Star Ski Touring Club in the Twin Cities, also couldn't wait for it to end. After about four and a half hours into the race, Holmquist crested the last hill on the trail and saw Telemark Lodge below. "It took me a prodigiously long time to recognize it for what it was: my destination," he said. "I always relish the thought of that view."[58]

That afternoon, Holmquist and other skiers soaked in the Telemark Lodge hot tub and heated outdoor pool, and then gathered around the huge fireplace in the lobby at 4 p.m. for an awards ceremony and fondue party, where Tony Wise addressed the crowd. Holmquist's first impression of Wise was a man with a round face, a short neck on wide shoulders, and a superabundance of energy. Wise spoke of "his vision of the future for cross-country skiing in America and said Telemark would be part of it," Holmquist recalled.

> He spoke in bursts, running words together, forcing his mouth to keep up with the ideas tumbling through his brain. Tony congratulated us for finding the stamina and determination to finish. Maybe the entry fee was pricey, but we'd been treated well, had finished in a crowd of people with our names blared out for all to hear, had been given a

> ribbon and medallion, like you might see on a four-star sommelier, along with a shower and hot tub, free beer and relaxation in a plush resort atmosphere. Weary and content now, I gave no thought to next year and another Birkebeiner.[59]

Holmquist, who was a geological engineer, went on to ski twenty-three Birkebeiners.

THE FIRST BIRKEBEINER was filled with surprises, and one of the biggest was that it was skied by a woman, Jacque Lindskoog. Technically, women were restricted to the short race, in accordance with the prevailing attitude that women were incapable of going longer distances. It was a bias that extended across different sports and events. For example, women were banned from officially competing in the Boston Marathon until 1972 (although they had competed unofficially as race "bandits" since 1966, drawing scorn and attempts to physically remove them). The world's longest-running ski marathon, the Vasaloppet in Mora, Sweden, didn't allow women from 1924 to 1980. And the Norwegian Birkebeinerrennet, dating to 1932, didn't allow women until 1976.

Jacque Lindskoog and her husband, Wayne, lived with their three young sons in Edina, Minnesota. Both in their early thirties, Jacque and Wayne had experience in long-distance biking and were members of the Twin Cities' North Star Ski Touring Club. Jacque had seen a film about the 90-kilometer Swedish Vasaloppet and was intrigued. So, when she and Wayne learned of the Birkebeiner, they both decided to enter.

"I just signed up and didn't even pay attention to women not doing it or the classification," Jacque said. "I didn't do it as a statement of women's lib or to crash it. I just wanted to ski a long distance. The Birkebeiner was a culmination of a lot of things Wayne and I had been doing." At the time, "women weren't doing long-distance athletic events," though she noted it wasn't for lack of skill: "There were a lot of really good [female] skiers" in the short race who "hadn't even thought of doing the long one but probably would have been just fine."

Some people later assumed race officials had misinterpreted Jacque Lindskoog's first name as the French spelling of a man's name. In truth, Bob Treland and Jeanette Vortanz said they knew Jacque was a woman when she came to register; they discussed the issue with her and then privately with Tony

Wise. At first, "Tony said no," Vortanz recalled, "but she was very determined and was going to race." After persisting, Jacque finally was told she could enter the long race but wouldn't get credit for completing it. Race records confirm the dispute. Jacque at first was on the women's race start list, but her 10 a.m. start time was crossed out and replaced with 9 a.m., the start of the long race. And in a handwritten start sheet of long race entrants, "Female" was written above Jacque Lindskoog's birthdate.[60]

Both Jacque and Wayne Lindskoog had done plenty of skiing but nothing as long as the Birkebeiner. The first time they ever saw cross-country skiing was in the 1960s, when they were downhill skiing in Michigan's Porcupine Mountains and watched as someone disappeared into the woods on a pair of unfamiliar-looking skis.

Jacque Lindskoog pressed race officials to let her ski the full Birkebeiner in 1973, despite rules preventing women from entering the long race. AMERICAN BIRKEBEINER SKI FOUNDATION ARCHIVES

Jacque, a registered nurse, and Wayne, a technical college counselor, soon got separated on the Birkebeiner racecourse, but she didn't get lost like some skiers did. "We were all spread out," she said. "It was a very lonely event; I just trudged along. We didn't know about 'hitting the wall' back then and all those terms about exhaustion." Jacque described a finish line that was far more modest than the modern-day Birkebeiner experience: skiers "finished at Telemark in the midst of all the people going downhill and walking toward the chairlift. They didn't even know what was going on."[61]

Unofficially, Jacque Lindskoog became the Birkebeiner's first women's winner, completing the race in 4:33—twenty minutes ahead of her husband and ahead of one-third of the male finishers. She wasn't trying to prove a point, but for those who were paying attention, she made one. Jacque's name didn't appear on the initial printed list of finishers that was shared among skiers that afternoon and evening in the lodge, and she didn't make an issue of it. Her name was handwritten later that night into the finishers' list. She doesn't recall Tony Wise, when they saw each other after the race at Telemark, further bringing up the issue of her participation. She took a sauna, and she and Wayne enjoyed the party atmosphere.

By one measure, the "very determined" Jacque Lindskoog was fifty years ahead of her time. It wasn't until 2023 that the World Cup stopped limiting women to a maximum of 30 kilometers and finally allowed them to ski a 50-kilometer race like the men. That historic event occurred on March 12, 2023, at the Holmenkollen course in Oslo, Norway; taking a bronze medal that day was Olympic medalist and American Jessie Diggins, a Minnesota native like Lindskoog. Diggins had skied the half-marathon at the Birkebeiner as a teenager. Another Minnesota native, Alayna Sonnesyn, was thirtieth in Oslo. Two weeks earlier, Sonnesyn won the 50-kilometer 2023 Birkebeiner while traversing some of the same terrain as the Birkebeiner female pioneer Lindskoog.

Lindskoog wasn't the only barrier breaker in the first Birkebeiner, which also required skiers in the long race to be twenty years old. Kenyon King, the outdoors director at Minnesota's St. Paul Academy, didn't know that when he rounded up several students to take on the challenge with him. Seventeen-year-olds Peter Alden and Bruce Derauf and fifteen-year-old Bob Levin had done plenty of downhill and cross-country skiing (Derauf had skied downhill at Telemark with his parents) and played hockey. Plus, King had taken them rock climbing, whitewater rafting, and on a nine-day skiing and camping adventure in the Boundary Waters. Why not a marathon ski? Two other students, June Reuben and DeDe Strouse, signed up for the short race; together, the group did some training in the weeks before the race and were excited to compete.[62]

Upon arriving for the start, however, the three boys learned they were too young to enter the main event. King pleaded their case, assuring Wise that his protégés could go the distance. Wise didn't exactly have a big turnout, so he may have figured why not, and the boys were in. They did just fine—Alden and Derauf finished together in 3:58 and Levin in 4:45. King, meanwhile, took third overall and won the 20-to-31 age class. Afterwards, Derauf said, "We took a dip in the hot tub and drove home."

The women's and juniors' race began at 10 a.m. The bus dropped the skiers off near Seeley and Highway OO, where Treland helped get the second event of the day underway. The trail groomers had hoped to reach Highway OO before the start of the short race, but the race started before the groomers arrived. The nineteen skiers lined up on a narrow, plowed road and headed to Telemark without striding tracks.

The women's overall winner was Carol Duffy, of Hayward, who finished in 1:56, defeating fellow Hayward resident Marlene Tremblay by two minutes. Duffy had been learning to ski in a Telemark women's program led by Ersson. Thus, teacher and pupil claimed the first Birkebeiner titles. June Reuben and DeDe Strouse fared well, too, taking first and second in the under-20 division in 2:15 and 2:35, respectively.

The junior race had several very young skiers. Jaymie Holte was eight, three days from her ninth birthday, skiing with her brother Ryan, age eleven. Bob Constalie was ten. They had parents in the long race, including Fred Constalie, who skied the first twenty Birkebeiners. All were from Westby (Norwegian for "western city"), a Norwegian enclave about two hundred miles south of Hayward.

The junior and overall short race winner was eighteen-year-old Duncan McLean, of Ironwood, Michigan. Completing the race in 1:08, McLean was the first skier in race history to cross the finish line. He even beat the trail groomers to the tape, thus having to set his own track on the plowed surface all the way—except for the tracked Telemark Lodge trails near the end.

When McLean reached the finish chute, no one was waiting there to greet him or record his time—just a Westclox. After looking around and seeing only alpine skiers using the chairlifts, McLean took off his Kongsberg skis, went into the chalet, and shouted, "There are racers coming!" The announcement drew quizzical looks from the alpiners but rousted a race official with a clipboard, Telemark employee Jeanette Vortanz. She had been at the start registering skiers, drove to Telemark, and was looking for a table to set up at the finish line. Vortanz quickly went to the finish line with McLean.[63]

Sure enough, other finishers were beginning to arrive, along with trail groomers Ward Williamson, Robin Williamson, and Steve Maznio. "We were in pretty tough shape," recalled Maznio. "Our feet [were] like a couple of ice cubes by the time we hit Telemark—it was cold as hell."

Maznio's experience in setting the track, cold as it was, didn't sour him on the race. He eventually finished ten Birkebeiners, became an accomplished Nordic racer, and continued to ski into his sixties near his home in Glenwood Springs, Colorado. Even after his family's Metro's Ski Inn closed in 2008, he's kept up with the growth of the Birkebeiner and is proud to "have helped get the whole thing started."[64]

One of the other earliest 1973 finishers was McLean's friend and fellow cross-country runner Barry Bolich. Both were new to the sport, initially thinking cross-country in the snow was just winter running. "We were clueless," McLean said. McLean and Bolich began skiing on an outdoor track at their school in Ironwood and through Bolich's pasture. They skied a short race at the Upper Peninsula Winter Games earlier that year in Escanaba, Michigan, with McLean using wooden army-surplus skis clamped to his Hush Puppy shoes.

When they heard about Telemark's "tracked" trails, they assumed this meant skiing around a running track. They visited the resort in early February, and an enthusiastic Fred Morgan cajoled them into entering the big race coming up. "We were unquestionably coming back in two weeks to ski the Birkebeiner," McLean said. "Whatever that was." McLean's father drove them to Hayward that morning. By the end of the race, McLean was hooked: "There was something that had to occur in the minds of all the skiers on that first Birkebeiner day: We were going somewhere. We were really going *cross-country* and doing it under our own steam."[65]

The thirty-fourth and final skier to finish the long race was Charles Weydt, age thirty-four, a technical college counselor from Rice Lake, Wisconsin. Weydt arrived ten to fifteen minutes after the race had started, wearing long underwear under blue jeans, a ski sweater, a quilted winter jacket, leather gloves, and a wool stocking cap. Using hickory mountain skis that were six feet nine inches long, with cable bindings that "probably weighed between fifteen and twenty pounds apiece," Weydt had an epic adventure. He got lost on the trail early in the race and, by his estimate, had skied close to 60 kilometers by the time he reached Telemark in the dark around 6:30 p.m., after nine and a half hours. Officials didn't even know he was still on the course until someone notified them and they went back outside to wait for him. "I half expected no one to be there," Weydt said, "but Bob [Treland] gave me my award and something to eat."[66]

Weydt, like all the other finishers in each event, received a bronze medal with a laurel wreath edge. On the front it simply said "Telemark" and featured the lodge's red, white, and blue insignia of a single Birkebeiner skier holding a shield and one long pole. On the back was stamped "1st Annual Telemark Birkebeiner, 2-24-73."

All in all, the experiment was a success, although far from proof that Wise had another hit idea. "Skiers were excited about it and . . . tolerated, in my mind, the fact that we were not very good at running a long-distance, cross-

Finishers in 1973 received a bronze medal (left) with one Birkebeiner warrior on the front. After various design changes in 1974 and 1975, the permanent first-year finisher's medal (above) debuted in 1976, featuring two warriors fringed by a wreath. (After their first race, finishers receive colored pins reflecting the number of races they've completed.) BRONZE MEDAL COURTESY OF DUNCAN MCLEAN. CURRENT MEDALS COURTESY OF AMERICAN BIRKEBEINER SKI FOUNDATION ARCHIVES, PHOTO BY LENORA LUDZACK

country ski race," Treland said. According to Vortanz, the simple fact that the Birkebeiner happened, despite its flaws and no matter the small number of skiers, "made Tony happy." There was no going back: Wise told Vortanz, Treland, and other Telemark employees to put the Birkebeiner on their 1974 business planning calendars.[67]

What happened to the thirty-fifth skier, the lone strider who didn't finish? He was Terry Marshall, age twenty-three, of Chippewa Falls, Wisconsin. Marshall and some friends had been backcountry skiing that winter in the Chippewa County Forest, and he thought the Birkebeiner sounded like fun. In preparation, he bought his first pair of wool knickers but otherwise was "basically clueless about this thing I was going to get myself into." He described his fellow non-elite skiers that day as "hippies, lunatics, and people from Minnesota."

Marshall was enjoying the race, guessing he was in the middle of the pack, when around the 30- or 35-kilometer mark he came down a steep hill with a turn at the bottom. His stiff wooden skis didn't turn as he expected, and his six-foot-two-and-a-half, 175-pound frame slammed into an oak tree, head on. "I was knocked pretty goofy," he said. He hit the tree so hard, he would have "the impression of oak bark on my forehead for five or six days." Woozy and with a cracked ski, he brushed himself off and went on—until a race official saw him struggling, pulled him out, and transported him to Telemark. Marshall nursed his wounds with a few bottles of his hometown Leinenkugel's beer, packed up, and went home.

Marshall never came back to the Birkebeiner, and as he left Telemark he didn't expect anyone else would either. "It began as a local thing and ended that day as a local thing," Marshall said more than thirty years later. "I don't remember anybody saying, 'This is the start of something big.'"[68]

The 1974 start at the Lumberjack Bowl was one of the coldest in race history at 13 below zero.
AMERICAN BIRKEBEINER SKI FOUNDATION ARCHIVES

FOUR

1974–1979
THE BIRKEBEINER TAKES OFF

IF THE FIRST BIRKEBEINER hadn't been so small—little more than a curiosity to locals and to the ski world—then the second race might have been a letdown. Entries almost doubled, but that still resulted in just sixty-four skiers lining up at the Lumberjack Bowl and another thirty-four at Highway OO for the short race on February 23, 1974. How would this upstart race, albeit part of a trending sport, grow significantly in popularity and prestige, drawing top skiers from around the world, by the end of the decade?

Small as it was, the second race made an important statement to the doubters—the Birkebeiner officially was an annual event, not some one-and-done experiment (such as the 1938 St. Paul Winter Sports Carnival Arrowhead Derby, a 153-mile race from Duluth to St. Paul). Four of Wise's ideas—Telemark alpine, Telemark Lodge, Historyland, and the World Lumberjack Championships—already had taken off. Maybe this one would too, if given a chance.

Wise made a change in the 1974 race that was barely noticeable at the time but that foretold his vision. He changed the name from the Telemark Birkebeiner to the American Birkebeiner, even though a poster promoting the race called it by the former name. It was an audacious move for a race that was not yet sanctioned by the International Ski Federation (FIS), was scoffed at by some competitors because of its distance, and was anything but national in scope.[1]

The low turnout in 1974 could have been attributed at least in part to the weather. It was thirteen degrees below zero at the start (some skiers claimed it was as cold as nineteen below) and windy—similar to the conditions during the famous Ice Bowl on December 31, 1967, in Green Bay, the coldest championship game in NFL history. Skiers trekked from the Lumberjack Bowl toward the woods, exhaling clouds of breath along the stark white, lonely trail while trying to ward off frozen extremities. Even Karl Andresen, who liked to call one degree "a summer day in Norway," wrote in his race notes after suffering frostbite, "Cold that day."[2]

The 1973 track-setting duo of Robin Williamson and Steve Maznio did not return for the 1974 race. Ward Williamson again drove a snowmobile to set the track, but he doesn't recall who or what was behind him; race photos show a single set of tracks.

Two skiers who knew how to dress for the cold, and who definitely knew how to ski, were twins Dave and Don Quinn, natives of Cloquet, Minnesota, just south of Duluth. They layered up, Don with wool socks over his ski boots, and wore white tops and hats with dark pants—a pair of speedy penguins as they led the break. The simple fact that they were at the race must have encouraged Wise: the brothers—both national competitors—had chosen to bypass an FIS-sanctioned race that day in their hometown to compete in the Birkebeiner instead. Former Olympians George Hovland of Duluth and John Burton of Minneapolis, as well as Minnesota ski legend Charlie Banks, also were in the field that day. Quietly, the ski world was taking note.

The Quinns had been Minnesota high school cross-country standouts, Dave winning the 1966 state title and Don taking fifth. They also dominated US Ski Association Central region junior races, going one-two in each one, and making junior nationals three times. They received scholarships and skied under Sven Wiik at Western State College in Gunnison, Colorado, Dave taking eleventh in a national championship and Don sixteenth. "We always enjoyed training together," Don said. "That's what pushed us. Endurance sports are work ethic sports."[3]

After graduating in 1971, the Quinns continued competing while giving lessons and guiding tours at Wiik's touring center in Steamboat Springs. They also entered Wiik's new race, the 32-kilometer Rabbit Ears Cross-Country Sprint, in 1972. Dave won and Don took third place in a field of about fifty skiers.[4]

Don Quinn leads brother Dave in the snowmobile-set single track on the 1974 racecourse. Dave took the title that year, with Don runner-up. AMERICAN BIRKEBEINER SKI FOUNDATION ARCHIVES

In early February 1974, the Quinns were back in Cloquet. Dave had returned from Anchorage, Alaska, after missing a spot on the US team for the FIS World Championships to be held in Sweden, and Don returned from training and racing in the east. They were skiing at the local Pine Valley trails when they saw an ad for the second Birkebeiner and decided it would be a good challenge. They started training. The distance wasn't new to them: in 1973, Dave took fifth in the 50-kilometer US national race near Minneapolis.

With the cold start, the twins corked hard green wax—as the science of ski waxing is inextricably linked to temperature—over pine tar binder on their Norwegian-made Splitkein wood skis, which had synthetic bottoms and Lignostone protective edges. The Quinns were among the race favorites. Their former coach, employer, and mentor, Wiik, was back for his second Birkebeiner, but the twins expected their toughest competition would come from Lars Arnesson, a Swede who was the new Nordic director at Telemark and had been winning regional races that winter.

The Quinns, at age twenty-five, quickly separated themselves from Arnesson. They took turns in the lead for about 35 kilometers, until Dave pulled away in the single track. Don lost sight of him and fell even farther behind when a group of mischievous snowmobilers—the race again was on snowmobile routes—removed the trail blazes at a corner, covered the tracks, and told Don to go the wrong direction. "They were kind of laughing," Don recalled. He realized the ruse about a half mile later, doubled back, and knew the race was lost to his brother. He still hoped to beat Arnesson, however.[5]

Dave finished in 2:59; Don in 3:08; and Arnesson in 3:10. Dave became the first American to win the American Birkebeiner. He received a laurel wreath, which he proudly wore while standing in the sun outside the Telemark chalet, and the Haakon Haakonsson Award, a carved wooden Birkebeiner warrior. The brothers returned to Colorado, where in early May at Wiik's Rabbit Ears race, Dave took second and Don third in the lengthened 42-kilometer event.[6]

Though Wiik had taken second in 1973, he fell to fifteenth place in 1974, finishing in 4:06, but apparently he had good reason. Traveling from Chicago, Wiik arrived late for the start and didn't have time to wax his skis. He began to catch up to some skiers, however, soon after crossing the lake. One of them was John Gannett, of Minong, Wisconsin, also in his second race. Gannett couldn't understand why the chatty Wiik was asking where the leaders were. "I saw what looked to me like a short, paunchy, middle-aged fellow who would probably have trouble finishing," Gannett said later. "When he hurried past, I was convinced he would burn himself out and I would see him on one of those canvas stretchers alongside the trail."[7]

Jacque Lindskoog once again was the only woman in the field in 1974, against regulations but this time without any pushback. She was acknowledged in the results, but because there was no women's division in the long race, she was listed in the men's 20-to-34 age class. "She refuses to compete in the women's class [short race] because she feels men and women should compete equally," Wise told a newspaper at the time. "Jacqueline's an example of what we're trying to do with the Birkebeiner." She finished in 4:53, right in the middle of the field.[8]

Jacque and her husband, Wayne, ended up doing thirty-nine and twenty-seven Birkebeiners, respectively. Jacque skied twenty-four of the first twenty-five Birkebeiners (missing one because of an injury) and about a dozen more after Wayne died in 2002. "It just got to be part of your life," Jacque said.[9]

After the first Birkebeiner, Wise must have figured that Ernie St. Germaine had proven himself. From 1974 to 1979, St. Germaine worked as a weekend cross-country instructor at Telemark. He wasn't planning to ski the race in 1974 because of his less-than-encouraging experience in 1973, until Wise mentioned that he wanted Ernie to be part of his race ski patrol. So Ernie trained, but there was no ski patrol and he realized it was Tony's way of making sure he entered. Ernie's buddy Dave Landgraf also returned despite vowing not to the year before. Landgraf didn't have much fun in 1974 either—his sweat quickly froze in the sweatpants he was wearing and made for another miserable experience.

In the 20-kilometer race, Duncan McLean repeated as champion, shaving almost two minutes off his time for a finish of 1:06. Tony and Sheila Wise's daughter, Frances, who had downhill-racing experience at Telemark, won the women's title in the short race in 1:35, edging repeat runner-up Marelene Tremblay of Hayward by fifteen seconds. Frances was greeted by her proud but disbelieving parents, who didn't realize she had that kind of skill in a sport that was new to her.

McLean, of Michigan, would become a Birkebeiner fixture. He would be named the citizen champion in 1976 (ninth overall) and top elite American in 1980 (tenth overall), would become a Telemark Academy skier and instructor, and would finish more than forty Birkebeiners. The event and sport would become a major part of his life during his career as a physical therapist and collegiate coach. "In the Midwest," McLean said, "it almost didn't matter how well you did [in ski races] anywhere else; it was how well you did in the Birkie."[10]

IF PROOF WAS NEEDED that the Birkebeiner truly was going to succeed, it arrived in 1975 with the entrance of 324 skiers (220 in the long race and 104 in the short), more than triple the 1974 field. Critical mass was building. Once again, the race featured top talent thanks to Wise. He asked US Ski Team Nordic director Jim Balfanz to send some skiers to the race. Balfanz came for a visit and agreed, entering A Team members Chris Haines and Larry Martin. Wise also contacted the Norwegian Birkebeinerrennet and proposed that it send their champion skier from 1974, and Wise would send the top American and top citizen racer to the next Norwegian race in return. The Norwegians agreed, opening the door to further cooperation. The Birkebeiner no longer was just a Wisconsin or American event—it was international. Wise, pushing ahead as usual, called these developments the race's first big breakthroughs.[11]

The 1975 racecourse brought a few changes. Like 1974, it had one set of tracks, but they were set by a weighted sled pulled by snowmobiling Ward Williamson. The start was on Lake Hayward instead of the Lumberjack Bowl, with Historyland's Cook Shanty used as the headquarters. Wise had asked Wiik to rework parts of the course, resulting in a figure-eight loop on the lake, more forest roads, more climbing, and an additional 7 kilometers to make a 55-kilometer event. The short race, renamed the Citizen's Race, was lengthened from 20 to 27.5 kilometers.[12]

As promised, Norway sent its Birkebeinerrennet champion, Dag Anmarkrud, to compete. Anmarkrud was the favorite. Haines, Martin, and 1974 third-place finisher Lars Arnesson were the challengers. The group of four broke away early, and then Haines, from Alaska, broke away from them. He finished in three hours, beating Anmarkrud by four minutes. Haines surprised the finish-line crowd, not only because he beat the Norwegian champion, but also because he wasn't striding in the tracks as he approached the finish. He was doing something no one there had seen before—he was skate skiing. Haines wasn't trying to be innovative; he was simply going the fastest way he knew on the icy Telemark trails, which hadn't been regroomed after a thaw and freeze. The start temperature was nineteen degrees, and it warmed into the low forties, making it a challenging day for waxing. Haines's skate finish previewed a new (and, at the time, controversial) form of the sport that one of his US teammates—nineteen-year-old Bill Koch, winning a junior race at the time in Finland—would help to popularize in the years to come.

In 1975, women were officially allowed, but there were no age classes like the men's division. The winner was Vigdis Snekkevik, of Wausau, Wisconsin, who finished in five hours, while Lindskoog finished second in 5:31.

BETWEEN THE 1975 AND 1976 RACES, both the Birkebeiner and Tony Wise were recognized at the highest levels. In May 1975, the race received sanctioning from the US Ski Association, raising its status from rogue event to an official part of the national Nordic program. During the Lumberjack Championships in July 1975, Wise was presented the King Olav Medal for his work to promote Norwegian culture. The award granted him an audience with the king of

Chris Haines skate skis across the 1975 finish line in front of the Telemark chalet. He used his Birkebeiner win as a springboard to the US Olympic team in 1976 in Innsbruck, Austria—the beginning of a family tradition. Chris's sister, Betsy Haines, skied in the 1980 Olympics at Lake Placid, New York, and their niece Kikkan Randall paired with Jessie Diggins in 2018 to win the first US Olympic gold medal in cross-country skiing.
AMERICAN BIRKEBEINER SKI FOUNDATION ARCHIVES

Jeanette Vortanz places a laurel wreath around the neck of 1975 winner Chris Haines, as Tony Wise and others look on. Vortanz began working for Wise in 1964, washing dishes in the chalet. "I did everything but make snow," she said. "Whatever Tony wanted, that's what you were doing."
AMERICAN BIRKEBEINER SKI FOUNDATION ARCHIVES

Tony Wise stands in front of the original International Bridge, which skiers crossed near the race's finish line. Telemark Lodge can be seen in the distance. COURTESY OF THE WISE FAMILY

Norway (which wouldn't happen until 1977) and reflected Telemark's growing international reputation. In October 1975, the race finally received official FIS sanctioning after additional efforts led by Bob Treland. Tony Wise's Nordic vision was coming true.

The 1976 race tripled in size again to 993 entrants and was held on Washington's Birthday weekend during the bicentennial year. The race that year featured a number of firsts: the first elite wave start, thanks to the number of top-level competitors from the US and Norway; the first start at Telemark, featuring a climb up the 370-foot Valhalla and Morgedal downhill runs (the easiest way to get enough vertical climb for the FIS sanction); the first race sponsor, NorTur, a Minneapolis importer of Norwegian ski products; new bibs bearing the race name for the first time; the start of a tradition, a prerace smorgasbord, at the Hayward Armory; new finisher medals designed by Josten's of Minneapolis; and a declaration by the race's newsletter, the *Birch Scroll*, that the American Birkebeiner was the longest—and close to becoming the largest—Nordic race in the nation.

The sport was taking off. Telemark's cross-county complex had grown to 93 kilometers. The trails had drawn nine hundred skiers in 1972–73 and four years later drew fifteen thousand. "It took about 10 years for downhill skiing to become fashionable, the sport of Beautiful People," Wise wrote in December 1975. "In five years, cross-country will have its own fashionable, exciting image."[13]

It ended up happening much sooner than that. Sixteen days before the Birkebeiner, twenty-year-old Bill Koch won a silver medal in the 30-kilometer race at the Olympics in Austria (after nearly making the US Nordic combined Olympic team in 1972 as a sixteen-year-old). In doing so, Koch became the first American to make the podium—or even come close—in a sport dominated for fifty years by the Europeans. Cross-country in the US suddenly had a young hero to help inspire the masses.

All that was more than enough to create a stir on Birkebeiner weekend in 1976. And yet, there was more. Incredibly, a month before Koch's historic achievement, he was training and qualifying for the US Olympic team during tryouts at none other than the Telemark Lodge trails. How did that happen? Wise had been pushing to get Telemark on the Nordic map, in part by attracting world-class skiers to the race. Sometime in 1975 he called US coach Marty Hall about coming to see the trail system, "but I put him off," said Hall, an easterner who had heard of Wise but knew nothing about Telemark. Then, that fall, when the US Ski Association was holding a coaching clinic with the US team in Minneapolis, Wise saw an opportunity a commuter flight away and invited the entourage to visit for an evening after their meetings had concluded. They balked, but Wise made an offer they couldn't refuse: he'd charter a plane, fly them to the front door of Telemark, show them around, give them dinner, and have them back by bedtime.

It was a shot in the dark, and at first Hall wasn't impressed with Telemark because all the trails Wise had hastily shown him were flat, although the Telemark special meal did impress. "I told the coaches, 'It will be a cold day in hell before I go back to that place,'" Hall said after leaving.[14]

However, the impromptu tour soon paid off. On Thanksgiving Day, new USSA Nordic director John Bower called Wise on behalf of Hall and explained that the US team had left its training site at seven thousand feet in Cooke City, Montana, and was scheduled next to train in Quebec City, Quebec, Canada, but snow there was lacking. "All of a sudden our well-thought-out training program for the Olympics was right side up," Hall said.

Wise assured Bower that Telemark had plenty of snow, but Hall wanted to make sure. With the team on a short holiday break, Hall called up team member Doug Peterson, from Minneapolis, who had skied alpine at Telemark with his family while growing up. "Marty said he wanted me to go up to Telemark and see what they have for snow," Peterson said later. "I drove up the next day, and Tony rolled out the red carpet for me. They had more than enough snow." Peterson reported back to Hall. "Marty, you won't believe this," Hall recalled Peterson saying. "They've got the whole damn city out there shoveling." The decision was made, although it was the busiest time of year at Telemark. "Tony said, 'Come on, move in,'" Hall said. "It was like talking with God."[15]

The team flew into Duluth, Minnesota, drove ninety minutes to Telemark, and was greeted with open arms—even as celebrities, which they definitely weren't accustomed to. Traditionally unsuccessful, US Nordic teams had spartan budgets compared to alpine and other US Olympic teams. "They'd been living like peasants," Wise later wrote. "It was the first time in their life they were treated like kings. We even had all of their pictures up on the wall."[16]

To Hall's surprise, when he saw the full Telemark trail complex, he realized there were plenty of hills to help get his team into Olympic shape, and he soon fell in love with the place. Best of all, "We could walk out the back door and be in the tracks. It was great," he said. "The real plus was we had been at altitude, and it helped us shift our training to low altitude and pick up our speed."[17]

Hall realized he had found a new friend and cross-country enthusiast. Each man was revolutionizing the sport, Wise for the citizen skier and Hall for the competitor. "We really melded," said Hall, who became noted throughout his career for his innovations in training, waxing, grooming, technique, and equipment. "All you had to do was walk into that lodge, and with Tony there was never a no. What he was saying he would do, he did. He came on as a big talker, but he backed it up."[18]

Wise's good fortune compounded. What was supposed to be a few days' stay at Telemark for the US Nordic team turned into about six weeks once they discovered that Lake Placid, New York—the scheduled site for the US trials—also lacked snow. Thus the team stayed put, and for four days in late December and early January the lodge hosted the US Olympic trials. Wisconsin governor Patrick Lucey, staying at Telemark for the holidays, was the honorary starter. It was the first time the US trials had been held in the Midwest since 1924, the year the Winter Olympics began.

The star was Koch, no surprise after his hot streak in junior events in Europe. He won two of three trials races, the 15- and 40-kilometer, and took second to Tim Caldwell in the 10-kilometer. Koch finished first overall to lead the men's team into Austria. On the women's side, also red-hot Martha Rockwell won all three events to lead the qualifying. "All of my memories of Telemark are totally positive," Koch said. "Being in a minor sport, we were just scrounging around and trying to make it work. Tony just rolled the red carpet out for us. It was amazing." He left Telemark confident, and that confidence was reinforced with podium finishes in two subsequent international races. "I went into the Olympics thinking, wow, this is the same competition. That gave me a lot of hope that maybe I was peaking at the right time."[19]

The training camp and trials, held on short notice, were a resounding success. Media from across the US attended and praised the facilities. Bower called Telemark "the leader of the future of cross-country development in the United States" and the Midwest "the accelerating giant of cross-country skiing in the United States." The Canadian Olympic team, also seeking snow, paid a visit to train and race against the Americans. After the success of hosting the US team, Wise received a commendation from USSA, which declared Telemark an official training site. Hall said he'd be back. Koch and Caldwell even broke a barrier during their stay, with an over-distance 100-kilometer (62-mile) training day—they'd done 85 previously—possibly the first in US history, in six hours, twenty minutes.[20]

Bill Koch skis in the Olympic trials at Telemark in 1976. Four weeks later, he won a silver medal in the Olympics, the first for the US in Nordic skiing. AMERICAN BIRKEBEINER SKI FOUNDATION ARCHIVES

A month after leaving Telemark, Koch made American cross-country skiing history with the Olympic silver medal. He added a sixth place in the 15-kilometer and a thirteenth in the 50-kilometer. The US further surprised the Nordic ski world when the relay team took sixth—just fifty seconds from a bronze medal out of fourteen teams, with Koch, Caldwell, Peterson (lead-off), and Ronny Yeager. "The Europeans saw how close we were to winning a medal as a team, and it was shocking," Peterson said.[21]

A few weeks later, several Olympians returned to Telemark, as a band played for them, to compete in the fourth Birkebeiner. Two of them were assigned bicentennial-themed bib numbers: 1776 for Haines, in honor of his Olympic team berth and as defending champion, and 1976 for Jana Hlavaty, who was born in Czechoslovakia and had become a US citizen just prior to the Olympics thanks to a special congressional effort.[22]

(Was there any question Wise and staff knew how to make things happen? Between February 10 and 15, after the Olympic trials and before the Birkebeiner, the lodge hosted three music icons for concerts, Buddy Rich, Tommy James, and Chubby Checker.)

The 1976 race drew enough high-level competitors for a 141-skier elite field, including US team members John-Mike Downey and Larry Martin, who both just missed making the Olympic team. The field also included Norwegian Olympic team member Tore Gullen and other Norwegian standouts like Bjorn Arvnes and Audun Kolstad. It was the first truly international field—albeit from just a few countries—but it impressed upon Wise that coordination was needed between countries holding ski marathons. "We had to develop some sort of worldwide series of races," he said.[23]

Kolstad—a lieutenant in the Norwegian army who, like Downey, had barely missed his Olympic team—became the first Norwegian to win the American version of his country's seminal race. He finished in 2:40 on his hot new fiberglass skis from Epoke, outdueling Downey by two seconds, with Arvnes just another two seconds back. The race was tight from start to finish, despite a lead group getting lost for four to five kilometers late in the race. Miraculously, Bob Treland was patrolling on a snowmobile and found the wayward skiers; he redirected them down a side road and back to the main trail, without losing any time.

(A few weeks later, Kolstad would go on to win the Norwegian Birkebeinerrennet in a field of 2,800 and would win again in 1977. On his heels once more would be Downey, who won the trip to Norway as the top American Birkebeiner finisher.)

Duncan McLean, now twenty-one, who had graduated from the short race to the main event, also won the trip as the top Birkebeiner citizen finisher. Hlavaty won the women's Birkebeiner title by five minutes, in 3:05, over Olympic teammate Lynn Vonder Heide of Alaska. Just a year after women were officially allowed to ski the long race, forty-three of them entered. Hlavaty, like Lindskoog, more than proved they belonged by taking an eye-opening eighteenth place overall.[24]

The 617 skiers in the touring division enjoyed sunshine, a fast course, and temperatures in the twenties. The enjoyment came *after* the challenging new start up and over the big alpine hill. After taking off from the eighth fairway on the Telemark golf course, they skied toward the lodge, then turned left and herringboned or V-stepped up—some side-stepped, it was so steep—

and across the Valhalla alpine run, over the imposing Morgedal run headwall (named for a village in Norway's Telemark region), and about three hundred yards down the wide Stormoen run (named after first Telemark ski instructor Ola Stormoen) on the back side. It was a fast, frenetic downhill marked by defensive snowplowing, out-of-control skiers beelining down a slope usually slalomed by alpine skiers, and numerous crashes. At the bottom, skiers made a sharp righthand turn onto the narrow trail and followed a sweeping curve back toward the lodge before heading south. "I'd have to say that I've never been involved in such a mixed up and confusing chaos in my life," citizen finisher Dan Sullivan said. "I'd also have to honestly say that I've never had so much fun in my life. It may well rank as my greatest achievement ever."[25]

The 1976 race was an unqualified success. Wise had engineered a massive transformation in the focus of his twenty-nine-year-old operation. "A new image is emerging at Mount Telemark," the *Minneapolis Star* reported. The "ski center well-known for its downhill skiing since 1947" was "now well on its way to becoming a world-class cross-country ski center as well."[26]

Wise had one more big idea to close out 1976. That spring, he announced that Telemark was negotiating with FIS to host the first-ever World Cup international ski race held outside of Europe. By July the Telemark Games—renamed in the fall the Gitchi Gami Games in a nod to the Ojibwe name for nearby Lake Superior—were approved. On December 21, many of the world's best male and female skiers descended on Telemark for two days of races. Skiers took on two new, rugged 5-kilometer loops and a new 10-kilometer trail designed by US coach Marty Hall (he also was helping to design a new Birkebeiner trail).[27]

Although it was initially billed as a World Cup event, by race time it was being called an unofficial World Cup race and then simply the American Cup (or Wise's branded Gitchi Gami Games) at the insistence of Scandinavian journalists who had started the fledgling World Cup series three years earlier and didn't look favorably on US skiing. However, it was on the official World Cup schedule that year, was sanctioned by the FIS, and met one of the criteria—having at least ten of the season's top twenty race points leaders; Telemark had sixteen. *Sports Illustrated* brushed off the semantics squabble, flatly calling it a World Cup event and "the most prestigious Nordic ski-racing contest in the United States since the Squaw Valley Olympics in 1960. The [Telemark] games attracted a field of European cross-country skiers the like of whom never assemble outside their native continent except when an Olympics demands it."[28]

A promotional poster for the 1976 Gitchi Gami Games
AMERICAN BIRKEBEINER SKI FOUNDATION ARCHIVES

In the end, the Europeans couldn't complain, as they dominated the men's competition. Finland's Matti Pitkaenen, who had won an Olympic relay gold ten months earlier, led the men's 15-kilometer race, and Canadian twins Sharon and Shirley Firth topped the women's 5- and 10-kilometer. The Americans, meanwhile, made a reputable showing. Koch, despite having a cold and recovering from a severe reaction to asthma medication, managed to eke out a still-respectable twenty-seventh place in a field of seventy-eight. Stan Dunklee finished tenth (his international personal best), and Tim Caldwell finished fifteenth. Doug Peterson was twenty-second and led the US relay team to an impressive third-place podium finish, out of twenty-four teams. The Americans, under Hall, had a breakthrough year in 1976, and Telemark was an integral part of it.

The event, put together in short order, was first-class. The trails were praised—John Caldwell called them the best in the US, and Koch said there was just one system in the world that was better, in Seefeld, Austria. The one hundred–plus skiers, coaches, and officials were treated to three days of lodging, food, entertainment, and events, including an Ojibwe ceremonial dance, and gifts such as Indian-made deerskin gloves, western hats, and denim clothing.

"The Europeans really loved the experience," Peterson said. Skiers crossed a wooden International Bridge near the lodge lined with their nations' flags.[29]

The catch: Wise paid most of the up-front costs, figuring it was an investment in Telemark's future. The race was originally estimated to cost $60,000, a figure that was later revised to $100,000 and then $160,000. "I bled profusely after that expenditure," Wise said in 1977. But he also promised to make it an annual event, proclaiming that "we've finally found our niche in skiing in the Midwest." In one year, Telemark went from an obscure trail system to one of the most respected in the country. Wise was promoting the sport at a level few others had done. "Cross-country was so brand-new, and it was just sitting out there for someone to stimulate it," Hall said. "I can't say I realized it then, but I was processing that here's a guy our sport needs. I came into the sport in 1969, and the old-fashioned sport had ended. I started a lot of things, and Tony was doing the same thing. We both had a lot to give."[30]

AFTER THE SUCCESSES OF THE 1976 RACE, the Olympic trials, and the World Cup event, the fifth Birkebeiner kicked off in February 1977 with a huge wave of momentum—maybe too much for some of the amped-up elite skiers. Entries more than doubled to 2,206, and for the first time the field included a large contingent of citizen skiers from Norway—almost four hundred of them—who flew to the United States on two commercial jets. Tour buses escorted the Norwegian skiers from the Minneapolis airport to Telemark Lodge—they even received a lights-flashing sheriff's escort once they reached the Sawyer County line. The Norwegians were eager to experience part of their culture in America, and many used their designated winter vacation week to make the trip. Ernie St. Germaine said he would never forget the year of the so-called Norwegian invasion, in part because the second-most important thing to them while visiting was experiencing American Indian culture. St. Germaine proudly took part in a powwow planned by tribal leaders that week at Telemark.[31]

The 1977 race also marked the debut of the new Birkebeiner trail between Telemark and Hayward, two years in the making. The day before the race, the new trail was formally dedicated. The old trail had few big hills; the new one was loaded with them—more than four thousand feet of climbing through the Bayfield and Sawyer County forests. Gone were the logging roads, confusing junctions, and snowmobilers. This was a trail designed by and for skiers.

An aerial view of the 1977 start, with the leaders cresting Morgedal and beginning the run down Stormoen. AMERICAN BIRKEBEINER SKI FOUNDATION ARCHIVES

In addition, the shorter Citizen's Race was renamed the Kortelopet and, for the first time, started at the same time and place as the main event. Kortelopet skiers finished at the Highway OO trail crossing, where the original short race had begun. The new name came about when Frances Wise asked original race entrant Karl Andresen, who was born in Norway, how to say "short race" (*kort løp*) in his native language.[32]

When race morning dawned, it was sixteen degrees, but things heated up quickly. At about 8:50 a.m., FIS technical delegate Lars Kindem walked in front of the start line on the golf course and announced on a megaphone in English and Norwegian that it was ten minutes to race time. Most of the elite skiers and other high-level skiers were in place, but other skiers still were arriving. One of the elite skiers was Sten Fjeldheim, who was born in Norway and emigrated to Minneapolis with his family first as a child and then a second time at age sixteen. Kindem had been Fjeldheim's high school history teacher and ski coach. Fjeldheim overheard a nearby Norwegian skier ask another, in Norwegian, what Kindem had just announced. The second skier replied, "Ten seconds to start." Fjeldheim knew what was about to happen, quickly clipped into his skis, and told his friend Duncan McLean to do the same. US Ski Team member Mike Gallagher, who also knew some Norwegian, overheard others talking about starting the race early and quickly got ready. Heightened race tension with the highly competitive Norwegian skiers, coupled with confusion about the start time, put skiers on edge. Norwegian Bjorn Arvnes, in the front, felt pressure from behind and was pushed forward. "When one started to move, everyone started to move," Arvnes said. Fjeldheim, near the front, heard more chatter and saw skiers raise their poles in the air while letting out a Viking war cry. "It was nuts," Fjeldheim recalled many years later.[33] A mass of skiers surged past a plastic start gate, and the race was on—eight and a half minutes early.

Fjeldheim, who had skied in the Olympic trials a year earlier at Telemark, later claimed there was no intention to gain a competitive edge, what's called a "thief" start, just miscommunication coupled with start-line tension. Kindem, however, believed the Norwegians did intentionally start early. Later, a letter from a Norwegian skier offered an apology but said there was no such intent.[34]

In 1977, the Birkebeiner still employed a mass start, where all skiers began the race at the same time (starting waves wouldn't be instituted until 1984). When Kindem gave his ten-minute warning, some skiers were inside the alpine chalet and lodge, or climbing out of cars and buses, or using the portable toilets. When it was clear the race had started early, many skiers had to sprint for the start line.

Race officials initially were unsure what to do, especially because it was the first year race results were going high-tech using Cybernet, Control Data's international network of computers. The computers weren't set to start until 9 a.m., so eight and a half minutes had to be added to every skier's finish time. "The Norwegians were wearing these black and yellow [Epoke] suits—we called them the bumble bees," said Harold Treland, Telemark's chief of start. "They were hootin' and hollerin' and we didn't know what was going on." Officials had to make a quick decision. "Jerry [Berard] looked at me and said, 'Shoot the cannon!'" About a quarter kilometer past the start, Fjeldheim heard the minicannon blast behind him.[35]

EPOKE

Arvnes, who had placed third in the 1976 Birkebeiner, was in the lead after the early break but lost it soon thereafter when he fell on an icy downhill. About four inches of fresh snow had fallen before the race, but it covered an icy base caused by freezing rain earlier that week; two citizen skiers suffered broken legs and others were injured on the new trail, which was technically challenging with a continuous mix of hills and curves. Arvnes quickly recovered and regained the lead with a teammate before pulling away with about 5 kilometers to go. He powered into the Lumberjack Bowl in three hours and three seconds, nearly two minutes ahead of countryman Kjell Pettersen. Norway, not surprisingly, swept the race in 1977, with Berit Mørdre-Lammedal, a police officer and former two-time Olympian and gold medalist, taking the women's race (out of 107 females overall) in 3:29. Lammedal, age thirty-six, defeated much younger skiers, including runner-up Alison Spencer, age twenty-four, a 1972 US Olympian, by three minutes.[36]

The Norwegians—who took thirty-two of the top fifty places and won two-thirds of the age class awards—were serious about their skiing. Dave Landgraf, the Hayward native and friend of St. Germaine's who had transformed from 1973 neophyte to elite skier, mixed it up on the trail with a testy Norwegian who wouldn't yield the track and didn't want to be passed. With Landgraf on his tail, the Norwegian began jumping in an effort to break Landgraf's ski tips. Landgraf pulled to the side, and they began exchanging blows with their poles "like two swordsmen" before Landgraf pulled away, Tony Wise said. "Those guys were so aggressive and competitive," Wise said of the Norwegians. "Everybody [from the US] who saw that race said, 'We'd better step up our training.'"[37]

The Norwegians, however, made far more friends than enemies and brought a new level of excitement and economic impact to race week. Lodging maxed out, with race entries for the first time exceeding the populations of Hayward and Cable. Merchants were happy as Norwegians snapped up souvenirs and filled the restaurants and bars. Among them were Norwegian skiing legends and longtime friendly rivals Oscar Gjøslein, age seventy, and his brother-in-law Sigvard Egge, age seventy-three, the latter with ski-like ruts creasing his weathered face. They finished strong in their age groups, closed down the Telemark lobby bar, and won plenty of hearts with their stories, friendliness, and

Facing page: FIS technical delegate Lars Kindem embraces skier Sten Fjeldheim of Michigan at the finish line in 1977. AMERICAN BIRKEBEINER SKI FOUNDATION ARCHIVES

inspiring performances. When Gjøslein finished the race, he said, "I could ski another 55 kilometers." Ditto, said Egge, who would return to Telemark in 1983 at age seventy-nine and win three gold medals in the World Masters Championships, including the 50-kilometer.[38]

The Birkebeiner lived up to its name as *the* American ski race beginning in 1977, prompting *Ski Magazine* to say, "There is no question that Telemark's Birkebeiner, with its splendid course and its exuberant horde of competitors, should become an American classic, an event no serious skier can let his life go by without entering." Tony Wise, who understood the power of the media, had to be beaming.[39]

The growing event was in the capable hands of Jerry Berard, who had taken over as chief of race—race director—in 1975. Berard, general manager at Telemark, had run Wise's successful World Lumberjack Championships since 1960, the Olympic trials, the World Cup event, and all of Wise's ideas in between. He was Wise's general *and* manager. "Tony wouldn't have gotten as far as he did without Jerry," Bob Treland said. "He had a very sharp business mind. He was the glue that made it all work."[40]

Except when the glue didn't work. Berard had started the skier clothing bag drop at the start, beginning a race tradition. However, in one early race most of the numbers glued to the bags by the US Postal Service fell off because it was so cold. Chaos ensued at the finish, and many skiers never found their belongings, leaving piles of clothes and gear that had to be donated to charity.[41]

A Hayward native, Berard was hired by Wise at age fifteen for $1 an hour in ski rental and went full time at age seventeen in 1954. He was Telemark's first full-time employee. "Telemark was a fun place to work; we sold fun," Berard said. He earned a bachelor's degree eventually but said, "I got my college degree working for Tony. He put a lot of responsibility on me when I was very young. I was a raw kid. He taught me a lot of things that a father would do."[42]

BETWEEN THE 1977 AND 1978 RACES, life was far from dull for Tony Wise and the staff at Telemark. In mid-March, Wise and daughter Frances visited Norway, Finland, and Sweden for eleven days; they received complimentary flights from Pan Am as a thank-you for the 1977 race filling two planeloads of Norwegians. Tony and Frances attended the days-long Holmenkollen ski festival events—Frances skied in the 42-kilometer citizen race—that drew one hundred thousand spectators; met with US Ambassador William Anders (a former Apollo 8 astronaut); and flew to Helskinki, Finland, and back to talk with ski officials there.

On the sixth day, Tony met with Norway's King Olav V at the Royal Palace in Oslo, as part of the King Olav Medal that Wise received in 1975. "That was one of the fantastic adventures for me," Wise said months before he died. At the time, he wrote that he wore a white shirt and black tie and met first with a palace official about how to act when with royalty. "The prime minister of Bangladesh preceded me," he said. "I talked with the king for almost 10 minutes about skiing, its growth in the US, the American Birkebeiner and the king's years in the US and Canada during World War II." The king loved sports and was a skier. While Tony and the king talked, Frances toured the royal palace.[43]

Their itinerary continued at a rapid pace. They flew to Sweden to meet with Vasaloppet race officials and, back in Norway, watched the Norwegian Birkebeinerrennet (meeting skiers who had competed at Telemark a month earlier). Next, they explored their Norwegian roots, visiting family in Hamer for a reunion and traveling with cousins from Rena north to Øversjødalen, where their ancestors had settled a farm in the late 1700s. They stayed overnight in the house where Tony's paternal grandmother Gjertina was born.[44]

However, the trip's success was quickly overshadowed by misfortune. A day after Tony and Frances returned to the US, on March 24, 1977, the Telemark alpine chalet went up in flames. The midmorning blaze—caused by an electrical short in a kitchen exhaust fan—quickly engulfed the twenty-thousand-square-foot building, valued at $750,000 with contents. Luckily no one was hurt. Employees and skiers fled to the base of the ski hill and watched what had been one of northwest Wisconsin's and the Upper Midwest's first big winter attractions, a star of the North where memories had been made by the thousands, melt into a black scar on the snow.[45]

Wise promised to rebuild. By October, he had sketched out his vision and, not surprisingly, it was big. Initial plans detailed a "futuristic" $3 million, three-level underground coliseum. The building would be cut into a hillside with a "curtain" of south-facing windows and solar panels, skylights, a restaurant on the mezzanine level, an athletic field on the roof, indoor tennis courts, convention space, and a banquet facility seating two thousand. In the meantime, Wise put up a temporary chalet on the old chalet's foundation and used the adjacent American Youth Hostel for ski rental and waxing.[46]

The Gitchi Gami Games returned in mid-December, with just Finland, Norway, and Canada—out of the fourteen nations invited—joining the US team. A star of the event was Billy Carter, brother of President Jimmy Carter. Invited by Wise, the southern peanut farmer tried skiing for the first time with his son William "Buddy" Carter; Telemark instructor Bob Woodward provided lessons. Billy was an official starter for the Games' 15-kilometer men's race and posed for a photo with a ceremonial Ojibwe headdress from Jimmy "Pipe" Mustache, also known as Running Elk.[47]

It was a whirlwind year, even by Tony Wise's standards, and it ended on a tragic note. On Christmas Day 1977, Dave Quinn, the 1974 Birkebeiner champion, died of cancer. The summer after his victory he and his twin brother, Don, were competing in a bike race in New England when Dave crashed on his back. He experienced shortness of breath over the next year, but nothing was

Spiritual leader Jimmy "Pipe" Mustache (center), a mentor to Tony Wise, and Becky Taylor (far left) of the Lac Courte Oreilles Band take part in a ceremony with skiers at Telemark Lodge in the late 1970s. AMERICAN BIRKEBEINER SKI FOUNDATION ARCHIVES

found until 1975, after Don uncharacteristically beat Dave easily in a ski race as Dave struggled to breathe, and Dave unexpectedly didn't make the US Ski Team. Tests revealed a large tumor in Dave's upper back and a collapsed lung. He briefly returned to racing during treatments and had begun teaching and coaching in Frisco, Colorado, but he died in Duluth, Minnesota, near his hometown of Cloquet, soon after sending Christmas cards to those who had impacted his life. Dave Quinn was twenty-nine. Sven Wiik called him "the best kid you could find to coach . . . and the finest of persons."

A younger brother in the Quinn family, James, who also had gone to Western State in Colorado but as an alpine racer, died tragically as well, at twenty-one, after a bike crash in May 1974. "Those things really put life into perspective for me," said Don, who continued the brothers' ski legacy by teaching, coaching high school skiers in Leadville, Colorado, and racing, including the Birkebeiner, into his seventies.[48]

WHILE THE 1977 RACE featured the Norwegians, the 1978 race was the first broadly international Birkebeiner. Skiers from five different nations finished in the top five. The winner was twenty-nine-year-old Alfred Kaelin of Switzerland, a former Olympic relay bronze medalist. He finished in 3:10 and was followed by skiers from Italy, Finland, Norway (defending champion Bjorn Arvnes), and Sweden. The race was the closest to date, with six seconds separating the top four skiers as they sprinted into the Lumberjack Bowl, Kaelin winning by two seconds. The women's race was won by Valborg Ostberg, a forty-seven-year-old grandmother from Norway who took an impressive thirty-seventh overall in 3:41. Ostberg had also won the women's Norwegian Birkebeinerrennet in 1977. Female participation in the American Birkebeiner was growing quickly—women comprised close to 20 percent of the field by just the fourth year that female skiers were officially allowed.

With three inches of snow overnight and more falling as the race began at twenty-one degrees, groomers quickly set two new tracks in the morning by pulling two skiers behind a snowmobile. Skiers from Canada, Germany, and Austria, along with thirty-one US states, also competed. The race grew again, up 500 entrants for a total of 2,717, with more than 2,000 skiers in the main race for the first time. The *Milwaukee Journal* called it "one of America's most spectacular mass participatory sports events."[49]

Valborg Ostberg, 47, of Norway, was the 1978 women's champion and took thirty-seventh overall. AMERICAN BIRKEBEINER SKI FOUNDATION ARCHIVES

The variety of nations competing in the 1978 Birkebeiner wasn't an accident. Tony Wise had invited officials from top ski marathons in eight countries, plus each nation's top national skier, and paid their way. He wanted to discuss his latest big idea—forming a worldwide series of elite ski marathons. Most of the officials didn't know Wise and were somewhat taken aback by the overture. Still, would it hurt to see what he had to say? Even the most skeptical countries, Norway and Sweden, came.

Wise's idea expanded on one already in place. A miniseries of ski marathons in Europe called the Alpentris had started with three national races in 1973. It grew to five countries in 1974 and was renamed the Euroloppet (*loppet* is the Scandinavian word for a long race). Wise wanted to bring the series to North America. In fact, he had floated the idea during his 1977 trip to Norway, with side trips to Finland and Sweden to garner support.[50] Just five years after Wise started the Birkebeiner, he saw an opportunity to align it with the world's best such events. It would validate the American Birkebeiner as *America's* ski marathon. "He wanted something that would single out his race as the only one of its kind in America," said Tom Kelly, his publicist.[51]

It looked like a hard sell but wasn't, maybe because Wise could sell. During two days of prerace meetings, officials were receptive to Wise's idea and hashed out issues despite language challenges. The group adjourned in general agreement and reconvened on June 10, 1978, at the annual Euroloppet meeting in Uppsala, Sweden, where they formally created the World Loppet League, later known as the Worldloppet. The league initially included one race each from Austria, Canada, Finland, Italy, Sweden, Switzerland, West Germany, and the United States. Norway, however, didn't attend because of concerns of how the partnership might affect its event. Wise and Telemark employee Dick Simono headed there afterward, reassured the Norwegians they wouldn't have to change their race, and Norway was in, too. Suddenly, Wise was influencing the race that had been his inspiration. Of the designated races, only Sweden's Vasaloppet (1922) and Norway's Birkebeinerrennet (1932) were significantly older than the American Birkebeiner.

An early pamphlet was already promoting the Birkebeiner as "the nation's longest cross-country ski race." AMERICAN BIRKEBEINER SKI FOUNDATION ARCHIVES

Wise was named the league's first secretary general, overseeing promotion and coordination of the series. He suggested that each participating country contribute $1,000 per year to fund the league and get promotion rolling, but he offered to pay everyone's fee the first year.

The first Worldloppet races, beginning with the Dolomitenlauf in Austria, were held in 1979. To participate in this world vision, at a time when the Cold War and geopolitical divisions across Europe still were prominent, skiers would get a race "passport." A page for each race would be stamped upon completion, with the lifetime goal of completing them all and receiving a medal and certificate. The first year of the races, 315 passports were issued. By 2008, the series had expanded to include races in fourteen countries on four continents. By 2023, the Worldloppet calendar had twenty races and sixteen thousand–plus passport holders. As the number of races grew, skiers could achieve "Worldloppet Master" status by completing ten races on at least two continents. Some skiers achieved this multiple times over. Hannes Larsson of France, for example, did it thirty-four times—the result of completing 340 Worldloppet marathons, including the Birkebeiner at age eighty-six, where he finished in three hundredth place. Another passport holder was retired Olympic champion Bjorn Daehlie, who described the Worldloppet as "the most important and beautiful cross-country ski races in the world." Just like the American Birkebeiner, the Worldloppet grew out of Tony Wise's "vision and entrepreneurship," said Epp Paal, Worldloppet's CEO, in 2024. "All races have evolved thanks to this international connection, which has taken the form of family. This is what we call it among our members."[52]

The Worldloppet's early success brought at least one moment of comic relief. Frances Wise remembers her dad laughing hysterically one day in his Telemark office when a friend called. The friend was confused because he thought his Worldloppet passport could be used as an actual passport and was being detained by security at an airport.[53]

The 1978 Birkebeiner not only attracted widespread international competition for the first time—it also featured the first major successes for the new Telemark Academy, a skier development program led by former US Ski Team member Peter Davis. Winning the Kortelopet were academy skiers Terese Maznio of Cable and Kevin Brochman of Minnesota, who also won a US Junior National title a week later in Jackson Hole, Wyoming.[54]

Also for the first time that year, local civic organizations were involved in the race effort. Bob Treland and Dick Simono hatched the plan and recruited thirteen volunteer groups, which then assembled two hundred volunteers to manage the route's nine aid stations. It was the start of a tradition that relieved pressure on race organizers and began to endear the community to the race and vice versa. Local support extended to the race sponsor in 1978, Silva Ski, a division of S.C. Johnson & Son in Racine, Wisconsin. The family of company founder Sam Johnson owned vacation retreats near and at Telemark. It was the beginning of decades of race support by the company and the Sam Johnson family.

One of the happiest skiers in 1978 was Mitch Mode of Rhinelander, Wisconsin, who took eighteenth overall in 3:28 and won the citizen championship trip to the mother race in Norway. Years later, as a *Birch Scroll* columnist, Mode recalled the joy of skiing in the late 1970s Birkebeiners and going up Morgedal, the 370-foot slope at the start of the race:

> Those early days—man! Were they something. You'd line up out on the golf course, and the first thing you had to do was ski up the downhill run. Then you had to ski down the other side. We'd charge out like madmen, stride up that hill as far as we could, and then herringbone the rest. . . . That uphill was still the best way to separate the field that has ever been. Cross-country skiers can't ski downhill worth a darn. That downhill slope was a disaster for many. Skiers would crash, others would run into the fallen, still others would wobble their way around the pileups, and eventually all the survivors would find their way onto the double-tracked trail that led to the finish line. It was glorious mayhem.[55]

The charge up Morgedal captured the attention of the *Milwaukee Journal*'s *Insight* magazine, which described the scene as "lung-gasping bedlam . . . [and] a return of the Oklahoma land rush. A swirling mass of skiers in racing bibs, struggling in herringbone ascent. Some slip on the steep hill, entangling the stampede of sprinting racers—a flailing mass of skis, poles, legs and elbows. Bound for glory!" Skier Karl Andresen, one of the original entrants, remembers once having to jump over a fallen skier on the way down Stormoen. "I managed to keep my balance, but just barely," Andresen wrote. "What a race, I thought, that makes me pull a Birger Ruud (my childhood ski jump hero from Norway) on these thin skis!"[56]

Alas, as the bruised egos, broken equipment, and fallen bodies on Stormoen mounted, it became obvious something had to be done about the stressful, dangerous start. "One year there was a lot of fresh snow and you couldn't even see people fall—just a ball of snow," skier Adrian Watt said. One race photo shows a group of about fifty skiers, thirty-five of them snowplowing and the other fifteen on the ground. Initiated to add elevation to an otherwise flat course as part of FIS sanctioning, the uphill start no longer was necessary because the new trail had more than enough hills.[57]

Multiple skiers wobble and fall in the "glorious mayhem" of skiing down Stormoen during the race start in the late 1970s. AMERICAN BIRKEBEINER SKI FOUNDATION ARCHIVES

In late 1978, Telemark hosted another World Cup event. The original series of races, including Telemark's in 1976, had been organized by European journalists but wasn't officially sanctioned. FIS had sanctioned an alpine World Cup beginning in 1966 but originally balked at a Nordic series. But by 1978, FIS agreed to a two-year trial program. Telemark was the first race on the twelve-event, eleven-country schedule, billed as the first official cross-country World Cup race ever held—a claim later disputed by FIS because of the trial period. "It is fitting that the first-ever competition be held at Telemark," John Bower, US Nordic director, said that year. "Telemark has developed the most sophisticated cross-country ski touring and racing facility in the United States and has exercised the leadership role and promotion of the sport."[58]

The race, also called the Telemark/Finlandia Vodka World Cup and Gitchi Gami Games, featured an elite field of 130 skiers from nine nations. Jerry Berard was the chief of competition and Bob Treland chief of course. Norway's Ova Aunli won the men's 15-kilometer. The American men didn't win individual medals but were impressive, with Bill Koch finishing sixth, Stan Dunklee

Alison Owen-Spencer competing at Telemark, where she won two World Cup races in 1978.
AMERICAN BIRKEBEINER SKI FOUNDATION ARCHIVES

eighth, Tim Caldwell twelfth, and Doug Peterson fourteenth. In the relay, the US took a silver behind Italy, with Koch (in comeback mode after taking a brief hiatus from the sport because of the post-1976 Olympics attention) hammering home the final leg in an event-best thirty minutes, eight seconds over the 10 kilometers. American Alison Owen-Spencer had a career-defining performance by winning the 5- and 10-kilometer women's races. She later hailed it as a highlight of her Hall of Fame career. Marty Hall called it a "breakthrough" for the fledgling US women's Nordic program, along with former teammate Martha Rockwell's pre-1976 World Cup–level win.[59]

The event further cemented Telemark's status as a leading world-class Nordic center and Wise as a new leader in the sport. For skiers, Wise held a powwow, offered a log-rolling demonstration in the Telemark pool, and provided traditional Ojibwe-made gifts such as moccasins for the winners and free cowboy hats for all. Peterson called it "more enjoyable than any Olympic experience I had. We all felt special—it was a testament to what Tony did. Europeans were blown away." Owen-Spencer said she remembered "feeling a piece of gratitude for everything it took to pull our sport to that level. The trail design, the people, the sponsors—I felt awed that so many people liked our sport enough to do that." Koch, who joined the dancers in the powwow, said, "Tony's contribution between the Worldloppet and the World Cup can hardly be overstated. He brought international respect to our sport in the US, that kind of high-level respect that would have probably taken a lot longer to come by, and he did it in an unlikely place."[60]

US skier Bill Koch (dark shirt and beard) attends a traditional feast at Telemark during the 1978 Gitchi Gami Games. At left is US Head Olympic Coach Rob Kiesel, and at right are Susan "Susie" White and Jan Goldman, members of the Lac Courte Oreilles Band. According to LCO member Ernie St. Germaine, feasts like this were held to celebrate the skiers. "People from the tribal community brought dishes of food to share in their honor," St. Germaine said. "The food is placed on blankets on the floor. It appears here that they also sat on the floor to eat, but it is not always done that way. Guests first fill their plates and return back to their places to eat as everyone then follows." AMERICAN BIRKEBEINER SKI FOUNDATION ARCHIVES

THE WORLD CUP ATTENTION focused on Telemark in late 1978 assured that the seventh annual Birkebeiner, on February 24, 1979, would be a record setter. The entrants numbered 4,459—nearly 1,800 more than in 1978 and double that of 1977.

The race, with a starting temperature of nine degrees and clear skies, featured a strong international field and another exciting finish. The top nine skiers, representing five countries, finished within forty seconds of one another. The finish line had been moved a short distance from the Lumberjack Bowl to Wise's Historyland, where he had re-created Old Hayward Main Street. Rain two days before, followed by a freeze, had hardened the 55-kilometer track, resulting in a record time of 2:47 by first-place finisher Arnt Haarstad of Norway. Haarstad broke from a pack of about ten skiers on the lake; with about 100 meters left, he pulled away from countryman and 1977 champion Bjorn Arvnes by six seconds. A lumberjack, Haarstad became the race's youngest champion at age twenty-two. At first, Haarstad's win caused confusion.

Skiers in the 1979 race break from the starting line on the Telemark Golf Course and head for the climb up Morgedal for the last time. AMERICAN BIRKEBEINER SKI FOUNDATION ARCHIVES

Announcers didn't recognize him as he skated out of the tracks (like Chris Haines in 1975) and down the homestretch lined with flags of Worldloppet nations. Who was he? His name wasn't on a list of top skiers because he was a late entry. The women's winner was an American and even younger, US team member Judy Rabinowitz, age twenty, of Alaska, in 3:10, skiing a marathon for the first time. (She would go on to ski in two Olympics, earn a law degree from Harvard, and work for the US Justice Department.)[61]

The record number of skiers caused traffic jams before the race and numerous skier traffic jams on the course. Skiers often were backed up for twenty minutes or more while they waited for a set of tracks to clear on a hill, and some resorted to taking off their skis and running around the backups in the deep snow. Some didn't make the racecourse cutoff times because of the backups and wrote letters voicing their displeasure.

Was the race getting too big? There were calls to limit entries. Wise listened but wanted the race to continue to grow. He announced several major changes. The Valhalla-Morgedal-Stormoen start would be altered for better flow. Skiers would go across Valhalla, zip down part of Morgedal, and flow behind the lodge—eliminating Stormoen—to a trail fifty feet wide on Nordmor Road paralleling the east-west Cable Airport runway. There would be nine sets of tracks for the first 7 kilometers, then narrow to six (three times as many as in 1979). Wave starts, which were suggested because of the number of inexperienced skiers holding up others, were considered but not yet implemented.

Most importantly, Wise announced just hours after the 1979 race that the trail would be widened from fifteen to thirty feet. He considered moving the Kortelopet, which started an hour behind the main race, to Friday of race week (forty years before it actually was moved). However, he didn't need to once the trail was widened. Instead, the Kortelopet start was delayed until two hours after the main race.

Wise bristled at criticism that he was only interested in making money as his race continued to grow. "Such is not the case. We have lost money each year we have held this event," he said, noting losses totaling $190,000 from 1977 through 1979. He argued that his motivation came from someplace deeper. "X-C skiing is like a religion to Telemark," the *Birch Scroll* proclaimed after the 1979 race. "It is the most exciting activity we have ever been involved in and we intend to give every ounce of energy and money to make it available to as many people as possible."[62]

As was becoming the norm, the race was just part of the party. Ice sculptures by Engelbert Hattenberger of Austria, who worked at the 1976 Olympics, greeted skiers at Telemark. (He also created the metal sculpture of the Norwegian warrior above the fireplace.) Opening ceremonies were held for the first time. After the race, four bands played at the lodge. The three major television networks, ABC, CBS, and NBC, reported on the race, thanks to Silva and parent company Johnson Wax.

Tragically, however, the Birkebeiner that year experienced its first race fatality, William Grainger, age fifty-seven, of Prince George, British Columbia, Canada who suffered an apparent heart attack near the 31-kilometer mark. Grainger was awarded the Birkebeiner finisher's medal posthumously.[63]

WITH THE BIRKEBEINER leading the way, ski marathons began to multiply across the US, enough to start an "Ameriloppet" of sorts, the Great American Ski Chase in 1978–1979 with four other races. One of the races in the series challenged the Birkebeiner for bragging rights. The American Ski Marathon began in 1978 in Goshen, Vermont, hosted by the Blueberry Hill Inn with icon John Caldwell as the first official starter. The race name claimed national status, and it was longer than the Birkebeiner at 60 kilometers (the 1980 Minnesota Finlandia went even farther at 100 kilometers). However, the American Ski Marathon topped out at about one thousand entrants before ending more than a decade later. Competition from these new marathons was another reason Wise pushed to create the Worldloppet and exclusively make his race part of it.[64]

Halfway through the year, on July 5, 1979, groundbreaking was held for the $3.3 million, sixty-four-thousand-square-foot replacement for the alpine chalet that had burned down. The Colosseum, as it was named, no longer would be an underground structure and was scaled back because of cost and grants that didn't materialize. Then, the fourth Gitchi Gami Games were held at Telemark in mid-December. While not a World Cup event, it doubled as the North American Championships and Olympic trials for the US and Canadian teams. "It's hard to comprehend what all took place at Telemark between 1976 and 1980. It was considered *the* place," said Bob Woodward, who became a noted Nordic journalist, including cross-country editor at *Ski Magazine*, after leaving Telemark.[65]

Tony Wise (blue suit coat) proudly oversees the Colosseum groundbreaking on July 5, 1979, with US Senator Gaylord Nelson (left) and Wisconsin Lieutenant Governor Russell Olson. AMERICAN BIRKEBEINER SKI FOUNDATION PAPERS. NORWEGIAN AMERICAN HISTORICAL ASSOCIATION, NORTHFIELD, MINNESOTA

Longtime Wise "generals" Berard and Treland, along with manager Jim Bauer, moved on in 1979. Berard and Treland took full-time positions with the National Guard, where they had served for years with Wise. Berard had made colonel and would continue rising through the ranks, becoming adjutant general—commander—of the Wisconsin National Guard in 1996–97. Treland completed Officer Candidate School, became a company commander, and served on Berard's staff in Madison. Berard had won a US Ski Association Silver honor, the Paul Bacon Award, in 1978 for event management. He was chief of timing for cross-country at the 1979 pre-Olympics World Cup and for the 1980 Olympic cross-country events at Lake Placid.[66]

Berard was at the center of Wise's highest-profile operations and had a front-row seat when both Telemark Lodge and the Birkebeiner took off from 1973 to 1979. It appeared to be an incredible success story, but under the surface the financial foundation was eroding beyond Berard's control. Warning signs had begun to appear. Notably, the loan Telemark received in 1978 for the Colosseum was for $5 million, but $2 million was designated to support debt restructuring.

Had the debt accumulated gradually over five years of new lodge operations, or had it spiked with Wise's cross-country push? It may have been both, but the cash outlays for cross-country were huge, and the payback hadn't arrived. Revenue for the 1978 calendar year was $215,000 for alpine but just $53,000 for lower-priced cross-country, although cross-country had a higher profit margin because the skiers didn't need the chairlift infrastructure. The alpine-to-cross-country disparity in number of skiers was 3 to 1, and in rental and ski shop sales it was 5 to 1.[67]

The push into cross-country included expensive promotional outlays to bring in big-name skiers and media. "We lost money every year on the Birkie," Berard said in 2022, noting that many lodge rooms were complimentary for officials, elite skiers, and members of the media. In 1978, the race lost $49,000—almost half of which covered media expenses, as well as food and lodging for guests and racers. In addition, Berard said, Wise "brought in press people from all over the world [and] would pay for their airline tickets." For the 1978 World Cup, for example, Wise paid $40,000 in airfares.[68]

Wise was operating beyond his means. "Tony's nature was brinksmanship. He pushed everything to the edge," said Telemark accountant Fred Vortanz. For example, Wise had agreed to escrow the money he made selling the lodge condo units with First Wisconsin Bank but instead used it for other needs, Vortanz said, adding that Wise arguably could have gone to jail if First Wisconsin had stood firm.[69]

By March of 1979, Wise's epic optimism was idling. He sent a Western Union Mailgram to officials from 115 ski industry companies and asked for financial support, $1,000 each, and a chance to meet with them at an industry show in Las Vegas. He cited the success he'd had raising the profile of the sport on virtually his own dime, including spending nearly $300,000 on the two World Cup events. (He had floated the idea of industry support three months earlier at the expensive Gitchi Gami Games, saying in a *Nordic World* magazine interview he needed help to get out of the red.[70]) "I have out-run my supply lines, and my company needs refueling," he wrote. "Now I need financial assistance from the cross-country ski industry in the amount of $100,000 if I am to survive."[71]

Skiers on the Birkebeiner Classic Trail, which opened in 2007 and brought more striders back to the race. AMERICAN BIRKEBEINER SKI FOUNDATION ARCHIVES, PHOTO BY KELLY RANDOLPH

FIVE

THE BIRKEBEINER TRAIL

THE AMERICAN BIRKEBEINER was the sixth idea to spring from the fertile mind of Tony Wise and make a significant impact on the sport of skiing, the region, or both. The list included Telemark ski area, Historyland, the Lumberjack World Championships, Telemark Lodge, and the Worldloppet, cementing Wise's legacy as a one-man visionary force.

Often overlooked, however, is a seventh idea that easily ranks among the greatest of what Wise created: the American Birkebeiner Trail.

In 1975, Wise reached out again to Sven Wiik, designer of the first Telemark Lodge trails, and began the process of developing a long, point-to-point, public ski and recreation trail that would help take the race—and eventually silent sports (e.g., nonmotorized) in northwestern Wisconsin—to new heights.

The idea was born of Wise's can-do attitude and his belief that his fledgling event would grow significantly and need a permanent racecourse. He knew the limitations of the hardscrabble route that Bob Treland and Ward Williamson had ably cobbled together for the 1973–75 races. Skiing single file at the base of railroad tracks and down rocky, bumpy Civilian Conservation Corps logging roads on routes shared with snowmobilers simply couldn't be part of a strategic growth plan.

Feedback from a skier survey published April 1, 1975, in the debut issue of the *Birch Scroll* race newsletter was all the proof Wise needed: the start area was too small, the tracks narrowed too quickly, there was congestion at a railroad crossing, skiers got lost, the track at the start of the short race was sandy, it was hard to pass slower skiers, some roads where the track was set were icy, snowmobilers were on part of the course, and the food stops were inadequate. Wise knew he needed a better trail.[1]

In 1975, the race drew just 324 skiers—hardly enough to justify what Wise had in mind. Still, he decided to create a wholly new trail roughly along the same corridor between Hayward and Cable, a trail with three sets of tracks that could hold *thousands* of skiers. That's confidence. And, like all his big ideas, it had shock value. "Tony used to tell us one of his ideas, and we'd say, 'My God, Tony, you can't do that!'" Bob Treland said. "When he said, 'Let's cut a trail through the woods,' then we thought he was really crazy. It was a humongous project. We were going to cut over 40 kilometers of trail."[2]

So began the American Birkebeiner Trail. In early May 1975, before receiving official permission to use public land, Wiik and Treland began a weeklong process of hiking through the woods with compasses and *National Geographic* topographical maps. The Chippewa lobe of the last Ice Age glacier ten thousand years earlier had deposited hills of till several miles wide on the east side of the Namekagon River valley. According to Wiik's estimation, this was a prime piece of sharply carved, postglacial landscape, land that he believed was some of the best in the country for the sport.

After studying the topography, the two men began near Fish Hatchery Creek, slightly northeast of Hayward, and marched north into the forest. Wiik would call out to Treland, left and right, which trees he wanted cut; Treland would mark them with ribbons. At the end of each day, they would march back over the new section to where they parked their truck. They advanced three to four miles a day. The energetic Wiik, old enough to be Treland's father, moved so quickly "he about killed me," Treland said. Plus, "there were a lot of bugs."

In designing a trail that would be at a minimum fifteen feet wide, Wiik's goals included avoiding sidehill cuts to minimize erosion, saving desirable trees, keeping the trail straight enough to help skiers maintain rhythm, widening downhill sections and turns to maintain flow, helping reduce skier falls, appealing to recreational users as well as elite skiers, and, ultimately, achieving the immersive feel of skiing through a forest under your own power.

Eight days and twenty-five miles later, Wiik and Treland emerged near the west end of the Telemark Lodge trail system. The route they had marked was "the most scenic possible," the *Birch Scroll* reported. "The terrain it crosses undulates with a regular rhythm mixed with short sections of level ground. The new trail should prove to be one of the finest ski touring trails in the country."[3]

BEFORE: The original trail, shown here in 1975, was pieced together on logging roads and other backwoods segments, often with a single track and so narrow that skiers lined up single file. AMERICAN BIRKEBEINER SKI FOUNDATION ARCHIVES

AFTER: The new and much-improved trail, 15 feet wide with multiple sets of tracks, during its debut race in 1977. AMERICAN BIRKEBEINER SKI FOUNDATION ARCHIVES

The concept needed official approval, though, and Wise was on it. He presented the plan to the Sawyer County Forestry Committee on May 7, and on May 20 the Sawyer County Board passed a resolution allowing it. Initially the trail was known as the Sawyer County Skiing and Hiking Trail. Bayfield County approved a resolution September 30, 1975, that provided a short easement to the Telemark trails but not the right to clear the land Wise wanted. As part of the plan, public use of motorized vehicles—including snowmobiles—would be prohibited, a significant concession at a time when silent sports were just beginning to grow. The deal came with a catch: Telemark Lodge would be responsible for grooming and maintaining the trail.[4]

It was a go. However, there was the matter of cost, a projected $96,534 (the equivalent of about $600,000 in 2024), including $5,000 for Wiik's services. The counties, at first, weren't offering to help. Wise saw the greater impact of the trail and prudently waited for government grants. They didn't materialize in 1975. As a result, the 1976 race was run on virtually the same jigsaw course as 1975 (with a new start at Telemark), which Wiik had updated slightly and lengthened.

While the project dragged on, the Telemark Lodge trail system grew by 10 to 15 kilometers in late 1975, Wiik again doing much of the designing. With the two trail systems, eventually 100 kilometers at Telemark, Wise oversaw planning and development of about 150 kilometers of ski trails in little more than a decade.

By May 1976, after much lobbying, the money for the trail was in hand: $50,000 from the US Bureau of Outdoor Recreation, $30,000 from the Upper Great Lakes Regional Commission (UGLRC), and $20,000 from Sawyer County. William Bechtel, who served on the UGLRC as a member of the Wisconsin Local Affairs and Development Department, was a key advocate in securing the funding. He seemed to be of the same mindset as Wise. "We have a very strong concern for the recreational potential in northern and central Wisconsin," Bechtel said, noting that the trail could spur future development. He regarded it as responsible development, meeting recreational needs without compromising the environment.[5]

With the funding secure, Wise asked Marty Hall, whose US Olympic team had trained at Telemark in December 1975 and had just returned from a successful Olympics in Europe, to review Wiik's design. On May 1, 1976, Hall, Wise, and Bob Treland met at the Lumberjack Bowl Pancake House and studied maps. Then, Hall and Treland—with the help of Treland's brother, Harold, also a Telemark employee—went into the woods, looking for the year-old colored ribbons. The foliage was so thick, they had trouble finding them. "We couldn't see from one trail ribbon to the next," Hall said.[6]

US Olympic Coach Marty Hall (left) and Bob Treland of Telemark study maps as they mark the new trail between Telemark and Hayward. Hall oversaw adjustments to the route, which was largely designed by Sven Wiik. AMERICAN BIRKEBEINER SKI FOUNDATION ARCHIVES

Hall "liked the trail as it was set" but recommended some changes to help the racecourse get FIS certification, which Wise wanted to help attract elite skiers. Wiik had designed the course assuming the race direction would remain the same. However, after the start was switched to Telemark in 1976, Hall made further changes to account for skiing the opposite direction.[7]

Hall believed the trail—still about three-fourths Wiik's design—would be more difficult than the first four races, hard enough to challenge elite skiers but not too hard for citizen skiers. "We're taking full advantage of the available terrain," Hall said. "There won't be any long, boring stretches. It's really an exciting trail. Skiers will be so involved in the course they won't realize they've gone 55 kilometers."[8]

Construction—logging and grading to create the corridor—was supervised by Bob Treland and coordinated by Bob Kinney, a University of Wisconsin–Extension agent from Hayward. Work began in mid-August 1976 and was scheduled to be completed by November—in time for the first snow. The trail was divided into nine segments, with a different local logging company hired to work on each one. The substrate, mostly sand and gravel from the glacier, turned out to be ideal to work with.[9]

As fall came on and progress continued, Wise heralded the new trail to increase interest in the 1977 race, not that more interest was needed. The Norwegians were coming en masse for the first time, part of a record number of 2,206 registered skiers, double the previous year.

The new trail was dedicated on Thursday, February 24, 1977, in Hayward, two days before the fifth annual race. Mayors Robert Anderson of Hayward and Kare Halvorsen of Rena, Norway, skied across the finish line together in a light snow. Then they clasped hands with Wise in front of US and Norwegian flags, the high school band played "On, Wisconsin!" (the state song), and ski enthusiasts—including Norwegian media—celebrated an important development in the sport they loved. Anderson signed a city resolution February 15 declaring Lillehammer as Hayward's sister city. Jack Revoyr, of the Wisconsin Department of Business Development, presciently observed that the new trail could turn the region into "the cross-country skiing center of the nation."[10]

Debut day—Saturday, February 26—on the new trail was crisp and sunny. Preliminary reports from skiers who had trained on the new route warned of new "gut-busting" climbs and "suicidal" downhills, both of which were partially true. Steep uphills often were followed by steep downhills and, in some spots,

The new trail, which cut through county forest lands, took almost two years to plan, fund, and build. AMERICAN BIRKEBEINER SKI FOUNDATION ARCHIVES

sharp curves, causing crashes, pileups, and backups among citizen skiers. New snow over an icy base was part of the problem, especially on downhills where skiers snowplowed off the new snow. Two skiers suffered broken legs, one after hitting a tree when he couldn't make a curve. "We'll have to make the trail easier or put in bypasses so it won't be blocked by so many skiers," Jerry Berard noted. A section of trail wasn't ready, routing the race onto a Telemark trail for about 2 kilometers.[11]

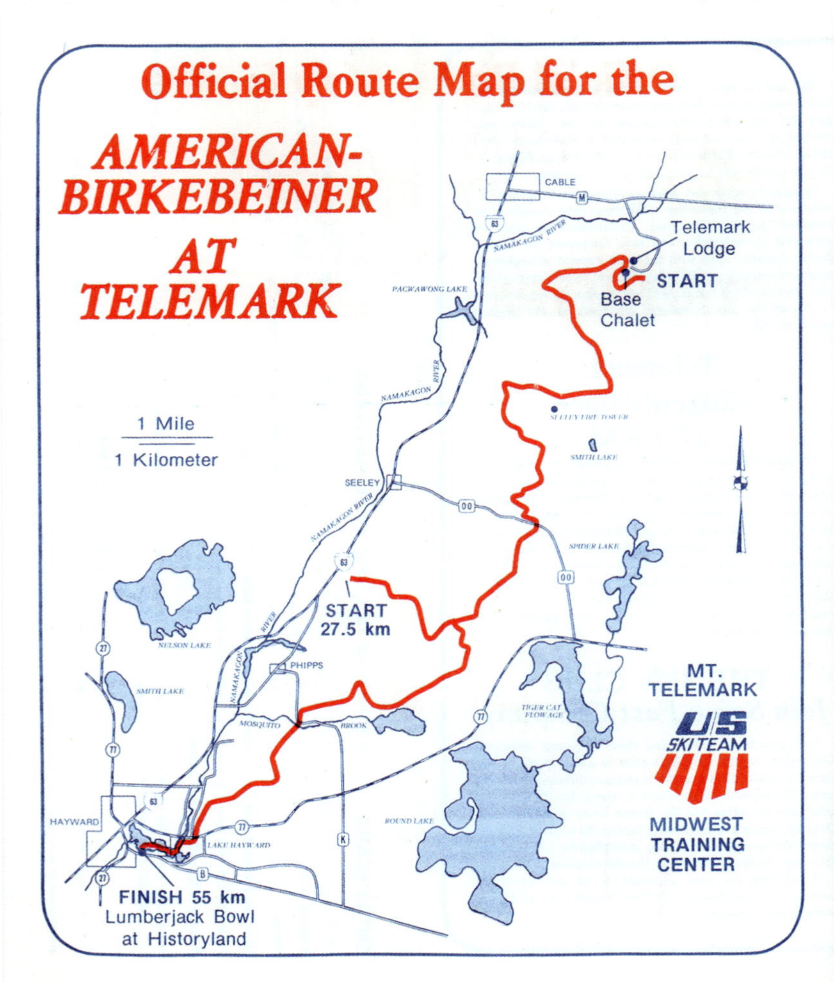

A map of the new Birkebeiner Trail, as revealed in the 1977 race brochure.
AMERICAN BIRKEBEINER SKI FOUNDATION ARCHIVES

The 1977 race start up Morgedal. Telemark Villages and the red poles of the ski lift can be seen in the background. AMERICAN BIRKEBEINER SKI FOUNDATION ARCHIVES

The Norwegians were expecting the relatively flat trail of 1976, based on what they'd heard from countryman and defending champion Audun Kolstad. "We were told before leaving Norway that the trail should be fairly easy compared to those we had at home, but I should say the trail was of a tougher side. This is something we appreciate. It shouldn't be easy," said fifty-five-year-old S. Christian Sommerfeldt of Norway, who earlier that week had completed a 90-kilometer race near Oslo, Norway. The rolling terrain of northwestern Wisconsin was uniquely challenging compared to the long climbs and descents in the mountains of Norway. Bjorn Arvnes of Norway, the 1977 winner who finished third in 1976, called the trail "very good and much harder" than the old one. "Technically, the race arrangement is as good here as in Europe."[12]

Wise's vision that a big trail would be needed to hold untold thousands of skiers came true, and quickly. Oddly for him, he didn't dream big enough. In 1979, more than 4,400 skiers began the race. Backups formed at the tops of steep hills and at other bottlenecks. Soon after the race, Wise announced that the trail width would be doubled—from fifteen to thirty feet with double the number of tracks. It would cost nearly as much to widen the trail as it had to build it, $90,000.[13]

Wise again lobbied for grants and got $30,000 from Sawyer County (a Conservation Committee member was Donald Landgraf, father of founding skier Dave Landgraf), $4,000 from Bayfield County, and $60,000 from the UGLRC. Getting permission to widen the trail wasn't a hard sell. After the 1979 race weekend, three area banks reported that deposits were $1.2 million more than after a typical February weekend.[14]

The project, again, was a big one. It included widening the first 8 kilometers of trail on Telemark and private property to fifty feet or more; and widening the next 42 kilometers of trail to thirty feet, including kilometers 48 to 50, which were on private property. The original trail also was modified with newly cut segments from the 8 to 12 kilometer marks and from the 45 to 47 kilometer marks. The work began in September and finished in November 1979, thanks in part to modern logging equipment that grabbed, sheared, and stacked the cut trees like toothpicks.[15]

Marty Hall, who had become a fixture around Telemark and designed other Telemark trails during the process, supervised the widening. "What's really amazing is that the trail did keep all of its undulations and dips despite being twice as wide," Hall said. He experienced it firsthand, finishing ninetieth in 3:04 in 1980 after returning from the Olympics. He noticed a couple of hills and corners that still needed some modifying, "but generally I was extremely pleased with what I saw in the race."[16]

The trail—now two and one-half US highway lanes wide, allowing skiers to see farther down the track—had lost some of its intimacy but remained a through-the-woods experience. Vermonter and two-time Olympian John Morton, who designed dozens of trails from coast to coast, described skiing the Birkebeiner for the first time in 1991:

> The course rocked and rolled, twisted and bobbed through the woods like a dance. It had rhythm. I could power up the hills, sensing they would be challenging but skiable; and sure enough, just as my legs began to burn, we would get a break. I also knew that I could go into the downhills full bore, confident a corkscrew turn in the trail wouldn't send me into the trees. The Birkie trail was a joy to ski.[17]

The Birkebeiner Trail in 1981, after being widened to thirty feet to accommodate continued race growth. AMERICAN BIRKEBEINER SKI FOUNDATION ARCHIVES

The widened trail, as planned, eased congestion in 1980 and beyond as the race continued to grow, but the corridor remained a work in progress. Wise proposed changes for the 1984 race, including creating alternate routes around some of the largest hills for less experienced skiers. He also looked into starting the race south of Hayward to ease congestion and accommodate more skiers. Those changes didn't happen, but in 1985, the manufacturing company Louisiana-Pacific in Hayward provided a bulldozer and driver to smooth out problem turns and downhills, including near Bitch Hill, the steep Bobsled downhill north of Highway OO, and six other spots.[18]

Year by year for dedicated skiers, the trail gradually became more than a means to an end but a sanctuary. They had sweat equity, in a sense. In spring 1995, when Sawyer County began logging off—some called it clear-cutting—fifty-two acres north of Fish Hatchery Creek, skiers protested. Trees not only provide a scenic backdrop for skiers but also serve an essential function, helping trails retain snow cover by blocking sunlight and wind. The county apparently disregarded its own 1991 policy requiring a 150-foot buffer on each side of the trail and defended its right to thin out mature and undesirable trees in that zone. A trail advocacy group formed, Friends of the Birkie Trail. Its members kept an eye on the trail and offered input on long-range management. Two years later, the Friends group and two other organizations that used the trail, the Chequamegon Fat Tire Festival and the Chequamegon Area Mountain Bike Association, came together to help with trail upkeep.[19]

The trail, a northern Wisconsin recreational success story, commands high-level attention. Race officials partner with the counties and state Department of Natural Resources on forest management and logging issues that could affect usability. Founding race skier, Wisconsin Conservation Hall of Fame member, and forestry expert John Kotar has been a liaison between the counties, race, and skiers. He recalled "some tough times in the early days" between skiers and loggers. "The Birkie would have been in danger of not being run because there was so much antagonism"—such as people putting logs across the trail to protest. Kotar helped bring the parties together, he said, "to come up with a reasonable management plan that serves both purposes, forest management and the trail. It's all doable, but people have to talk to each other." What's the unforeseen impact of cutting a two-hundred-foot tree? How should the canopy be managed? "I helped with ways that would not harm the trail," Kotar said, "which is dear to thousands of people."[20]

For the skier, the trail flows streamlike through the woods, with landmark hills. The rolling Power Line Hills, for example, are in an actual power line right-of-way. Other hills include Timber Trail, Fire Tower, Boedecker, Highway OO, Gravel Pit, Mosquito Brook, Bitch, Sunset, and Duffy's. A few treacherous hills keep even veteran skiers on edge, such as Heckler's at about kilometer 10. Its two nearly ninety-degree downhill turns—first left, then an immediate right—can cause mayhem, such as the year there was a pileup of close to forty skiers. The hill's other nickname, Bobblehead, is a reference to the helmeted snowmobilers who traditionally gather between the two curves to watch and hold up signs to rate the falls. In later waves, skiers have to pick a luge-like chute where previous skiers have snowplowed the trail to the bare, icy base.[21]

That turn still bothered Marty Hall more than four decades after he oversaw changes to the original design. "Ninety-nine percent of the trail is good,"

Facing page: Skiers climb the Power Line Hills in 2023. The racecourse was routed around the hills in the mid-1980s but returned to stay in 1988 based on a skier survey. A cluster of spectators at the top of the hill cheers for skiers as they make the grueling series of ascents early in the race. AMERICAN BIRKEBEINER SKI FOUNDATION ARCHIVES, PHOTO BY KELLY RANDOLPH

said Hall, who designed other trails in the US and the 1995 World Championships course in Canada, but "one thing they need to fix, and I don't know why they haven't, is snowmobile corner." In fact, in August 1980, Hall wrote to Wise from Vermont and diagrammed how the trail should be reconfigured to take out the first curve and make it one gentle right curve. Hall had hoped the hill could be fixed that fall, but it never was.[22]

For better or worse, the ubiquitous hills are a mark of distinction for the Birkebeiner, a feature that sets it apart from most other races in the US and even in Europe. When the trail was completed prior to the 1977 race, the total climb was measured at 1,240 meters over 55 kilometers—or 4,068 feet over about 34 miles. Since then, the climb has gotten even steeper. By 2022, the trail offered two courses, one for skate skiing and one for classic. The skate course climb that year was 1,398 meters over 50 kilometers, or 4,587 feet over 31 miles. That's an increase of about 500 feet in 5 fewer kilometers and nearly a mile of climbing. The classic course, meanwhile, was 1,379 meters over 53 kilometers (or 4,524 feet over almost 33 miles).

Even legendary US skier Bill Koch and his 1976 Olympic teammate Doug Peterson call it a challenging course. "What's amazing to me about the Birkie is that . . . for such a brutal course for a citizen's race, thousands still come," Koch said. "And knowing fully what they have been through for four, six, even eight hours, I'm amazed that so many return again and again to try and better their time. The Birkie shows no mercy, and so many who complete the course come in totally spent." Peterson added, "It's the more challenging trail of all the Worldloppet races. There's a lot of vertical. It's a true test even for the very elite skiers."[23]

Indeed, when someone has finished the Birkebeiner, they have skied a World Cup–level course—almost. FIS rates the course at 1,204 meters of climb (less than the race's own elevation analysis). Certified FIS 50-kilometer racecourses for the World Cup and the Olympics must be between 1,250 and 2,100 meters of climb—or at least 25 meters of climb per kilometer average.

Thus, for the citizen skier who may lack technique, top equipment, training time, or be well past their prime physically, it's a brutal test to train on the local trails or flats all winter—or hardly at all in warmer regions with little snow or no trails—and take on a World Cup course. "I can't think of an overall more challenging trail because of the terrain," said Ron Bergin, who skied twenty-five Birkebeiners and other marathons in the US, Canada, and Norway and was

The hills in the first half of the course are daunting, and they spike again toward the end.
AMERICAN BIRKEBEINER SKI FOUNDATION ARCHIVES, PHOTO BY MARK MILFORD

owner and editor of *Cross Country Skier* magazine. The payoff is at the end, as skiers glide across Lake Hayward toward downtown. "There's nothing like coming down Main Street and the feeling of the crowd," Bergin said. "You feel like a rock star just finishing the race."[24]

What makes the Birkebeiner course so difficult isn't the size of the hills but the number of them. There are four FIS-certified A-level climbs, the first at 10.3 kilometers (Fire Tower), followed at 15.7, 20, and 42.1 kilometers with climbs of 138 feet, 112, 105, and 131, respectively. A-level climbs must have an average steepness of at least 6 percent; these four range from 5.9 percent at Fire Tower to 11.9 percent at Boedecker Hill at the 15.7-kilometer mark. The course also has twenty-six B-level climbs, ranging from 33 to 66 feet.

The A and B climbs account for nearly 43 percent of total climb on the course, while one C-level climb of about 20 feet and undulating terrain make up the rest.

The infamous Bitch Hill, at about kilometer 40 for skaters, is named for its severity but also the costumed characters that over the years have coaxed

Skiers snowplow down a hill to control their speed in heavy traffic during the 1983 race.
AMERICAN BIRKEBEINER SKI FOUNDATION ARCHIVES

weary skiers to the top. It's worthy of its name "in part because it is located late in the race, and it is the biggest leg burner with 66 feet of climb at 14.6 percent average slope and 17.8 percent maximum," said Allan Serrano, an FIS technical delegate who has measured and rated the course. Serrano, originally from Anoka, Minnesota, and a former high school teammate of Olympian John Bauer, raced the Birkebeiner while part of a development team in the early 1990s. He also was director of race operations for several years beginning in 2015.[25]

The Birkebeiner starts with 12.5 kilometers of steady elevation gain. The climbs become mixed with more descents later in the race, resulting in the trail's rolling feel. Most B-level climbs are challenging but often follow "an equally steep descent," Serrano said. "A strong skier with good technique can easily charge up these climbs because they can maintain the momentum they gained on the descent."[26]

The physical challenge of the Birkebeiner Trail—including the technical ability required to ski efficiently on the uphills and fearlessly on the downhills, curves, and amongst the masses—commands the respect of those who tackle it. "It's a particularly tough course for the Worldloppet circuit, one of the toughest if not the toughest," Bill Koch said. "Most of the other ones are characterized by flatter terrain. In that sense it's a much better test for competition for a World Cup skier. The ups are quite steep."[27]

While the Birkebeiner trail is tough, World Cup and Olympic skiers most often face stiffer marathon tests. A standard-bearer for difficulty is the Holmenkollen course in Oslo, Norway, with thirty-six climbs of at least 75 feet in the 50 kilometers; the Birkebeiner has five. The highest climb at Holmenkollen is nearly 250 feet at 6.1 percent slope, and skiers do it six times on the 8.3-kilometer course. To match that, Birkebeiner skiers would have to go up a hill nearly twice as high as Fire Tower—the highest on the course—six times. The 2022 Olympic course in China had twenty-four climbs higher than 75 feet, none as high as Fire Tower but all about twice as steep.

For the world elites, difficult courses are needed. They can double pole up slopes that are 15 percent or less grade. The Birkebeiner has just three hills that top 15 percent average grade; there are twelve at Holmenkollen, and there were six in China.[28]

For pure skiing enjoyment, other great trail systems exist in the US, such as West Yellowstone, but there's nothing comparable to the long Birkebeiner

Trail with its varied terrain and, beginning in the late 2000s, a parallel classic trail for the first half (see Chapter 9). "We get a lot of lamenting [in the East] that there's not an opportunity anywhere near that," Serrano said. "Regardless of the fact it's such a huge homecoming event for thousands of people with a skiing experience that's unique, there's also a certain appreciation of being able to ski on the Birkie Trail."[29]

About fifty years after marking the trail with Wiik, Bob Treland sat on the edge of the Lumberjack Bowl where he directed the start of the first two Birkebeiners. He realized even in 1975 that the proposed trail "was going to be something big." Just like the Birkebeiner itself. "I'm very proud to have been part of it. It's grown into something fantastic, a premier event."[30]

The trail is a point-to-point wilderness experience passing through no towns or commercial areas—a testament to Wise's vision. Wise, however,

The Birkebeiner Trail, shown here in 2005, "favors an experienced skier with lesser fitness over a fitter skier with less experience," says FIS technical delegate Allan Serrano. "The ability to move among the crowd in these conditions is a big asset." AMERICAN BIRKEBEINER SKI FOUNDATION ARCHIVES, PHOTO BY KELLY RANDOLPH

wouldn't have feigned originality as a trail maker or in his land ethic, although he acted as a steward of the region's natural resources in building Telemark and supported the National Wild and Scenic Rivers Act that helped preserve the Namekagon. He would have deferred to Native Americans, who had created much more environmentally sensitive trails centuries and millennia earlier across North America on a scale that dwarfed the Birkebeiner trail. In fact, what remains of the ancient Chippewa Indian Trail, with its southern terminus at Chippewa Falls and northern end near Bayfield some 270 kilometers away, crosses the present-day race trail near Mosquito Brook.[31]

The Native peoples' latticework of two-foot-wide, well-worn footpaths across the northland often became templates for present-day highways. Yet these trails bear no resemblance to a highway—nor were they "a romantic wandering through the woods," says Ernie St. Germaine. "Paths and trails were called *mikana*. The rivers were our interstates and our routes to everywhere with occasional portages, which were the trails. There were also well-worn trails around every lake." Indeed, by linking one waterway to another, such trails served an essential role in a complex transportation system. "Every river had a name at the turn, or bend," St. Germaine explained. "This was how the people were able to keep track of locations, [much like] roadmaps."[32]

The spirit of preserving the woodlands as much as possible was part of the Birkebeiner Trail from the beginning. According to the proposal that Tony Wise submitted on May 20, 1975, to the Sawyer County Board:

> Upon completion, the trail should not bear any scars to remind the public of the work accomplished. All work . . . will be done in such a manner as to preserve the natural beauty of the surrounding environment. Every effort will be made to preserve and leave undamaged trees and plants out of the trail right of way. There cannot be any unnecessary earth moving or cutting of trees. . . . The trail should be laid out as naturally as possible, following the terrain as it exists.[33]

As natural as the trail appears, however, it's the result of much human work. Maintaining it for public use is a major commitment and six-figure annual expense for the American Birkebeiner Ski Foundation. The trail needs year-round attention, with winter grooming heading the list. Backcountry skiing and breaking trail mostly went the way of the black-and-white television in the

1960s—today's touring skier and citizen racer expect set tracks and a groomed skate deck. "You can't do the sport right by just going into the woods," Wise said. "You have to have prepared tracks. Otherwise it's like playing golf in a pasture."[34]

The original trail agreement specified that Telemark would be responsible for grooming, but the work was costly, time-consuming, and not done reliably in the early years, except during race week. Sometimes nonrace trail grooming consisted of locals Kurt Proctor, Gary Penman, and others snowmobiling over fresh snow or pulling drags and homemade track setters just so they could ski. Wise prioritized grooming his Telemark system instead, where skiers paid $4 a day to ski or bought an annual pass. Telemark trail revenue was about $60,000 during the winter of 1976–77—one-tenth of the revenue from alpine lift tickets. Wise spent $20,000 on grooming that winter, plus $32,000 on a new machine, a smaller version of the alpine groomers that could set parallel tracks.[35]

Beginning in 1985, the new Birkebeiner Ski Foundation took over year-round maintenance for the Birkebeiner Trail. They groomed the trail once every two weeks from December to mid-February, with snowmobiles double-tracking it, as well as before and after the race—about eight times a winter—and mowed twice a summer. This was progress but hardly the stuff of good tourism. If a storm hit the day after grooming, tough luck for the next two weeks. Still, there was reluctance to groom the trail at all, with the prevailing attitude that it wouldn't bring enough skiers to Hayward to justify the work.[36]

Trail-grooming technology advanced significantly from the snowmobile-pulled weighted sleds of the 1960s and 1970s to large, tank-tread machines with heated cabs. With plows in the front and rollers in the back, they packed the base and laid down crisp corduroy for skating and sculpted striding tracks. In the mid-1980s, Logan Manufacturing Company of Logan, Utah, maker of LMC groomers, brought in machines and drivers to groom the trail for the race. PistenBully of Germany joined the grooming effort for the 1988 race with a smaller groomer. The Birkebeiner's first commercial groomer designed for Nordic trails was an LMC 3700 Snow Cat. The foundation purchased it for $61,000 prior to the 1989 race and spent another $11,500 to build a structure to house it.[37]

Facing page: A groomer sets tracks on the Birkebeiner Trail in an undated photo likely taken in the late 1970s or early 1980s. AMERICAN BIRKEBEINER SKI FOUNDATION PAPERS. NORWEGIAN AMERICAN HISTORICAL ASSOCIATION, NORTHFIELD, MINNESOTA

Grooming and track setting were spotty using the LMC 3700. This didn't appreciably improve until the early 1990s when the foundation bought a PistenBully 100 and sent Kurt Proctor to the Canmore Nordic Centre in Alberta, Canada, for training. Proctor called the trip "an awakening." Afterward, he said, "I made sure we set some good-quality tracks."[38]

Eventually, larger PistenBully groomers, with six-figure price tags, became the norm. They could set multiple tracks and skate lane corduroy at the same time or plow off most of a heavy snowfall if needed, like the ones that hit several days before the 2022 and 2023 races. By 2023, the Birkebeiner had four of the big, German-made machines and one Italian-made Prinoth that could groom the whole trail and spur trails, more than sixty miles, in eight hours.

The trail was more than thirty-five years old before the foundation recognized its original potential to draw skiers all winter—not just race week—if groomed regularly. This would require money, however. Trail use donations only totaled $28,000 a year, and it cost $4,000 each time groomers went out. In 2013, new foundation Executive Director Ben Popp hired a full-time trail supervisor and proposed a mandatory trail use fee—$10 a day or $50 annually—to support improved grooming and year-round maintenance. Such fees had been common for years on public trails around the Midwest. The Sawyer County Board narrowly approved it. Within four years, trail fee income approached $100,000.[39]

Year-round trail work and high-tech groomers with floating rubber treads have made it possible to ski on four inches of packed snow. However, maintenance performed the other nine months of the year—mowing, picking rocks, brushing back the forest, planting grass, installing drains and culverts, reengineering slopes, adding ditches, building erosion bars, and building up low spots where water collects—helps make that possible. "We put in more hours during the summertime than we do in the winter," Proctor said. "Mother Nature is constantly trying to take that trail back."[40]

Trail upkeep isn't just for skiing. In 1983, the trail hosted the Chequamegon Fat Tire Festival mountain bike race, which has now become nationally recognized. Its founders (including four Telemark employees) used the race to elevate a sport that was becoming popular—much like the Birkebeiner did for cross-country a decade earlier. The trail also hosts other ski races, such as the Pre-Birkie, the Seeley Hills Classic, and in 2015 the International Paralympic Committee Nordic World Championships, as well as the Birkie Trail Run and Fat Tire Birkie. Adjoining trailheads with spur trails, some with lights, have been added, along with log cabin shelters that double as race food stations. Adjacent housing developments advertise back-door access to the trail. Take away the Birkebeiner, and the trail still would be a year-round destination.

AMERICAN BIRKEBEINER SKI FOUNDATION ARCHIVES

In 2016, the trail drew one hundred thousand users and was named the number one cross-country ski destination in the nation by *USA Today* in a reader's choice survey, outpolling trails in nine other ski-centric states. During that decade, the Birkebeiner, in part owing to the trail, was named by *National Geographic*, *National Geographic Adventure*, and *Outside* magazines as one of ten amazing races in the world, "most vaunted ski race" in the country, and a top twenty-five American race; the area was a Nordic mecca.[41]

Has the trail become too important to fail? More than fifty years after Tony Wise conceived it; after Sven Wiik, Marty Hall, and Bob Treland revealed it; after Telemark, the foundation, the counties, the Department of Natural Resources, the National Guard, the US Forest Service, Wisconsin Conservation Corps, and volunteers have maintained and improved it; and after hundreds of thousands of people have traversed it under their own power, the American Birkebeiner Trail has endured, inspired, and helped the Birkebeiner become a race of worldwide importance. In other words, exactly what Tony Wise envisioned.

Two skiers take a spill on a crowded downhill during the 1985 race, the first one run by the new Birkebeiner Foundation.
AMERICAN BIRKEBEINER SKI FOUNDATION ARCHIVES

SIX

1980–1989
FALLING AND RECOVERING

WITH A BIG NEW TRAIL, a lodge that was humming, and entries on the rise, the Birkebeiner was a juggernaut on skinny skis as the 1980s began. Tony Wise and team could do no wrong, it seemed, other than some year-to-year growing pains. Telemark was a true international phenomenon in the Nordic world. What could stop the progress?

It seems Wise answered that question when he quietly forecast his own financial ruin in 1979. By the mid-1980s the futures of Telemark and the race were in the courts and in doubt—and almost collapsed altogether—despite the emergence of a popular new ski technique that took the sport itself to new heights.

The February 23, 1980, race was held during the final weekend of the Winter Olympics, which were in Lake Placid, New York. As skiers headed to Telemark on Friday, the US men's hockey team was thrilling the nation in an upset win against the Soviet Union—the "Miracle on Ice"—en route to winning the historic gold medal. Birkebeiner officials, trying to capitalize on the Olympic fervor, dubbed their race the Citizen Olympics. In fact, the Birkebeiner had enjoyed a presence at the Olympics that year, a sign of the respect that the race and Telemark had gained. Race officials past and present, including Jerry Berard (chief of timing), Harold Treland (chief of start), Tom Kelly (media specialist), and former race announcer Peter Graves (ABC Sports analyst), worked the cross-country events at Lake Placid, and Tony Wise was a special guest of the US cross-country team. Berard's daughter, Diane, who had learned to ski at Telemark, was an alternate on the US alpine team.[1]

Entries for the 1980 Birkebeiner dropped by less than one hundred to 4,387. Out front on the course that day were the Norwegians again (a consolation prize after their teams were fifth in the Olympics). Per Knotten, the 1973 Norwegian Birkebeinerrennet winner, won in a record 2:24 over 52 kilometers, holding off 1979 champion and countryman Arnt Haarstad. It was the fifth straight American Birkebeiner win for a Norwegian skier. Norwegian Gry Oftedal, in her first marathon, won the women's race in 2:53. It was twenty-two degrees at the start, with snow falling at the finish.[2]

A race within the race played out behind the leaders. Who would be the first person in history to complete a Worldloppet? Six skiers were attempting to go the distance in the first year of its existence by competing in all nine events, in Austria, Italy, Germany, Canada, Finland, Sweden, Switzerland, Norway, and the US, in that order. The races totaled 587 kilometers—364 miles. In the mix were Tom and Carol Duffy, both 45, of Hayward. The Duffys' European odyssey included Carol—with Tom joining her—having to ski a special preliminary race in Sweden's 90-kilometer Vasaloppet because women weren't yet allowed in the main event. They did it three days after finishing the 75-kilometer Finlandia Hiito.

Because of a scheduling conflict that resulted in the Birkebeiner and Finland race on the same weekend in 1979, the Birkebeiner deferred. The first chance to complete all nine races and become a Worldloppet Master came at the 1980 Birkebeiner. The first of the six Worldloppet skiers to cross the finish line in Hayward was Gunnar Sarring of Sweden, followed by Carol Duffy, the Birkebeiner's original women's short race winner (wearing bib No. 1), who was two minutes ahead of Tom (bib No. 2), the third finisher. Waiting for the Duffys in Hayward with flowers were their eleven children.[3]

Berard had recently stepped down as race director and Telemark Lodge manager, so Wise took over in 1980 with help from Don Plante, Marty Hall, and the US Ski Association's Harry Brown. After the problems with trail and traffic backups and injuries in 1979, race officials were determined to have a smooth race. The newly widened trail helped significantly, as did the new start going around—instead of over—the Valhalla and Morgedal runs to reduce backside Stormoen crashes, plus the five hundred volunteers on hand to provide support.[4]

1980 women's top three skiers (left to right): Jennifer Caldwell, third place; runner-up Anna Bjorgan; and winner Gry Oftedal. AMERICAN BIRKEBEINER SKI FOUNDATION ARCHIVES

Tom and Carol Duffy of Hayward, pictured here after their 1980 Birkebeiner finish, were two of the first three skiers ever to become Worldloppet Masters by finishing all nine Worldloppet races. AMERICAN BIRKEBEINER SKI FOUNDATION ARCHIVES

The race in 1980 unveiled two additions: a ski patrol, in part because of the skier death in 1979; and, in a sign of the future, the use of a computer system. The ski patrol had three members, Toby Markowitz, Howard Holtz, and John Pitman, all from the Twin Cities area. Markowitz would go on to lead the patrol for years, recruiting certified ski patrollers from all over the country. When the Kortelopet was on the same day as the Birkebeiner, Markowitz would ski the short race, change clothes, then join his wife, Dorothy, on the ski patrol, helping injured and ill skiers with basic first aid or more serious medical attention. The procedures he set up remained in use as late as 2024, and he would continue to volunteer at the race into the early 2020s.

The new computer system belonged to Minnesota Micro Systems of Minneapolis, which was hired for the event. This was the first time a computer was used on-site to track and report results. Advances in technology were allowing companies to take "micro" computers that cost $10,000 to $15,000 apiece into the field. The computer model used in 1980 was made by Vector Graphic, an early microcomputer company from Westlake Village, California. Race announcers in Hayward also used computer terminals to punch up information on finishers. Previously, race-timing officials had used phone lines connected to an off-site computer system to relay the results.[5]

TWO MONTHS BEFORE THE 1981 BIRKEBEINER, Tony Wise made another kind of Nordic history—the world's first indoor ski races. Held December 16–18, 1980, at Telemark, the fifth annual Gitchi Gami Games featured members from the US and Canadian men's and women's ski teams racing through Telemark's brand-new $3 million Colosseum.

The Gitchi Gami Games were part of the Colosseum's weeklong grand opening. A few days earlier, an indoor tennis exhibition featured touring pros Tim and Tom Gullikson, twins from Onalaska, Wisconsin, who were ranked in the top fifty in the world. The Gullikson brothers praised the new facility, which had Dynaturf courts like one installed at the White House.[6]

At least in size, the Colosseum indeed was grand compared with the alpine chalet it replaced. Wise named the facility after the graceful, two-thousand-year-old elliptical amphitheater he'd toured during a recent stop in Rome, Italy. However, the two structures couldn't have been more dissimilar. Wise's sixty-four-thousand-square-foot Colosseum (one-fourth the size of its namesake) was low, rectangular, and industrial in appearance, with a black metal roof that looked like a stovetop range hood—an odd departure from his Norwegian-themed lodge and race. A plywood replica of the Roman original, however, stood indoors for the grand opening, and Old World murals decorated the interior. It housed four tennis courts and convention space, plus a ski shop, bar, and cafeteria. But it seemed out of place compared to the homey old chalet and the Wright-influenced lodge, to which the Colosseum eventually would be connected by tunnel. Still, the new Colosseum could do things the chalet and lodge couldn't—like handle a crowd of more than fifteen hundred for a concert by Jerry Lee Lewis and conventions with room for large displays like fire trucks—and that was the need.

For the Gitchi Gami Games, race officials opened two large doors on opposite sides of the vast building to create a partially indoor route: a 2.5-kilometer loop on artificial snow (real snow was lacking), with skiers going in and out of the building up to six times. Spectators indoors sat on bleachers and could watch other parts of the race on closed-circuit televisions. The temperature inside hovered between forty and fifty degrees, and the snow was treated with ammonium nitrate to prevent melting. Spectators in the Colosseum watched as Tim Caldwell beat his friend Bill Koch to the outside finish line in the 15-kilometer race. Wise had been campaigning to get national television more interested in the Birkebeiner and the sport. "Our goal," Wise said, "is to show the public, and especially television, just how exciting cross-country skiing can be."[7]

Koch, at age twenty-four, was in his prime and had competed in his second Olympics earlier that year. It may be a footnote in his storied career that Koch skied in the world's first indoor race, but it was no surprise to see him again at Telemark, where he had become a regular. In fact, Koch had visited Telemark in the summers of both 1979 and 1980—he was designing his first major ski trail. Koch hadn't liked how some of the steep trails at Telemark forced cross-country skiers to break stride and herringbone up the hills. He shared this critique with Wise, who was ready with a solution. "Tony just asked me to design a trail," Koch later recalled. "He said, 'Anything available is yours.' I found a really nice [glacial] esker, a low ridge. I played off the esker, which was one hundred foot vertical or less. That fit for me; you didn't have to herringbone."

The Bill Koch Trail came together over the course of two years—just as a Bill Koch Ski League (the genesis of the future Barnebirkie children's race) was starting in Hayward and Cable, with seventy children learning how to ski

Workers spread several tons of snow over plastic and Styrofoam sheeting to create a three-hundred-foot lane—with two sets of striding tracks—straight through the Colosseum for the world's first (partially) indoor cross-country ski race in December 1980, part of Telemark's Gitchi Gami Games. AMERICAN BIRKEBEINER SKI FOUNDATION PAPERS. NORWEGIAN AMERICAN HISTORICAL ASSOCIATION, NORTHFIELD, MINNESOTA

To design his trail at Telemark, Bill Koch spent ten days there in summer 1979 walking the terrain, going over maps, and marking trees he wanted cut. AMERICAN BIRKEBEINER SKI FOUNDATION PAPERS. NORWEGIAN AMERICAN HISTORICAL ASSOCIATION, NORTHFIELD, MINNESOTA

under the direction of the Telemark Academy. Trail planning took place during the winter of 1978–79, marking in summer 1979, and final shaping in summer 1980. Koch aimed for one-third uphill, one-third flat, and one-third downhill. The result was a 15-kilometer intimate striding experience at the minimum FIS standard of just over eight feet wide—tough enough to challenge Olympians but with hill bypasses that made it suitable for all levels of skiers. "It's the first trail I can remember getting paid for, the first big job that I had," Koch said many years later. "It's one of the best I designed."[8]

HEADING INTO THE 1981 BIRKEBEINER, Wise and his team expected more than seven thousand entries, which would make the race the fourth largest in the world. However, just 180 skiers lined up for Birkebeiner IX—at least initially. Snow cover had been spotty all winter, so race officials had stockpiled it near Telemark just in case. A warm front the weekend before the February

21 event laid bare much of the trail. The mild weather continued, and officials scrambled to save the race in some form, with volunteers planning to truck in snow or find a different route through the woods where snow remained. None of it worked. By early Wednesday, three days before the race, heavy rain and temperatures in the midforties wiped out the rest of the snow. That afternoon, officials announced plan B—the main race would be postponed for two weeks until March 7.

Plans C, D, and E came next. Many elite and foreign skiers already were on-site when the race was rescheduled, so officials got creative. That Friday, a 48-kilometer race for 60 elite skiers was held in six loops around Telemark, with a second 42-kilometer event for 120 foreign citizen skiers. The elite winners were sweat-stained Jean-Paul Pierrat of France in 3:09 and Marianne Hadler of Vermont in 3:57. Competitors slogged through slush and water and up the Telemark hill—which was covered in artificial snow—as temperatures rose to sixty-five degrees, which forced about half of them, including Bill Koch, to drop out. Unexpectedly, a third race of 42 kilometers was arranged on Saturday for a small group of skiers who had traveled long distances and didn't arrive in time for Friday's citizen race. They finished in the rain.

On Saturday night, the rain turned to snow. Between twelve and twenty inches fell, and finally the cold weather held. Two weeks later, on March 7, 3,400 skiers gathered for the rescheduled ninth Birkebeiner, where Tim Caldwell became the first American champion since 1975. The 55-kilometer course was in great condition, and Caldwell covered it in in 2:34, three minutes ahead of former champion Bjorn Arvnes of Norway. Muriel Gilman of Bemidji, Minnesota, won

Jean-Paul Pierrat after winning the slush-filled race in 1981. AMERICAN BIRKEBEINER SKI FOUNDATION ARCHIVES

the women's race in 3:22. Start temperatures for the four races helped tell the weather story—forty, forty-eight, forty-five, and ten degrees. Total entries were 6,356—less than the 7,000 expected but still smashing the previous record by nearly 2,000. The strange year included the race briefly changing its name to the Norwegian American Birkebeiner because the Norwegian Ski Council was the sponsor (dignitaries included the Norwegian ambassador to the US, Knut Hedemann).[9]

It was a rough Birkebeiner, but the worst was yet to come. On April 30, 1981, the big northland balloon that was Telemark Lodge lost some of its air. Payroll checks were bouncing, and creditors had begun to line up because they weren't getting paid. Bayfield Electric was threatening to shut off Telemark's power. Telemark accountant Fred Vortanz summoned Wise to the lodge that afternoon for a come-to-Jesus meeting with several creditors, including the Colosseum's major funder from the federal Farmers Home Administration. The goal was to help Wise get his spending under control, but "he wouldn't give up the checkbook," said Vortanz, who kept the books but didn't write the checks.

Then, someone entered the meeting and passed Wise a note. Wise glanced at its contents, then made a stunning announcement. "Gentlemen," he said, "we just filed Chapter 11 in Eau Claire. Thank you." Everyone got up and walked out. Wise had just put up a wall: the federal bankruptcy court action for debt reorganization meant Telemark could continue to operate without the fear of creditors like those in the room taking legal action. He had to submit a payment plan acceptable to the courts, if not necessarily his creditors, which totaled six hundred and fifty in all.[10]

In the fall 1981 issue of the *Birch Scroll*, Wise wrote that Telemark was "saved" by the filing. The admission must have shocked anyone paging through the publication who had witnessed the Birkebeiner's rapid growth and the ballyhoo surrounding the nine-year-old lodge and new Colosseum. Debts were $7.1 million (and rising) and assets $2.2 million. Tony and Sheila Wise owned Telemark Enterprises, which consisted of Telemark Management, Telemark Company, Telemark Land, Historyland, and THAW (a payroll company that allowed Wise to avoid paying overtime to seasonal workers, many of whom worked six days a week and holidays). Wise promised business as usual and that American Birkebeiner X in 1982 would be the greatest one yet. The long-term outlook, however, wasn't good. "Tony needed to win the lottery," Vortanz said, "and that probably wouldn't have been enough."[11]

The morass of Telemark's debt included the big Colosseum loan. The first loan payments were coming due, but Chapter 11 stopped them cold. "We never made a payment on the Colosseum," Vortanz said. Another creditor was the Telemark Lodge Owners Association, whose members had signed long-term leases on condo units. Lease agreements required Telemark Management to pay owners (a group that included the Vortanzes) 20 percent of revenue from their room bookings. Wise had been making payments on the owners' units from the start—even before the lodge was profitable, driving himself further into debt—but still owed the association $400,000, or about $2,000 per owner, which never was repaid.[12]

At the time, Telemark employed about four hundred people, or 4.3 percent of the region's workforce. In allowing the reorganization, the courts may have considered the economic impact if Telemark had closed—unemployment would have risen 14 percent in Bayfield County, 16 percent in Sawyer County, and up to 24 percent in both counties if other Telemark-related job losses were counted.[13]

Wise blamed the financial problems on two bad winters in a row, but his telegram in 1979 seeking industry support to survive indicated the problem wasn't new. Previous debt, combined with the Colosseum payments and the tough winters, had tightened the screws. "He'd make a quarter, and he'd borrow a dollar against it," Bob Treland observed many years later. "Unfortunately, that was his undoing." Wise's Nordic vision had stretched his operation so thin that it was melting from the heat generated by his devil-may-care management style. One time, when a housing lot sold, an employee flew to Wausau, Wisconsin, to get the check so it could be brought back immediately to pay the power company.[14]

Lodge workers were well aware of Telemark's bankruptcy and millions of dollars in debt, yet many admired Tony for his drive to serve others. He "was a purveyor of hospitality and good times," recalled employee Gary Crandall, "and not for Tony, but for the community." Ironically, by 1981, the lodge had just begun to turn a profit by approaching the 50 percent occupancy rate, and Telemark was grossing almost $3 million a year in food and liquor sales. And in 1981, Wise, with seven restaurants at Telemark and Historyland, was named Restaurateur of the Year by a regional tourism organization.[15]

AS WISE HAD PROMISED, the Birkebeiner's tenth race in 1982 (the same year its Norwegian counterpart marked its fiftieth) was the greatest Birkebeiner to date. The opening ceremonies on Friday, February 26, included skydivers with international flags unfurling from their feet, hot-air balloons, a 140-member University of Wisconsin marching band, a parade of states and nations, Norwegian folk dancers, a Lac Courte Oreilles tribal powwow, a reenactment of Norse explorer Leif Eriksson meeting Indigenous people on the coast of Newfoundland in 1005, and Norwegian officials presenting to Birkebeiner officials a gift of snow brought from Lillehammer and Rena. A giant Viking warrior ice sculpture by Austrian Engelbert Hattenberger greeted skiers as they arrived. Thousands of people attended. That night, a torchlight parade was held outside the Colosseum. The postrace Birkefest festivities were similarly grandiose, with a $7.95 smorgasbord of American-style salads, entrees, and desserts, an awards ceremony, fireworks, and a concert. Wise, by all appearances, had not pulled back on his spending.[16]

That year, Wise honored ten skiers who had completed every race, thus initiating the race's ten-year-award tradition. He called them the Founders. They were Karl Andresen, Fred Constalie, John Gannett, John Holmquist, John Kotar, Dave Landgraf, Wayne Lindskoog, Nils Meland, Ernie St. Germaine, and Rick Scott. Two others who just missed being on the list were Jacque Lindskoog, the first women's winner who had switched to the Kortelopet one year because of knee surgery, and Duncan McLean, who had competed in—and won—the first two Kortelopets because of the age restriction and hadn't missed a Birkebeiner since he was eligible. Some people referred to Jacque and Duncan as the Forgotten Founders. Also honored was the first Birkebeiner winner, Erik Ersson, who returned from Sweden to compete in the race and took 116th place. He received engraved birchleggings commemorating his 1973 victory and a carved wooden Telemark shield.

Entries were down slightly, though only by eight skiers, to 6,348. For the first time since 1975, the race started in Hayward, and for the first time it involved Main Street. This was somewhat of an accident. In previous years, a school gym near Cable had provided overflow housing for up to one thousand

Facing page: A skydiver at Telemark during the opening ceremonies for the tenth anniversary race in 1982. AMERICAN BIRKEBEINER SKI FOUNDATION PAPERS. NORWEGIAN AMERICAN HISTORICAL ASSOCIATION, NORTHFIELD, MINNESOTA

skiers. It wasn't available that year, but a school in Hayward was. However, busing approximately one thousand skiers from Hayward to Telemark would complicate logistics and add to prerace road congestion—so Wise decided instead to reverse the course and find a place to start in Hayward. He briefly considered using the Lumberjack Bowl or Historyland as the start area, but the race had grown so large that this was no longer feasible.

In early January, Wise was at one of his favorite Hayward eateries, the Moose Café, when he mentioned the issue to owner Norm Cooper. Cooper suggested a solution: why not start the race downtown? Wise loved the idea but was skeptical because he had mentioned the idea years before and it was rejected. Cooper, however, quickly got the Chamber of Commerce on board. The idea galvanized in late January, when the city approved Wise's request to close Main Street and other nearby roads for several days and to have the course cross Highway 63, causing a detour on race day. Presented with the opportunity, city officials clearly recognized the value of making Hayward an integral part of the growing race, a decision that would set a precedent and pay dividends in the decades to come. The new reversed route was finalized: skiers would start west of downtown, ski along Main Street and across Highway 63 to the lake, cross the lake, then head north through the woods to finish at Telemark's Colosseum.[17]

The Main-by-accident start was serendipitous. The sight of 6,348 colorful skiers gliding through downtown Hayward on the twenty-four-degree, cloudy morning after a dusting of snow overnight, with spectators jamming the sidewalks, was unforgettable. The first person to ski down Main Street was the same person who first crossed a Birkebeiner finish line—original Kortelopet winner Duncan McLean of Michigan. Then they came in droves, the hours-long spectacle undeniable proof that the Birkebeiner had become even bigger than people realized. It had taken over an entire downtown, this low-key sport coming out of the woods to the people.

Wise had invited a special guest to watch the race: 106-year-old Canadian ski icon Herman "Jack Rabbit" Smith-Johanssen. Together, Wise and Smith-Johanssen stood on the balcony of the Hayward Inn, at the southwest corner of Main and Highway 63, taking it all in. Moved by the sheer size of the race and pageantry of the start, Smith-Johannssen called it "one of the greatest things to happen to the cross-country ski sport" and "the most exciting day of my life."[18]

The 1982 start marked the first time Main Street was used for the race.
AMERICAN BIRKEBEINER SKI FOUNDATION ARCHIVES

It also was a day to remember for Ola Hassis of Sweden, who edged Norway's Jan Borkheim by three seconds to finish in 2:42. Norway's Gry Oftedal won her second women's race in three years in 3:04. (Finish times were a little slower than previous years, in part because skiing north, generally uphill, was harder.) Thousands of spectators jammed the finish area around the Colosseum and cheered Hassis and Oftedal as they walked to a news conference. Amazed, the thirty-year-old Hassis, who had won his country's Vasaloppet three years earlier, said, "I've never seen anything like this." Hassis was the first Swede to win since Erik Ersson in 1973, and Ersson sought out his countryman later that day to personally congratulate him.[19]

Unfortunately, the Norwegian Ski Council sponsorship had ended after the previous year, leaving the Birkebeiner without a major backer, only minor sponsors—and further complicating Wise's financial problems. Another hiccup in the 1982 race was a problem with the computer bar code reader that delayed results for up to twenty-four hours.

In addition to lighting up Main Street on a winter day for the first time, the 1982 race was a harbinger of a new form of skiing when some lead skiers kept one ski inside the tracks but pushed the other ski to the side, a technique called the marathon skate. When the lead group crossed Highway OO, Howie Bean of the US abandoned the tracks completely and skated—full side to side—through. A revolution in the sport was underway, called skate skiing, or freestyle. It hadn't completely caught on, but top skiers were beginning to use it more and more, and many had been using it situationally for years to maximize speed.

One of the skate skiing pioneers was Bill Koch. In 1976, when he won his Olympic silver medal, he was filmed skate skiing in a Rossignol video *The Bill Koch Experience*. In 1980, he saw the marathon skate, or Siitonen Step, used by top skiers in the mostly flat Vasaloppet marathon in Sweden. It was named after Finland's Pauli Siitonen, a long-distance specialist who marathon-skated like ancient hunters had done centuries earlier, although hunters had a short ski (called an *andor*) as their pusher. "A light bulb went off in Koch's head," said FIS official Bengt Erik Bengtsson. "Why not apply skating to standard 15-, 30-, and 50-kilometer FIS-sanctioned races?" Bengtsson witnessed Koch skating that year—in fact, the same week as the Birkebeiner—in the World Championships at Holmenkollen in Oslo, Norway. Koch went on to win the World Cup title in 1982—four wins in the ten events—in part because he had taken the Siitonen Step to full skating.[20]

Skating was part of the striding technique used by classic skiers as far back as the 1930s, well before it became a popular form of skiing on its own. Sven Wiik, the Birkebeiner trail designer and Olympic coach, had used full skating for years while making turns, noting that the "skating turn increases your speed, a result of the pushing-off motion that propels you around those bends and corners in the trail." It was just a matter of time before someone would employ it for more than turns or a sprint finish, with the innovative Koch seizing the opportunity.[21]

As quickly as skating evolved from the Siitonen Step into both skis out of the tracks, it became controversial—at the competitive level because it was nontraditional and provided a seemingly unfair speed advantage without the need for kick wax, and at the recreational level because it chopped up the striding tracks. Rules and racecourse barriers around the Nordic world were put in place to prevent and restrict skating at the elite levels, including no skating near the start and finish lines. But it became a losing battle as skaters found ways around the new rules, even if the tradition-bound Norwegians "were opposed to the heretical new technique," Bengtsson said, and even if one expert predicted the death of the sport because of it. "The Norwegians just hated skating and did everything in their power to put a stop to it," Bill Koch recalled, but "they couldn't quash it." One skier who employed the Siitonen Step and skating in the 1982 Birkebeiner, taking eleventh place, was none other than Pauli Siitonen himself.[22]

BY 1983, AN FIS OFFICIAL PROCLAIMED "the skating step has come to stay." Skate skiing offered new retail markets for specialized equipment, and international governing bodies, manufacturers, and retailers saw it as a way to grow the sport. Skiers liked it too. It was faster, more athletic, and to some, more fun. "All the people who bike and run in the summer, they found a winter sport," said longtime race entrant Duncan McLean.[23]

Like the sport itself, Wise continued to push forward. Telemark was awarded the 1983 World Masters Championships (for skiers thirty and older), held in the US for the first time. The 15- and 30-kilometer events were held at the lodge the same week as the Birkebeiner and were sponsored by American Airlines. The World Masters marathon event intertwined on Saturday with

Opening ceremonies, 1983
AMERICAN BIRKEBEINER SKI FOUNDATION ARCHIVES

the main race. About 450 masters entrants from around the world, including several former Olympians, were part of a record 6,800 Birkebeiner entries. Meanwhile, even as the 1983 race was underway, Wise was creating a five-event endurance series patterned after similar events in Europe. The American Classic Competitions would include four marathons (biking, swimming, running, and roller skiing) between May and October 1983 and would culminate with the 1984 Birkebeiner.

The February 25, 1983, race once again was scheduled to start in Hayward and go down Main Street, but those plans were shelved because of mild weather, lack of snow, and thin ice. The start was moved east of Lake Hayward to Duffy's Field, which was fortified with 450 dump truck loads of snow, shortening the race from 55 to 50 kilometers. Wise had secured a much-needed sponsor, Maxwell House, and skiers were greeted by a giant promotional coffee can. It was sunny and twenty degrees at the start—a perfect day for Birkebeiner XI. In one of the closest races ever, Austrian police officer Rudi Kapeller won in 2:14, edging Sweden's Lars Frykberg by two-tenths of a second. Ola Hassis, the 1982 champion, finished just another three-tenths behind Frykberg, who broke a pole fifty meters from the finish. Jennifer Caldwell of Vermont (whose brother, Tim, and father, John, were former Olympians) won her first Birkebeiner in 2:39 and would go on to win the Great American Ski Chase marathon series. Jennifer's future husband, Howie Bean, took fifth.[24]

After the computer problems in 1982, the Birkebeiner bought its own computer system for the first time, from Northeast Sports Timing of Connecticut. It cost $30,000 (equivalent to almost $95,000 in 2024) and was supposed to ensure easy timekeeping for the 1983 race. When a skier finished, a magnetic strip was to be removed from their bib and fed into a computer to record their time. Wise called it the finest such system in the world, but on race day it was the worst. An electrical problem rendered the system useless, and officials had to count finishers manually. After the top few, it was a scramble to record bibs and times as skiers poured in. Wise bought a different system for 1984.[25]

Could Wise have delayed the computer system purchase with Telemark facing potential bankruptcy? He knew no way other than first-class. It's one reason the 1983 Birkebeiner made newspaper headlines in places like Baltimore, Boston, Chicago, Kansas City, Los Angeles, San Diego, Seattle, and Washington, DC, and in various other smaller newspapers in Florida, Massachusetts, New York, Pennsylvania, and as far away as Korea. "Make room for Cable on the stage of world-class attractions," the *Los Angeles Times* said. "Cable, Wis—population about 300."[26]

IN 1984, WITH MAXWELL HOUSE STILL THE SPONSOR, the race again began in Duffy's Field, where snow was trucked in because of a two-week thaw. For the first time, wave starts were used instead of the longtime skier honor system, by which skiers positioned themselves in the start area roughly according to where they expected to finish. Lars Frykberg was runner-up again, this time falling about fifty meters from the finish and losing by eight seconds to Bengt Hassis of Sweden, who won in 2:02 over 48 kilometers. Vigdis Roenning of Norway was the women's winner by six minutes, in 2:27. The race start was twenty-two degrees, and trail conditions were fast and icy after some warm days and cold nights. This led to at least thirty-nine injuries, including eleven fractures, five dislocations, and four concussions. The Swedes, however, had no issue with the hard track—they skate skied like metronomes all the way, looking like they had perfected the new, radical style.[27]

A record 7,150 skiers, grouped by wave for the first time, at the 1984 start in Duffy's Field
AMERICAN BIRKEBEINER SKI FOUNDATION ARCHIVES

The race grew by another 350 skiers to 7,150, surpassing 7,000 entrants for the first time. Bankruptcy aside, the Birkebeiner was on a roll, attracting both elite athletes and citizen skiers. Among those competing in 1984 was Beth Heiden-Reid, of Madison, Wisconsin, a 1980 Olympian with a bronze medal in speedskating. Heiden-Reid had embarked on a highly successful second career in cross-country ski racing at an opportune time—she knew how to skate. At the 1984 Birkebeiner, she came in third in her age class and was the sixth woman overall.

Cross-country skiing had truly caught on among Wisconsin's citizen skiers, too. The state hardly had a competitive skier a decade earlier, but by 1984 six Wisconsin skiers finished in the Birkebeiner's top fifty, including Hayward's own George Welk in eighth place. And both winners of Wise's first American Classic series were from Eau Claire, Wisconsin: weekend warriors Pat Quinn, an engineering executive, and Linda Bauer, a middle school athletics director.

Green Bay Packers placekicker Jan Stenerud (pictured at right, with Tony Wise) was a special guest at the opening ceremonies for the 1984 Birkebeiner, five months before he was traded to the Minnesota Vikings. Stenerud, a native of Norway, had been on skis only briefly in eighteen years; on a whim, he skied the 1984 race and finished in 4:11. AMERICAN BIRKEBEINER SKI FOUNDATION ARCHIVES

The 1984 Birkebeiner seemed to indicate that all was well at Telemark, despite bankruptcy reorganization three years earlier. Five days after the race, Wise opined in the *Birch Scroll* about all the good things happening. However, he ended his missive with a shocker:

> On March 14th Telemark Enterprises will face another of its many trials. [The company] will appear at a Chapter 11 hearing called by the I.R.S. in Eau Claire, Wisconsin. Much like the proverbial postman or cat with nine lives, Telemark has always successfully endured its previous ordeals. We hope we win our battle on Wednesday, because liquidation of Telemark Enterprises would cause great economic dislocation not only for our 400 employees but for the entire economy of Northwestern Wisconsin.[28]

Wise then asked the public for prayers for Telemark, an ominous sign from someone as supremely confident, optimistic, and nonreligious as Wise. As it turned out, Telemark wasn't meeting its debt-repayment obligations under Chapter 11 reorganization and, in fact, had fallen even further behind. As a result, the IRS had begun Chapter 7 bankruptcy proceedings—or liquidation bankruptcy, in which a debtor's assets are sold off and business operations cease—against the company in late 1983. Telemark Enterprises owed $277,000 just in employment taxes for the first three quarters of that year, and after the first quarter of 1984 it was more than $500,000 in arrears with the IRS.[29]

By spring 1984, Telemark was hemorrhaging. At the hearing on March 14, with Wise representing himself in court, the company requested a thirty-day extension to catch up on its debts—even while Wise knew he didn't have the funds. His method of operation was to write a check on Friday, let it bounce once, and cover it on Monday. He was paying $2,000 to $3,000 a month in overdraft charges. "We ran the bank," Fred Vortanz said. "We told them which checks to cover."[30]

Prayers for Telemark were not answered. Two months later, on May 17, 1984, Telemark was declared bankrupt (ironically, it was the same day as Syttende Mai, the national holiday of Norway). Wise's company and all he had built were in the hands of a court-appointed interim trustee, Lawrence Kaiser, who then appointed Sullivan Associates of Minneapolis to run the company, keep the lodge open, and begin the process of selling off the assets to pay the creditors. Wise was out and Paul Bremicker was named the temporary general manager, with Fred Vortanz retained as second in charge.[31]

Bremicker was a member of the Telemark Lodge Owners Association and ran a Cable lumber yard. He had been president of Commercial State Bank in St. Paul and had seen Wise default on early 1970s loans. "I fought for the last ten years to inform the association that, financially, Tony Wise couldn't get up in the morning and not be bankrupt," Bremicker said.[32]

Wise envisioned Telemark miraculously righting the ship like bankrupt carmaker Chrysler had done at the time, but US bankruptcy judge William King ruled that "there is no realistic possibility of rehabilitating this debtor" and that "reality must be confronted." Telemark's debts totaled more than $8 million (by some estimates closer to $10 million), including $6 million to Peoples National Bank of Hayward, which hadn't received a payment from Wise in three months. However, 90 percent of the Peoples National loans were guaranteed by the Farmers Home Administration, and it held the lodge and land as collateral. One line in a 1984 court document spoke volumes: Telemark Enterprises hadn't made an annual profit in nine years, since 1975, the third year of the fledgling Birkebeiner.[33]

Reeling from the impact of the court decision, Wise allegedly removed 305 physical items from the Telemark property, including a grand piano, three mobile homes, a computer, and more than $12,000 in cash. As a result, in July, Judge William H. Frawley banned Wise and his family members from the Telemark grounds (later, Wise said he returned most of the items). It seemed unthinkable just a few months earlier at the successful 1984 race: Tony Wise unable even to step foot on his beloved Telemark property.[34]

Two interrelated dramas played out over the next few months, regarding Wise's empire and the future of the Birkebeiner. Who would run the race? Sullivan Associates didn't necessarily want the responsibility of planning a major event along with stabilizing the troubled lodge; the race was on the verge of becoming collateral damage from the bankruptcy. Yet, this was America's Birkebeiner, and letting it die seemed unthinkable. The race became a cause célèbre for skiers and fans across the nation. Wise went to court to retain the race, Historyland, the World Lumberjack Championships, 140 acres near the lodge, and his Telemark liquor license. The lodge was a lost cause—Wise couldn't pay the debts. He argued that the rest of his empire, though, had been leased to Telemark and wasn't actually owned by the company. Frawley, however, found no evidence of that. Wise also proposed managing the Birkebeiner as part of his new American Classic Competitions. On October 3, 1984, in US Western District Bankruptcy Court in downtown Eau Claire, Judge Frawley ruled that everything Wise owned was under the Telemark Enterprises umbrella and therefore no longer his.[35]

Then, things went a little crazy. Anticipating as much, Wise summarily announced—within hours of Frawley's ruling—that he was starting a competing race, the Norwegian-American Birkebeiner, which would be held on the same day, February 23, 1985, as the American Birkebeiner. It would be 60 kilometers long, starting and finishing in Hayward. It would follow the main trail to Highway OO, turn south for 15 kilometers on Phipps Fire Lane, and reconnect with the main trail. A short race called the Kurzlauf ("short run" in German) would end at the midpoint. Wise published an issue of a new race magazine, the *Birch Log*, with event details, a course map, and registration information. He reenlisted Telemark publicity director Tom Kelly and announced that Bill Koch would be among the entrants. Previous Birkebeiner race entries would be honored. He even had the backing of the Worldloppet; in an October letter to Wise, Worldloppet secretary general Eugen Peter said the organization would only sanction a US race run by Wise. Sawyer County and City of Hayward officials said Wise could use the trail and downtown for his event.[36]

Two races on the same day on the same trail? Sullivan Associates filed a complaint on October 9, 1984, alleging interference by Wise. On November 2, Frawley ruled that Wise could not hold a competing race in February 1985 within one hundred miles of Hayward and Cable. Sullivan Associates tried to reach an out-of-court agreement by offering to sell the race for $1 to the Hayward Chamber of Commerce and hiring Wise to manage it. Negotiations with Wise failed, and he also reportedly turned down an offer to work for the race as a consultant for $30,000 a year.[37]

The race, region, and skiers were in limbo just a few months before the thirteenth annual event. A potential solution was in the works, however. Sometime in late fall 1984, a group of local leaders gathered in the back room of Karabali's restaurant in downtown Hayward for an informal meeting. Their goal: to gauge interest in forming a nonprofit foundation to take over the race. Local attorney Tom Duffy, his office just up Main Street, took the lead. Duffy was one of the first Worldloppet finishers and had handled some of Wise's legal matters in the past. He knew "the race was hanging by a thread," he later recalled, and said

The Birkebeiner not only awards the first people to cross the finish line—for many years it also awarded the last with the Bronze Broom Trail Sweeper Award. Here, Tony Wise hugs 1983 recipient Marilyn Dawson of Madison, who finished the race in 10 hours and 41 seconds.
AMERICAN BIRKEBEINER SKI FOUNDATION ARCHIVES

the idea for a foundation came from a group of Milwaukee attorneys who were friends and Birkebeiner skiers. Other such races around the world, including in the Worldloppet, were run by community foundations as well. One of the meeting attendees, maybe to the surprise of some, was Wise, who apparently was keeping his options open.[38]

Attendees roundly supported the idea. They knew it wouldn't be easy, but they also knew that wresting the race from unknown future Telemark operators—or possibly none at all if the lodge closed—and putting it in the hands of local residents who had a vested interest would be a win for the region. It was a testament to what Wise and his employees had built: the very communities Wise had sought to empower when he created his company post–World War II were now rallying to save one of his creations. The Birkebeiner "belongs to the people of this area," Duffy said at the time. "If we want to ensure that it continues as it has in the past, we have to take this action now." Wise, however, resented losing control of his beloved race and still held out hopes of either getting it back or organizing another competing race. He was proud to have helped bring prosperity to the region, but he was also stubbornly protective of the business interests in which he had invested so much. "My friends turned on me," he said.[39] A line in the snow had been drawn. Speaking to a group of community supporters, he said, "It really gripes me when I see people saying this belongs to the community."[40]

Wheels quickly spun into motion to create a state-approved foundation, first called the Norwegian-American Ski Foundation and then quickly renamed the American Birkebeiner Ski Foundation. On November 3—the day after Wise's Norwegian-American Birkebeiner was quashed—Duffy and others presented their plan to the Hayward Chamber of Commerce, which backed the idea. On November 5, the foundation planners applied for nonprofit status from the state. On November 9, a steering committee for the foundation met with Telemark trustee Lawrence Kaiser to discuss a plan for the foundation to take over the race. On November 12, one hundred area residents gathered for a public meeting in Hayward, where three-fourths of them voted in favor of the plan. On November 13, the Sawyer County Board revoked Wise's trail access for his now-forbidden Norwegian-American Classic race and instead gave it to the fledgling foundation to use for the Birkebeiner. The foundation had its first big win.[41]

Then it was one ski forward and one back. On November 28, the foundation and Telemark Enterprises announced they had received Judge Frawley's approval to jointly host the 1985 Birkebeiner. Upset that the race was slipping completely away, Wise upped the ante with new plans to take his business out of his beloved hometown. He announced on December 1 that he would hold a similar race at Giant's Ridge ski area in Biwabik, Minnesota, 110 miles away—outside of the court-ordered 100-mile zone—on the same day as the Birkebeiner. He also claimed it would be sanctioned by the Worldloppet, which would guarantee instant credibility and weaken the Birkebeiner. Excited Giants Ridge officials pledged $65,000 to help make it happen, in part because a government-funded local group had just put $6.9 million into the bankrupt Giants Ridge operation and turned it into a US Ski Association Nordic center.[42]

Who would win the ski duel between Wise and the new foundation? On December 6, 1984, the answer became clear. Two separate events happened that day: first, Kaiser wrote to Duffy, confirming "that an agreement has been reached between Telemark Enterprises and the American Birkebeiner Ski Foundation, Inc." concerning the 1985 American Birkebeiner and future races. Per the agreement, Telemark and the foundation would jointly run the 1985 race, and then the foundation would take over. Telemark would give the foundation the rights to the race and to the names American Birkebeiner, Birkebeiner, and Birkie, "on the condition that the Foundation will not further transfer the race without Telemark's approval and that the race will always run from Hayward to Telemark unless further agreement is made."[43]

Then came the dagger. The Worldloppet announced the same day in Switzerland, after a unanimous vote by members via telex, that its US race sanction would stay with the Hayward-Cable race and not go to Wise's race in Biwabik. It was a complete reversal in the Worldloppet's position. Behind the scenes, Kaiser and others had been lobbying Worldloppet members, via letters and numerous overseas phone calls, to keep the sanction with the Birkebeiner. In a letter to the Worldloppet's Eugen Peter, foundation board member Lea Justice of Clam Lake, Wisconsin, described the strong community support for the new foundation and included local newspaper clippings documenting Wise's financial and legal constraints. Peter cited Justice's letter as one reason for the Worldloppet's definitive decision. Duffy and fellow Hayward attorney Howard Hanson flew to Switzerland prior to the decision to help seal the deal.[44]

The sanction gone, Giants Ridge immediately pulled its support from Wise, his last hope of staging a competing race. Had he been serious about trying to hurt the race he'd created? Frances Wise later claimed her father was "just acting out" and hadn't actually meant to undermine the Birkebeiner. Despite the defeat, Wise vowed not to give up on getting the Birkebeiner back.[45]

The Worldloppet had a simple, if painful, reason to turn its back on Wise. Recommitting to an established race with a top-tier course, the promise of long-term financial stability, and an experienced support staff was the safer choice. Plus, even if Kaiser had not released control of the Birkebeiner, the foundation was prepared to hold a new, similar race called the Norwegian-American Classic starting and finishing in Hayward.

On the same fateful day, December 6, the foundation received letters and proclamations of support from officials in Hayward, Cable, area townships, the Lac Courte Oreilles Ojibwe Community College, and even the ten race Founders. Town of Cable chairman Bernard Radloff wrote that the board "is glad that the race is now owned by the people of this area."[46] Meanwhile, the official transfer of the Birkebeiner to the foundation wouldn't take place until February 1, 1985, a few weeks before the race.[47]

The Birkebeiner no longer was hanging by a thread. However, repairing the big rip in its Lycra wouldn't happen overnight. Could the new group pull off a successful event in 1985 and bring financial and organizational stability to the race? Efforts began immediately: in a half-page ad in the *Sawyer County Record*, the foundation invited residents to community meetings in early December in Hayward and Cable. "We need your help!" the ad read. "The American Birkebeiner now belongs to all of us! Be a part of the Birkie's future."[48]

The new race organizers were, in essence, many of the same people who had helped run and support the race over the years. Foundation president Dan Dilworth was director of the Hayward-based Louisiana-Pacific Waferboard Operations in North America and had played on the 1964 US Olympic hockey team with eventual Olympic coach Herb Brooks. Foundation secretary James Moe was a partner in the Anderson, Hager & Moe accounting firm. Foundation treasurer William Beckwith was vice president of Hayward's Peoples National Bank (Wise's largest creditor). And vice chairman William "Butch" Johnson was president of Johnson Timber. Other board members included Duffy; New Moon Ski Shop owner Steve Morales; Lakewoods Resort owner Phil Rasmussen; City of Hayward attorney Howard Hanson; Lac Courte Oreilles Community College president John "Little Bird' Anderson; Central Cross Country Competition chairman James McCarthy; and Dick Simono, the former Telemark employee who had helped Wise organize the Worldloppet. Now working as a local real estate agent, Simono took a three-month leave of absence from his job to serve as race director and foundation coordinator.[49]

The foundation's job, after hastily organizing, was fourfold: build public trust, raise money, prepare for the race, and run the race. On the first account, the foundation board pledged to "keep the tradition of the American Birkebeiner alive." It adopted the slogan "Alive in '85" and stated in the *Birch Scroll*: "It has not been an easy or clear-cut situation for anyone involved. The end of [the Telemark era] is a difficult one to accept for many of us. The extravagance, the grandiose dreams, and the undaunted determination are what made Telemark and the Birkebeiner, and for that Wise will not be forgotten."[50]

The foundation began a drive to raise $150,000 in less than three months, a tall order for a couple of small towns. The money was desperately needed because more than $120,000 in entry fees from the twenty-seven hundred preregistered skiers had disappeared into Telemark operations and no longer was available for the 1985 race. That put the foundation in a hole because it planned to honor those entries. A public fundraising thermometer sign was erected. The front page of the *Sawyer County Record* ran a photo labeled "Birkie Fund Started," showing foundation members holding checks, along with a story headlined "Birkebeiner 'alive and well.'" Local residents could support the effort by buying "Birkie is Alive in '85" buttons for $5.[51]

The foundation was supported at the top by six corporate and individual donors—called charter guardian benefactors—who each gave at least $5,000. They were Samuel C. Johnson II, head of conglomerate S.C. Johnson Co. based in Racine, who had a family retreat near Cable; Johnson Timber; Peoples National Bank; Reinicke Co.; Nardi Electric; and Louisiana-Pacific. Other initial supporters included twenty-four charter patrons who gave $1,000 or more (Samuel Johnson's son, Fisk, among them) and twenty-nine charter sponsors who gave $500 or more, a donation list that read like the Yellow Pages from the Hayward-Cable phone book. Several Louisiana-Pacific suppliers were among the donors. "Dilworth was really instrumental in raising a lot of that money," Morales said.

By late January the foundation had raised more than $85,000. By the week of the race, it had amassed $110,000 in cash and an additional $40,000 in-kind donations to reach its goal. The foundation sold 410 individual annual memberships to the organization at $25 apiece, raising $10,250. Many of these were purchased by longtime race finishers who had already entered but gave again, knowing their entry fee had disappeared. Another 160 individuals, businesses, and organizations contributed as well.[52] Simono called the groundswell of community support "the most gratifying thing I have ever seen."[53]

A new race committee was formed. Its nearly twenty race chiefs included many familiar faces, like Fred Vortanz and Harold Treland. Each member had from two to twelve years of race experience, or 137 years in all. "Sour attitudes won't be a part of the Birkebeiner Foundation because too many fundamentally good people are involved," wrote local news columnist and *Birch Scroll* editor Joe Chisholm. "North America's largest, grandest, and best organized cross-country event is ours and we are proud of it. It is a warm, human, good-time explosion in February in Wisconsin."[54]

AS RACE DAY APPROACHED on February 23, 1985, somehow the labor-intensive event was on as usual, despite nearly a year of uncertainty, acrimony, and major challenges. The Thursday of race week featured a new youth ski event—the precursor to what would become known as the Barnebirkie—in downtown Hayward for the local chapter of the Bill Koch Ski League. A special guest was Koch, now living in Eugene, Oregon, who was in town to ski. Friday's opening ceremonies at Telemark matched Wise's pomp and circumstance. Wise, meanwhile, lay low in his office on Main Street. He still maintained the race had been stolen and promised a "holy war" to get it back. Founding skier Ernie St. Germaine dedicated his race to Wise, his "uncle" and mentor.[55]

Prerace publicity had been sporadic and many skiers had been unsure whether the race would even happen. But at 9 a.m. on Saturday, a new era began with 5,464 skiers, down about 1,500 from the record-breaking 1984 (it would be eleven years before the race topped 7,000 again). The weather that week had unexpectedly warmed, causing a late-week meltdown on Lake Hayward, and planners scrambled to move the start to nearby Rosie's Field. It was twenty-eight degrees that morning—and would rise to forty-two degrees by the afternoon—as skiers pushed past an oversized American flag, two hot-air balloons tethered to the ground, and a giant, inflatable beer can from the main sponsor, Wisconsin's own Miller Lite, which had stepped up in a pinch.

Once again, top US and international skiers made up the elite group. Norwegian hero Oddvar Braa, two-time World Cup champion and 1982 World Cup 50-kilometer gold medalist, won in 2:07 over the fast, 48-kilometer course, four seconds ahead of Austrian Walter Mayer. Koch finished tenth overall and third among Americans in 2:11, while raising money for the Save the Children Fund. Muffy Ritz, from Minnesota, took the women's title by eighteen seconds in 2:40. Sixth among the women was Gabriele Andersen (formerly Schiess), a native of Switzerland, who drew international attention the year before by fighting off dehydration and heat exhaustion to stagger to the finish line of the first-ever women's marathon in front of 100,000 people at the Olympics in Los Angeles. It was her fourth Birkebeiner.[56]

Skating was still in vogue. Ritz decided the night before the race to go without kick wax for the first time in her life and skate the whole race. She was nervous, wondering if she could do it. She took a block of kick wax to the start line just in case she changed her mind—then threw it into the woods. "You can go so much faster because you're not dragging wax through the snow," she said. "But you have to have strength, especially on the uphills" to skate just with glide wax. All the lead skiers skated, including of course Koch, who was pictured on the cover of the *Birch Scroll* skating into the lead as the race began.[57]

Spectators watch skiers head for the finish line at Telemark during the 1985 race.
AMERICAN BIRKEBEINER SKI FOUNDATION ARCHIVES

At a meeting at Telemark a few months later, the foundation board reported postrace assets of $50,467, not counting $43,000 in the bank from more than twelve hundred skiers who had already registered for 1986. It likely was the first time the race had made money in its thirteen years. "We will be a worldwide, major cross-country ski event forever," Dilworth predicted. The foundation anticipated that the race would be self-supporting by 1986; no more fundraising drives would be needed. Board member Russell Haling of Hayward praised the community for coming together to meet a "great challenge" and save the race. Even the skiing Founders with ties to Wise complimented the foundation for doing "an excellent job in all phases of the XIII Birkie."[58]

The success of the 1985 race, the breakup of his company, and the loss of his lodge were just part of the pain Wise was feeling during this time. He felt abandoned by the same community he had long tried to help. "It tore his heart out," said Ernie St. Germaine. "They didn't help him when he needed it, and he had done so much for the Hayward area. Everything Tony did was for tourism." Frances Wise called it "beyond horrible. People betrayed him. He spent his life to improve the economy of the area, and as soon as the doors closed people shamed him. People reaped a lot of money because of him. They were heartless. At least show some kind of empathy. Where's the recognition for Dad? There wasn't any." Harold Treland, who saw Tony work hard and love what he did, said simply: "Everybody felt sorry the way it turned out." Former Telemark general manager Jerry Berard agreed: "It was sad because his life was gone."[59]

AFTER THE DRAMA OF 1985, the relatively quiet 1986 race was more than welcome. Entries were up a bit, to 5,500, and there was plenty of snow for the first time since 1982. The race went all 55 kilometers and down Main Street for just the second time in its history, reaffirming to the public and the media that the Birkebeiner indeed was alive and well.

Among skiers, the talk in 1986 was the trail. The time had come to groom for skaters because the number of them, both elite and citizen, was growing, and they were destroying the striding tracks. Elite skiers had won the two previous Birkebeiners by skating. A survey found that 21 percent of entrants were skating with another 33 percent using a combination of skating and striding. Now, for the first time, the trail was groomed to accommodate skate skiing. The left side of the trail was smooth, with one track on the far left for those who wanted to marathon skate, while on the right, multiple sets of tracks were set for striders.

Trail Committee chairman Steve Morales acknowledged that the "stars of the sport are all skating now," so the race had to get with the times. The new technique, he said, "will be a major part" of cross-country's future. In the 1985 World Championships in Seefeld, Austria, the sport changed forever. The top twenty-three skiers in the men's 30-kilometer race were skaters.[60]

New equipment designed for skate skiing—longer poles, shorter skis, special bindings, and higher, stiffer boots—began to appear at elite levels. In the 1986 prerace *Birch Scroll*, Swix advertised its Rainbow Glider Pack of glide wax and "virtually weightless" Boron skate poles for skate skiers. Morales owned Hayward's New Moon Ski Shop and quickly sold through his first shipment of skate equipment. When skating equipment became hard to get, elite skiers were "cutting the tips off the stiffest striding skis and just going for it," he said. Top trail systems in the US were not yet groomed for both styles of skiing—even though skaters were on the trails and cutting into the tracks. Theodore Wirth Park, one of the Nordic ski centers in the Twin Cities, ignored its own no-skating signs and began grooming a skate lane anyway because the trend had reached the weekend skier.[61]

The 1986 ice sculpture by Austrian Engelbert Hattenberger, whose work had been a fixture of the Birkebeiner experience since 1979. AMERICAN BIRKEBEINER SKI FOUNDATION ARCHIVES

Tony Wise, it might be said, went out when skating came in. Suddenly, the 1986 Birkebeiner was a skaters' race to win. Muffy Ritz, wearing a red ski suit with blue arms and shoulders, skated to a second straight title, the first woman to do so, in 3:26. She was three minutes ahead of the second-place women's finisher, fellow skating Minnesotan Lynne Cecil. Sweden's Anders Blomquist, wearing yellow and white, skated to the men's title in 2:53, six seconds ahead of countryman Hans Persson, with defending champion Oddvar Braa coming in fourth. Americans had a good showing in the men's race, too, with six in the top ten, including Audun Endestad of Alaska in fifth and Kevin Brochman of Minnesota, who surprised the foreigners when he led late in the race before fading to sixth.[62]

New snow that week, plus two inches overnight and another inch during the race, slowed the times overall. However, the skaters were comparatively still faster. Hayward-area skier and Indian Trail Resort owner John Dettloff stayed with classic that year while his training partners skated. He finished about a half hour behind them. "We were all in the same shape, but they were that much farther ahead," Dettloff later recalled. He would switch to skate skiing the following year (it "blew away all my previous times," he said) and would go on to ski more than forty Birkebeiners, many in the elite wave, but would never go back to classic. "Skating was freer and faster," he said. "I just embraced it." At the Colosseum finish in 1986, skiers skated and strided past Engelbert Hattenberger's sparkling ice sculpture featuring two life-sized skiers between two larger-than-life Viking Warriors.[63]

The 1986 race was named the Whoppers American Birkebeiner. The new moniker acknowledged a much-needed corporate sponsor. Sponsors pick up about 20 percent of the race tab, with registration fees covering the rest. Leaf, the parent company based in Finland, made Whoppers malted milk balls and other candy. It sponsored the entire eight-race Great American Ski Chase using four of its candy names, including the Whoppers North American Vasa in Traverse City, Michigan.

The successful 1984 Olympics in Los Angeles had ushered in a new era of corporations leveraging the advertising power of high-level athletics. Beatrice Companies, for example, spent $3 million to sponsor the Chicago Marathon in 1984, and the Boston Marathon signed its first major sponsor in 1985, John Hancock Mutual Life for $10 million. The Birkebeiner Foundation had taken note of the trend and was looking for title sponsors when Leaf landed on its

The Whoppers American Birkebeiner, 1986. AMERICAN BIRKEBEINER SKI FOUNDATION ARCHIVES

doorstep.[64] Not everyone loved this new development. Wise—whose first title sponsors were ski companies Silva and NorTur, the Norwegian Ski Council, and Maxwell House Coffee—thought it was tacky to change the race name for a mere $50,000. A few foundation board members didn't like it either and wondered if a different candy name could be used.[65]

Overall, year two for the foundation—the first year it was fully in charge without Telemark—couldn't have gone better. Race profits increased by about $12,000 to nearly $56,000, and total assets reached almost $116,000, more than double from 1985. Butch Johnson took over from Dilworth as foundation chair. The Bill Koch Ski League youth event was held for the second year, although the children skiing down Main Street wore leftover adult bibs from 1985 with sponsor Miller Lite in big letters on the front.[66]

THE MATTERS OF TELEMARK'S FUTURE and a court appeal from Tony Wise about his claim to land involved in the bankruptcy still hung in the air, the latter actually causing Telemark to close for the first time in its forty years. On December 31, 1985, the Northwoods Group of Cable purchased Telemark Enterprises for $5.06 million (far below its estimated value of $13 million), with $3 million for the lodge and about $1.5 million of partial debt repayment to major creditors. The sale was supposed to be finalized April 15, 1986, but was put on hold pending Wise's appeal, causing the lodge to shut down the next day "due to lack of operating capital," said Fred Vortanz, who thought it was a miracle the lodge had stayed open that long. The winter staff was down to fewer than seventy employees from its high of four hundred when Wise was owner.[67]

Wise represented himself in court as he had in 1984, because he said he couldn't afford attorney's fees (his only income was now a $500 monthly National Guard pension, and eventually $1,100 a month from Social Security). He again claimed that parts of his empire, including parcels of land at Historyland and in Cable, were separate entities from Telemark Enterprises. The government, however, presented evidence that Wise had managed all of his operations as one overarching business supported by money from a single general fund. (Fred Vortanz had advised Wise to keep the businesses separate, but he wouldn't. When the ski chalet burned down, for example, Wise funneled the insurance payout into the struggling lodge rather than fund the chalet's replacement, the Colosseum.) On May 14, 1986, a judge in Eau Claire ruled that everything remained in the hands of the new owners. The decision effectively meant the end of Wise's legal battle but allowed Telemark to reopen. He went home "in a barrel" as he said, with nothing but some souvenirs.[68]

Bob Treland experienced Wise's financial machinations firsthand. Treland would work twelve- to sixteen-hour days, sometimes seven days a week, managing Historyland and the Lumberjack World Championships during the busy summer tourist seasons. But Treland and his staff rarely were able to reinvest any of the profits at Historyland. Instead, Wise would declare with a wink that they didn't have a good summer as he took the profits and funded another arm of his operation that needed it more. "It was very discouraging and disheartening," Treland said. Still, like many people, Treland had far more good days than bad while working for Wise and ultimately saw the good because "of all the mouths he fed. He did so much."[69]

The various court decisions left the Wise family and friends hurt and reeling—feelings that would linger for decades. Janie Wise, a younger daughter who went to appeals court hearings with her dad, thought the decisions were predetermined. "They didn't have to close the door on him," Janie said in 2022. "They vilified him, and he never really got over it. Our family lost everything. We didn't get to inherit the Birkebeiner. We didn't get to shape the future of the race in the image of what he would have liked. They wanted him to lose it."[70]

But for the people who depended on Telemark, the final court decision brought relief. Northwoods Group president Robert Maddox pledged to put $2.5 million into the lodge, inspiring hope for Telemark employees and the nearby businesses that depended on lodge traffic for income. However, when Maddox struggled to get financing, his bid to buy the lodge fell through; three months before the 1987 race, the lodge closed again. Race organizers and employees worked diligently and spent tens of thousands of dollars (one estimate put it at $140,000) to reopen the lodge for the fifteenth annual Birkebeiner. Meanwhile, the people who depended on Telemark faced an uncertain future once more.

The fate of the lodge wasn't the only headache the foundation experienced in 1987. The weather—and a subsequent change in route—caused additional mayhem. Lack of snow pushed the start again to Rosie's Field (the fourth time in five years the lake couldn't be crossed), and the course was shortened to 44 kilometers. A two-hundred-foot well was hastily dug in the field to provide water to make snow for the new start area. More snow was dumped in big piles and spread onto various bare spots along the trail. At the improvised start area, skiers went down a wide hill and then quickly funneled into a trail of soft snow. But the trail narrowed too quickly to accommodate the vast number of skiers flying downhill, and a pileup of an estimated 150 elite skiers ensued, poles snapping by the dozens, skis popping off. Skier waves were up to one thousand people. FIS technical delegate Lars Kindem said the start area was "unsatisfactory" but that "organizers had no choice." Grooming was an issue as well. The icy trail base was broken up for safety, but temperatures rose the day before the race and softened the course, followed by two inches of snow during the race, making for slow conditions.[71]

The trail-related chaos likely contributed to an ultraclose finish. Konrad Hallenbarter of Switzerland stuck his foot across the line in 1:54, ahead of a tripped-up, head-first-falling Pal Sjulstad of Norway, to win by two one-hundredths of a second as thousands watched in front of the Colosseum. The finish was so close that officials had to review the tape. Konrad Undsgard of Norway was another eyelash behind. Two-time defending women's champion Muffy Ritz got caught in the start crash, lost her skis briefly, and finished third, ten minutes behind champion Ellen Justina "E.J." Holcomb of Idaho in 2:20. Holcomb thought the start looked crash-prone and started on the outside. She slipped around the blockage through some trees and took off—as did many others. Former Olympian Betsy Haines, sister of 1975 champion Chris Haines, took second.[72]

A new event in 1987 was the children's Barnebirkie (*barn* means "children" in Norwegian). The race was sponsored by the Sons of Norway, which worked with the Bill Koch Ski League chapter to organize it. The goals: make it one of the largest children's ski events in the world, help bring families together to celebrate race week, ensure the future of the race and sport, and add to the Birkebeiner's economic impact. Noncompetitive and designed for children ages three to thirteen, the Barnebirkie was held on Thursday, two days before the main event. Each of the approximately 250 young finishers received a medal and cookies.[73]

Young entrants in the first-ever Barnebirkie in 1987
AMERICAN BIRKEBEINER SKI FOUNDATION ARCHIVES

FIVE MONTHS BEFORE THE 1988 RACE, Telemark returned to the headlines. The lodge was sold again at auction, drawing a crowd of more than six hundred to Telemark on September 15, 1987, for the fifteen-minute event. The winning bid was $1.35 million by Impact 7, a nonprofit from Turtle Lake, Wisconsin. (Among the interested bidders were televangelists Jim and Tammy Faye Bakker.) The next day, however, Judge Thomas S. Utschig, presiding over the bankruptcy court in Eau Claire, ruled the bid insufficient to help pay the creditors. The judge reopened the bidding, and Lake Properties of Crossville, Tennessee, led by Minnesota native William Papaik, narrowly won with a $2.3 million offer. The bid was less than half of what Robert Maddox had agreed to pay. The deal included the eighteen-hole golf course, which Papaik quickly sold. However, three and a half years of Telemark uncertainty seemingly had come to an end. Among those who would get paid from the proceeds was Bayfield County, which was owed $780,000 in real estate taxes.[74]

Six weeks later, another part of Wise's empire was sold. Foundation board member Butch Johnson and his business partner, Ron Lambert, sold Historyland to a Minnesota company but kept the World Lumberjack Championships. They had bought both venues for $403,000 from Peoples National Bank, the major Wise creditor that was awarded both as part of the bankruptcy settlement.[75]

Lake Properties put $750,000 into the lodge that fall—and promised $2.5 million more, including building forty-eight new time-share condominiums and 104 more that would be sold—and the lodge reopened December 10, 1987, with Governor Tommy Thompson in attendance. Opening day took place three days shy of the ski hill's fortieth anniversary, December 13, 1947, when Wise and Hobart "Mac" Hewett opened for business.[76]

The lodge was open and crowded like old times for the 1988 race, which had a new $65,000 title sponsor, Curel, the skin lotion brand launched in 1984 by S.C. Johnson & Son Inc. Another nineteen sponsors, led by the Bank of Hayward with $15,000, boosted total sponsorship cash to a hefty $142,000 for the foundation.[77]

Snow was aplenty, too, bringing the 1988 start back to Main Street for just the third time. The second Barnebirkie, on a balmy Thursday, drew 548 children, making it the largest such race in North America. But the weather changed on Friday, with a strong wind from the northwest. It was one degree at the start

At the 1988 start on Main Street, three-fourths of the street was groomed for the ever-growing number of skate skiers. AMERICAN BIRKEBEINER SKI FOUNDATION ARCHIVES

on Saturday for the 5,621 skiers, with a windchill of forty below zero. Former sheriff Don Primley, chief medical officer, and his team handled hypothermia cases and more, but he'd seen it all before—he had helped at every Birkebeiner.

For the first time, skiers from the Soviet Union, eight of them from the Murmansk Ski Club, participated as part of the Ski for Peace program. Living five hundred miles north of the Arctic Circle, the Russian skiers likely felt right at home in the frigid air. Their visit was five years in the making. Wise had begun the effort when he and publicity director Tom Kelly visited Murmansk in 1983 for the forty-ninth annual Murmansk Ski Festival and 58-kilometer marathon, with help from the US Embassy and Wisconsin congressman Dave Obey.[78]

The 1988 race belonged to two Swedes, with Orjan Blomquist (brother of 1986 winner Anders) winning in 2:20, ahead of countryman Hans Persson by eight seconds. Kelly Kimball of Minnesota won the women's race in 2:52, more than a minute over Muffy Ritz. Defending women's winner E. J. Holcomb nearly quit because of the cold.

One of the most memorable stories of the day was that of defending Kortelopet champion Luke Bodensteiner, a seventeen-year-old from West Bend, Wisconsin. With the long- and short-race skiers in the same waves at the time, Bodensteiner was leading the entire elite field from both races as he neared the Kortelopet finish line at Highway OO—and then skied right on by. Later, he said he simply missed the cutoff. Could it be because elite team officials were blocking the turnoff, not expecting a Kortelopet skier to be leading? The Kortelopet finish did look different in 1988, ending between two new log cabins. When Bodensteiner realized his mistake, he figured it was too late or too hard to turn back, and he just pushed on. Eventually he was passed, but he hung on gamely at a distance he'd never before skied. He would have finished ninth in the Birkebeiner had his time counted (he had to be eighteen for the full race and wasn't registered). Bodensteiner would go on to ski in the Olympics for the US in 1992 and 1994. The skier who was behind him in the Kortelopet but ended up winning was a surprised John Bauer of Minnesota, who would join Bodensteiner on the 1992 Olympic team and make two more Olympics.[79]

The weather improved in 1989, with a mild start at thirty-three degrees. Orjan Blomquist (wearing No. 1 after his 1988 victory) proved he could win whether it was cold or warm. He finished in 2:19 to becme the first back-to-back men's winner in race history, outdueling Konrad Hallenbarter (wearing No. 2) by four-tenths of a second. Hallenbarter had won in 1987 in a similar sprint. "This time, it went the other way," he said. Betsy Youngman of Ohio, an alternate on the 1984 US Olympic cycling team, won the women's title by four minutes in 2:35 over defending champion Kelly Kimball. One of Youngman's skis popped loose when she got tangled with other skiers at the start, but she recovered. When Kimball fell at about 13 kilometers, Youngman said she "decided to put the accelerator down," and she took the lead for good.[80]

For the first time in five years, the race topped 6,000 skiers at 6,108. Plus, by 1989, Curel's commitment had more than tripled to about $200,000, covering about half of the cost needed to stage the race, according to new race director Linda Edgren, a former US Forest Service employee. She replaced Iowa native Marty Eckhardt, who became the race's first female director, in fall 1986. The foundation had taken over at an opportune time, as the growing interest in skate skiing expanded the momentum from the 1970s surge. Between 1980 and 1987, Nordic ski sales in the United States rose 42 percent, and by the late 1980s, an estimated 5.5 million Americans were cross-country skiing.[81]

As the tumultuous decade came to an end, the people and businesses around Hayward and Cable saw the Birkebeiner growing once again and Telemark poised to regain its luster. Hayward had held onto its national reputation as a Nordic hot spot, and the local economy received a $3.5 million annual boost, including $2.63 million in actual spending, during Birkebeiner week. Karabali's restaurant on Main Street, for example, used to bring in $2,000 during the entire month of February before the race began. By 1987, it was bringing in $14,000 during the three busiest race days alone.[82]

By the late 1980s, even the original Telemark condo owners, who had lost their investments during the bankruptcy, were happy again. Three weeks before the 1989 race, ninety-eight owners won a two-and-a-half-year court battle against their title insurance company, Ticor, of California. The $2.8 million settlement gave them each how much they had paid for their unit more than fifteen years earlier, up to $30,000.[83]

For most people, wounds had healed, and the American Birkebeiner had recovered from its existential crisis, leading the *New York Times* to provide the ultimate compliment, calling it the "Boston Marathon of skiing."[84]

Birkie Fever is on full display during Birkebeiner week, from entertaining events like the Giant Ski race, shown here in 2013, to the main races, spectators, and volunteers. AMERICAN BIRKEBEINER SKI FOUNDATION ARCHIVES, PHOTO BY DARLENE PROIS

SEVEN

THEY CALL IT BIRKIE FEVER

THE AMERICAN BIRKEBEINER took off like a well-waxed ski in the late 1970s as skiers became fascinated with the challenge—a veritable call of the wild that tested physical and mental limits, with a hint of danger in the depth of winter.

Media headlines created mystique and fed the race's popularity like a forbidden fruit: "Birkebeiner—It's Torture." "A Fine Madness." "They Must Be Masochists." "Exhausting Fun for Skiing Addicts." "Ski Race for the Strongest." "55 Kilometers of Glorious Agony." "The Unendurable 34 Miles of the Birkebeiner." A *Chicago Daily News* reporter wrote: "A 55-kilometer hike in the woods is a tough assignment. Anytime. But, in the middle of winter? On skis? Over snow-packed trails?" Even Tony Wise acknowledged it was too tough for some. "Many know they aren't going to finish," he said in 1976, "but they get a bib placed over their chest and the spirit of the chase."[1]

The challenge was mild compared to the epic tests undertaken by ancient explorers, but it was borderline quixotic in an age of convenience and creature comfort. Skiers must conquer an extreme distance, be athletic enough to employ efficient classic or freestyle technique, embrace weather challenges, overcome the infamous hills, and be able to ski in nerve-jangling traffic, while traveling at thirty miles per hour on icy and sweeping downhills. Then there's the X factor: finding the will to finish when your entire body aches (at least the parts that haven't gone numb from cold) and is telling you it no longer wants to trudge on.

The challenge has inspired many dedicated entrants who build their years and, in some cases, their lives around the race. These skiers have been afflicted with what is called Birkie Fever. The slogan was born in 1978 after

Bob Woodward, Telemark's 1977–78 cross-country ski school instructor and ski journalist, saw the popular film *Saturday Night Fever* in Duluth. The words seemed to fit the Birkie. "It was an obvious real fever that built up about ninety days before the race," Woodward said. The slogan was cemented in Birkie lore as the title of a tenth anniversary book by Tom Kelly, Telemark public relations director, who attended the movie with Woodward.[2]

What is Birkie Fever? It's a winterlong, all-encompassing motivation—waking on a February morning and instantly counting down to race day, thinking incessantly about the demanding trail and pushing your fitness level, headlamp skiing in the dark after work, embracing all snow, all cold, slowly feeling your body transform into a taut skiing machine, and dreaming of the ultimate payoff, flying victorious toward the finish line. John Kotar, who skied the first thirty-nine races, knew it well:

> Most first-time Birkie skiers don't realize they have the disease until several months later. . . . They fight it off by refusing to train but succumb anyway in the final days of February. On race day, they find themselves in the starting area, getting buzzed up by the energy generated by thousands of supercharged skiers. . . . At the finish they will be rewarded once more by the elation that only comes from meeting an extraordinary challenge.[3]

John Morton witnessed Birkie Fever the first time he attended the race. Morton was a collegiate ski champion, made the 1972 and 1976 US Olympic biathlon teams, took part in five more Olympics as a coach and team leader, and served as chief of the biathlon course for the 2002 Olympics in Salt Lake City. In 1991, at age forty-four, Morton had retired from coaching the iconic Dartmouth College ski team and had started his own business, Morton Trails, building recreational trails across the world. He decided to try the race he had heard so much about. Upon arriving at Telemark Lodge the night before the race, the New Hampshire native soaked in a scene the likes of which he had never seen:

> It seemed like a convention of everyone in America who had ever cross-country skied! The main lodge was mobbed with competitors, coaches, race volunteers, officials, and representatives from scores of ski companies. At the time, I had been to four Winter Olympics and

> several Biathlon World Championships, but never had I seen so much enthusiasm, excitement, and energy focused exclusively on cross-country.[4]

Jim Quinn, one of Morton's fellow competitors that year, caught Birkie Fever like so many other skiers when he completed his first race:

> The frigid wind blew snow in my face, stinging my eyes and causing icicles to form on my beard and mustache. Every muscle ached with a pain that went beyond exhaustion. Each hill seemed steeper than the last. My clothes were soaked with sweat despite temperatures in the mid-teens. For a few minutes, a sharp pain in the fingers of my left hand told me I'd come close to frostbite. This is fun? . . . You realize that finding the will to finish the race means reaching inside yourself for something you don't usually need and probably didn't know was there. It sounds crazy. It is crazy. There's no sane reason to get so tired, cold, and sweaty. I want to do it again.[5]

An exhausted skier, Peter Kling of Alaska, at the 2014 finish line
AMERICAN BIRKEBEINER SKI FOUNDATION ARCHIVES, PHOTO BY DARLENE PROIS

The cure for Birkie Fever seemingly can only be found upon finishing the race—again and again. The will to reach the finish line is strong. One year, a skier either broke or lost a ski early in the race but kept going on his remaining board—alternately hopping and sliding on the flats and riding downhills with both feet on one ski, like a skinny snowboard—finishing to boisterous cheers. In 2003, John Arntzen, of Roscoe, Illinois, broke a binding in a fall at 21 kilometers but vowed to walk the final 29 kilometers if he had to. Aid station volunteers and ski patrol members tried duct-taping Arntzen's boot to his ski, but, though he finished, he learned the hard way that duct tape doesn't glide. In 1977, a skier was hit in the mouth by a pole and broke off a tooth; he spit it out and kept going. Another year, a skier was huffing and puffing so hard as he crossed Lake Hayward that he blew his false teeth right out of his mouth.[6]

THE BIRKEBEINER IS A HORIZONTAL MOUNTAIN, the mountain Tony Wise never had at his Telemark alpine ski area. If a printout of the race elevation profile were stood on end, it would look like a rock climber's nightmare, a true cliffhanger. Race difficulty and lore have inspired many skiers to wax hyperbolically. "Skiing the Birkebeiner is like being born, living a long life, and dying—all in the same day," declared the *Milwaukee Journal* in the 1970s (later, the popular aphorism was modified with a new ending, "and going to heaven").[7]

Part of Birkie Fever comes from the primal challenge of propelling oneself for hours across a frozen landscape on modern versions of the boards and poles used during the Ice Age. What is it about this sport that provokes such dedication? *New York Times Magazine* writer Sam Anderson, who covered the 2018 Olympics, described it this way:

> Cross-country skiing expresses something deep about the human condition: the absolute, nonnegotiable necessity of the grind. Every single mile per hour must be earned. You pump your arms and legs against an endless and relentless resistance. . . .
>
> And yet consider the world that this suffering unlocks. Racers rake the stark landscape with their angular shadows. They slide into a whiteness beyond civilization, etching thin parallel tracks over the face of infinity, through places most of us will never go, past the pitter-patter of animal tracks in old-growth forest. This is one of the sport's

> great consolations: access to a landscape so stark it merges with the spiritual state of absolute exhaustion, a simultaneous emptiness and fullness that is essentially religious—topographical Buddhism.[8]

Cross-country skiing can be a pleasant glide in the woods, but skiing long distances across angular terrain ups the ante. Add bad weather, deep snow or ice, and the possibility of additional obstacles brought on by age or lack of conditioning, and completing the American Birkebeiner becomes, for many, a Sisyphean-like challenge.

In 1978, John Waugus of Marinette, Wisconsin, completed the race with a prosthetic leg, the first person believed to do so. His time was 7:10, but he was far from last place, finishing 1,417th out of 1,701 skiers. "Every time I came to a sign saying 'Caution: Steep Hill,' I said a prayer asking that I'd make it to the bottom, only to say another prayer so I could make it up the mountain in front of me," Waugus said. "I don't really know why I kept going. It sure felt good to cross that finish line."[9]

In 1979, forty-one-year-old Harry Cordellos of San Francisco became the first blind skier to attempt to ski the race. He was guided stride for stride with verbal instructions from Einar Odden, a Norwegian exchange student at University of Wisconsin–River Falls, but didn't make the Highway OO cutoff time. Cordellos vowed to return, and in 1980, again with Odden's help, he made the cutoff. He finished in 6:53, savoring the moment when the finisher medal fell over his shoulders. Cordellos already was an accomplished runner, swimmer, water skier, and more—he set the Boston Marathon record for totally blind runners in 1977 in 2:57—and would go on to run more than 150 marathons, finish the Hawaii Iron Man triathlon, write several books, and become a global advocate for the blind.

Two members of the US Disabled Ski Team finished the Birkebeiner in 1993. Michele Drolet, of Morristown, New Jersey, became the first blind woman to finish. She was guided by Mark Blaskey of Eau Claire, Wisconsin, who talked her through the twisting course in 4:02. Drolet had finished her second Kortelopet the year before but, like many who start with the half-marathon, wanted the ultimate Birkie challenge. "I definitely had Birkie Fever," she said. "It's a way to prove to myself I can overcome any obstacle. I don't consider myself disabled." The Birkie became Drolet's springboard: in 1994, she became the first US woman to win a medal in cross-country at the Paralympic Winter Games.

Jeff Pagels of Green Bay was a Wisconsin Department of Natural Resources worker, triathlete, champion canoe and kayak racer, and six-time Birkie finisher. Then, in 1984, a tree fell on Pagels, leaving him paralyzed from the midabdomen down. He kept competing, making the 1992 US Paralympic team and winning cross-country gold medals in the 5-kilometer and 10-kilometer. That same year, Pagels became the first person on a sit-ski—a low chair mounted on skis—to complete the Kortelopet. He aimed for the Birkie in 1993, propelling himself with his arms to the finish in 4:52. Two months later, Pagels and fellow sit-skier Mark Wellman crossed the Sierra Nevada, covering 49 miles in three days, including a nearly ten-thousand-foot pass. They skied ten hours a day, sometimes progressing at just six inches per push, while each pulling a sled filled with thirty pounds of camping equipment and food.[10]

Jeff Pagels, pictured at the 1992 Kortelopet, became the first sit-skier to complete the long race in 1993. AMERICAN BIRKEBEINER SKI FOUNDATION ARCHIVES

Many other skiers have finished despite serious health and physical challenges. In 2005, five weeks before the race, Mitch Eichman underwent surgery to remove two inches of his windpipe because of thyroid cancer. Mitch, age fifty-four, spent the first four weeks after surgery with his chin on his chest as his neck muscles recovered. The fifth week, he had planned to be the support crew for his brother, Tony, with whom he had skied thirteen Birkies. To his brother's surprise, however, Mitch brought his skis along and decided to ski the race, with no prerace conditioning. He and Tony once again skied and finished together.[11]

Fifty-nine-year-old Jim Tenorio of Menomonie, Wisconsin, had completed thirty-two Birkies by mid-January 2012, when he had an egg-sized, cancerous tumor removed from one of his kidneys. After a week in the hospital—during which "they caught the cancer early enough and removed it all"—Tenorio didn't know if he could finish the race, but he knew one thing: he was going to try. "I did not want to miss out on being with so many people with such a passion for the sport," Tenorio said. "Just to be in Cable and Hayward on race weekend is exciting. To be one of the racers is even better." He finished in 6:10, much slower than his usual time, but after more than three decades of Birkie racing, Tenorio knew that finish times weren't the only measure of success. "I've got to think that cross-country skiing kept me in good condition, which helped me recover from the surgery as I did," he said.[12]

Others have been driven to ski the Birkie despite similarly long odds. Hayward kindergarten teacher Barb Klippel overcame non-Hodgkin's lymphoma in 1985, a near-fatal head injury in 2005, and other health challenges to complete her nineteenth Birkebeiner in 2008—at age seventy-five. In 2012, she was the honorary race starter and went on to finish her coveted twentieth race at age seventy-nine. Klippel wore a bicycle helmet to protect her head, and several friends formed a protective cocoon around her as she skied. She became the oldest woman on record to have completed the race.[13]

Bob Britz, a teacher and coach from Shakopee, Minnesota, suffered extensive injuries—including a broken leg, pelvis, ribs, and arm—in a car accident in mid-1984 that left him incapacitated until January 1985. He still finished his ninth Birkie in February 1985, as part of forty-five straight while aiming for fifty. In spring 2015, elite skier Nathan Lillie of Altoona, Wisconsin, broke a leg—crushing the top of his tibia and tearing his meniscus—in a training collision on the Birkebeiner trail. His doctor, also a Birkie skier, didn't know if Lillie would ever ski again. But after surgery to install a metal plate, three months on crutches, and extensive rehabilitation, Lillie returned to the race in 2016 and finished just four places lower, 129th, than before his injury. In fall 2018, Steve Morales, the 1970s founder of New Moon Ski Shop in Hayward, broke a hip while roller skiing. Five months after hip replacement surgery, Morales finished fifth in the 70-to-74 age class in his thirty-ninth Birkie.[14]

Birkie Fever takes many forms. Weddings have been held and skiers' ashes have been spread on the trail. One skier proposed to his girlfriend on Main Street, taking off one ski and getting down on one knee before crossing the finish line. Another agreed to propose only if his girlfriend beat him to the fireplace at Telemark Lodge; she did. In 2019, Cate McKinney and Daniel Gerdts were married on the awards podium after finishing the race together (Cate skiing with a veil and Daniel a bow tie) almost in the same spot where they got engaged post-Birkie five years earlier. An older skier, upon finishing, was asked by a WOJB reporter how long she planned to keep skiing the race. She replied that she'd eventually like to cross the finish line and ski straight into her casket.[15]

Skiing the Birkebeiner has helped save at least one man's life and was the dying wish of another. In the late 1970s, Darrell Thompson, of Cable, was in his thirties and struggling with alcohol addiction when two friends, Tom Duffy and Bob Bergum, suggested that he "get off my dead butt" and do the Birkie. So, as Thompson recalled many years later, "I went to Telemark, bought a pair of skis and poles, and started skiing." He went on to do thirty Birkies. He started setting even bigger goals and began to do the Worldloppet, traveling multiple times to Europe and becoming a two-time master with twenty worldwide races under his belt. He found a whole new life in the beauty, solitude, and clarity that comes with sliding down a ski trail. "Without alcohol I found who I was," Thompson said at age eighty-eight. "I wouldn't be here today if it wasn't for skiing."[16]

Elmer Hassett, also from Cable, began skiing as a kid in 1935. As an adult, he was a member of the National Ski Patrol and helped with site development for the 1960 Olympics. Hassett's military career included serving in World War II and the Korean War, teaching military science at Dartmouth College, and teaching skiing and other winter warfare tactics to US soldiers. Hassett retired in 1970 as a lieutenant colonel and took up the Birkie in 1976, at age fifty, after seeing an ad at a ski shop in St. Paul. (He showed up at Telemark Lodge the night before his first race and slept in his Saab because the lodge was full.) Hooked, he went on to ski nineteen Birkies.

Lynn Larson carries Elmer Hassett's ashes in the 1997 race. AMERICAN BIRKEBEINER SKI FOUNDATION ARCHIVES

Hassett, at age seventy, had hoped to ski his twentieth Birkie in 1996, but treatments for prostate and bone cancer left him too weak to compete. As the 1997 race approached, Hassett knew he was dying. Before he passed away on January 15, 1997, he had one last request of his pastor at United Church of Christ, Lynn Larson, also a Birkie skier: Would Larson carry Hassett's ashes—in a backpack marked with his bib number—in the upcoming race? "I was deeply honored," Larson said later. Larson's eight great-grandparents were immigrants from Norway, where skiers carry a weighted pack in the Norwegian Birkebeinerrennet to represent Prince Haakon. "I was carrying a special bundle, too," Larson said, "my Prince Elmer." Hassett's ashes weighed more than ten pounds. "I found myself having conversations with Elmer's spirit and remembering him quite a bit," Larson said. "It almost felt like Elmer was right there with me. I found myself singing about Elmer. It was more than a race for me." Larson finished in 4:53, his best Birkie.[17]

It was a fitting last hurrah for Hassett, who had become a tireless Birkie volunteer over the years. He received a special bib, a coveted purple Birchleggings Club bib honoring those who completed twenty races, for his posthumous trip down the trail. After the race, Hassett's ashes were spread on the trail, and a plaque in his honor was placed about one kilometer south of Highway OO.[18]

SO SPIRITED ARE THOSE WHO LOVE THE BIRKIE that they write songs about it. On race morning, WOJB 88.9 FM, Woodland Community Radio, an independent public radio station in Reserve, Wisconsin, plays a loop of race-themed songs as part of daylong race coverage. The folksy tunes include "Birkie Fever (Get Me to the Start Line I'll Be Ready to Go)"; "Birkie Rag"; "Birkie Polka"; "Kortelopet Dreaming" (to the tune of the Mamas and the Papas' "California Dreamin' "); "Something I Must Confess (A Birkebeiner Love Affair)"; and "Where the Hills All Have Names" (to the tune of U2's hit "Where the Streets Have No Name"). The song "Let the Birkie Grab Your Soul" hit the airwaves in 2001. It was written and sung by John Schulz, a skier and Ashland anesthesiologist who composed verses between operations. "I tried to convey the sense that the Birkie is bigger than life," Schulz said.[19] Lyrics include:

> Let the Birkie grab your soul,
> Push you down the trail,
> Help you lock on your goal.
> Let the iron-thighed clusters keep the pace moving strong
> So Cable to Hayward won't last very long
> As you go through the snow
> With the seed of speed
> Being all that you need
> Let the Birkie grab your soul.

Birke 2000

From Cable to Hayward
A journey takes place
Known by all as the
Birke ski race
Wave upon wave
By the thousands they come
Some groping, each hoping
a small victory is won
A logistical nightmare
A staggering feat
To arrive at the start
The first challenge to meet
Landgraf, Andresen, Ernie St. Germaine
Among the strong founders who still remain
Year after year
This proud bunch comes through
Reminding the rest
You are what you do
A question is raised
Some want to know why?
Does failure escape those who will try?
Why do it?
Why suffer?
Why bring on the pain?
Why push till you're empty?
What is there to gain?
The answer, my friend, will enter your mind
As you pass through the gate
at the finish line

By

Mary Rufledt Gladitsch

Above: Icicle beards (and mustaches and eyebrows) a[r] a common and oft-photographed sight at the Birkebei[ner] finish line. AMERICAN BIRKEBEINER SKI FOUNDATION ARCHIVES

Left: A poem by Mary Rufledt Gladitsch captures the essence of Birkie Fever: "Why do it? Why suffer? Why bring on the pain? . . . The answer, my friend, will enter your mind as you pass through the gate at the finish lin[e]" AMERICAN BIRKEBEINER SKI FOUNDATION ARCHIVES, WITH PERMISSION FROM THE AUTHOR

While most skiers opt for performance-enhancing Lycra, others show their Birkie spirit in more creative ways. AMERICAN BIRKEBEINER SKI FOUNDATION ARCHIVES

Sten Fjeldheim of Marquette, Michigan, finished sixteenth in his first Birkie in 1977 and ninth in 1984, competed in four Olympic trials from 1976 to 1988, and went on to coach the Northern Michigan University Nordic teams. He returned to the Birkie in 2005 at age forty-eight when he took an impressive thirty-ninth in 2:15. "I realized the Birkie is such a huge celebration of our sport," Fjeldheim said, almost thirty years after his first Birkebeiner. "Nowhere else in the US do you have that sort of crowd just there to enjoy cross-country skiing. It's a big homecoming for a lot of people."[20]

Cross-country skiing also has numerous benefits as a full-body, aerobic workout. Elite skiers are known to be some of the most fit people on the planet, and citizen skiers do pretty well too. In a 2014 study, preventive medicine specialist Paul Anderson of the Mayo Clinic examined the health behaviors of more than five thousand four hundred Birkebeiner skiers, with an average age of almost forty-eight. The skiers' rates of smoking and obesity were far below national averages, and virtually all of them, 99 percent, were more fit than their peers across genders and age categories.[21]

The sport's low-impact, natural movements are kind to the body, making it possible to cross-country ski late into life. How else can the feat of Gunnar Lillieroth, of Umeå, Sweden, near the Arctic Circle, be explained? In 1997, at age eighty-two, Lillieroth finished the Birkie in a solid 5:55. He won his age class—largely because he was the only person in his age class—and at the time was believed to be the oldest skier to finish the race. Lillieroth recently had completed 70-, 65-, 60-, and 55-kilometer marathons in Europe. The week before the 1997 Birkie, he completed a 50-kilometer ski marathon in Canada, and he returned to Sweden the week after for the 90-kilometer Vasaloppet. In all, Lillieroth completed eight ski marathons that season on two continents.[22]

Some skiers seem to defy age with a vengeance. In 2023, former Olympian John Bauer, at age fifty-four, finished twenty-first in the Birkebeiner in 2:19, winning his age class by fifteen minutes. In 1993, Hermann Ritzinger of Austria, then fifty-two, also won his age class by fifteen minutes, also in 2:19, and finished fifty-second overall. That same year, Bjorn Lasserud qualified for the elite wave at age sixty-four—when most elites were in their twenties. Lasserud, who was born in Norway and had emigrated to Minneapolis, didn't take up skiing until he was an adult, remarkably qualifying for the US Central Division ski team at age forty-nine. In 1993, he finished in 2:44 and won his age class by twenty minutes. He was back the next year, at age sixty-five, winning his age class in 2:42. In all, Lasserud would complete twenty Birkies and would become an ambassador for the sport, before his death in 2020 at age ninety.[23]

A GOAL FOR MANY LONGTIME ENTRANTS is to become a Birchlegger. Upon reaching their twentieth Birkebeiner, skiers qualify for the Birchleggings Club and, from that year forward, ski with a prized purple bib. Skiers at thirty or more Birkies are girded with the warrior-like black Uberlegger bib.

The Birchleggings Club was created in 1992 by John Kotar, a Birkie Founder, and longtime skier Dave Balsiger. Kotar, who had skied every Birkebeiner to that point, noticed that skiers who raised concerns about race issues weren't always being heard, so he proposed the idea to the foundation. The vision was not just to honor twenty-year skiers but also to operate as a "body of experienced skiers exceptionally dedicated to the sport who will be in a position to contribute significantly to the future of the Birkebeiner," according to the club. At the time, only a handful of skiers had done all twenty races. By the fiftieth race, that number was around two thousand—including more than one hundred skiers who had done forty-plus races. "The people who come year after year form a kind of brotherhood system," Kotar said.[24]

Birchlegger Roy Carlsted, age seventy-eight, of St. Paul skis in the 2002 race. In all, he finished thirty-two Birkebeiners. AMERICAN BIRKEBEINER SKI FOUNDATION ARCHIVES

The Birchleggings Club, incorporated as a nonprofit in 2013, acts as a second benevolent foundation for the race. In addition to promoting skier retention, it funded the log cabin at the Mosquito Brook Road trail crossing; supported the Tony Wise Museum of the American Birkebeiner and the skier bridge over Highway 77; and supports youth ski programs in the region. In 2023, the club supported the Birkie Green sustainability initiative by repurposing used bibs to make shopping bags and raising funds to buy an electric snowmobile to film race leaders. "The club is a partner with the foundation. We need each other," Kotar said.[25]

Birchleggers are living time capsules for the race. Steve Carmazon completed his first race—the third Birkebeiner, in 1975—with no intention of doing it most of his life. He had been a high school track and cross-country athlete in Minnesota, graduating in 1971, and picked up skiing as a young adult. One winter, Carmazon and some friends skied 106 miles (170 kilometers) over four days on an abandoned railroad bed west of Minneapolis. When they heard of the Birkebeiner, 55 kilometers sounded easy—but, Carmazon said, "we didn't know about the hills." He enjoyed the challenge, the atmosphere, and the new circle of friends. After Carmazon's first Birkebeiner, he never even came close to missing another. His race involvement deepened further when he became an active member and vice president of the Birchleggings Club. As of 2024, Carmazon had skied forty-eight races, the second-most in event history, two behind Ernie St. Germaine.[26]

BIRKIE FEVER EXTENDS BEYOND ITS DIEHARD SKIERS. Every year, up to two thousand volunteers from around the region and country help the foundation pull off an event that would be a logistical challenge even for a big city. The Birkie draws about five times as many skiers as the combined population of Hayward and Cable, requiring an all-hands-on-deck effort. By comparison, the home of the world's largest marathon, New York City, has more than eight million residents to support its fifty thousand runners.

"Without the volunteers, there would be no race," said Kurt Proctor, longtime resident, trail groomer, skier, and business owner. Allan Serrano, director of race operations in the mid-2010s, said it's "staggering to think about the people who volunteer, including jobs like parking and lost and found. It's really special to see all those people having a good time providing something for other people and having an appreciation for how much people love the event."[27]

Ronda Tworek recruits volunteers for the Birkebeiner and ten other annual foundation events. Volunteers for the 2023 Birkie included 1,661 individuals and twenty-two nonprofit groups. Sixty-five percent of them came from outside of the Hayward-Cable area. "The greatest joy is seeing so many people come together to help," Tworek said. "There is a Birkie Fever all its own for the volunteers, a 'volunteer vibe.'"[28]

Support from volunteers has helped many a skier reach the finish line. "After one-fourth of the race, I was convinced I wasn't going to make it," one skier wrote to the Birkebeiner Foundation in 2005. "However, I was so pampered and replenished at the aid stations that I began gaining confidence. Maybe that is why I look forward to the Birkie every year. At no other time during the year will anybody that I know actually cater to me like that. I even had two wonderful women taking turns placing bananas in my mouth." Here, a volunteer feeds a slice of banana to another skier in 2011. AMERICAN BIRKEBEINER SKI FOUNDATION ARCHIVES

Longtime volunteer crew leaders James Krueger and Dave Johnson work the start area. "The best part is working with the skiers and volunteers, plus the challenge of pulling off successful starts," Krueger said. "Being able to contribute in a small way to such a big event makes a person proud." Johnson, a former Birkie skier himself, coached high school cross-country and taught science in Duluth. "Many of the skiers I coached are doing the Birkie," he said. "It's really meaningful in that way. I get to be part of all of their starts, a part of that cross-country joy for all of them. You just want to hug everybody who's there."[29]

Erik Hansen, the volunteer leader at the Mosquito Brook Road stop, stays up past midnight prior to the week's three long races to prepare eighty sack lunches each night for his volunteers, who include a dedicated group of students and parents from the Peak Nordic Ski Club in the Milwaukee area. Then he's at the food stop before dawn, bringing it to life. An architect who works for the state and a certified personal trainer on the side, Hansen skied about a dozen Birkebeiners before becoming a volunteer. "It is a real experience to step back and watch a finely tuned machine work and work well," he said. "The American Birkebeiner is an amazing thing, an international phenomenon done with extreme dedication by all the people who take part in it." One year, Hansen's crew rallied around a despondent first-time entrant who pulled in with a binding that had torn off the ski. The skier thought he'd have to drop out with 14 kilometers to go. The crew made some calls, used some power tools, and fixed his ski—and he finished the race. "When we sent him on his way, he was one very happy and grateful individual," Hansen said.[30]

Past the finish line—where more volunteers staff the food tent—Rhonda Tworek's husband, Dave Tworek, oversees skier bag pickup. His crew sorts and hands out twelve thousand bags over three days, for the open-track event on Wednesday, the Kortelopet on Friday, and the Birkebeiner on Saturday. In 2015, Dave streamlined the operation by building two hundred wooden sign holders for bag numbers, shooting laser lines to delineate rows, and ordering bags numerically (a process that takes more than three hours), all of which significantly reduced skier wait time. Since 2015, his team hasn't lost a single bag out of the more than one hundred thousand placed in its care. Dave does a marathon-like seventy-six thousand steps every Birkie day, proving that volunteering for the race can be just as intense as skiing it. "I had one volunteer who had done twenty-one Birkies and said this was harder," Dave said. "It's a long day."[31]

For some volunteers, the work starts several months before race week. Donna Hughes started volunteering in 1980. She begins each October overseeing the assembly of race packets, one for every skier. It's a labor-intensive operation that requires precision, especially during race week, when she works up to one hundred hours. Hughes's volunteer crew organizes ten thousand or more bibs by wave and number to make sure each skier is quickly and correctly matched when they pick up their packet. Hughes runs the operation like a command center, as even one bib assigned to the wrong person can cause problems, creating a domino effect for other skiers.[32]

A skier searches for his bag at the pickup area in 1986. Today, volunteers at the bag pickup area work as many as sixteen hours each race day, dramatically improving wait times for exhausted skiers. AMERICAN BIRKEBEINER SKI FOUNDATION ARCHIVES

Before bib pickup was moved to Hayward, Hughes and others would spend all night in Telemark's Red Arrow Room helping late-arriving skiers, some of whom then slept between the racks of bibs. Hughes would nap for a few hours in a sleeping bag, and then, on race day, she'd oversee late bib pickup and drive to Hayward to help at the finish. Her husband, Jim, also volunteered. He once drove an Austrian skier back to Ashland—forty miles away—on race morning after the skier realized he had forgotten his skis. Another time, Donna and Jim took in two German skiers for the week when it was clear their unheated recreational vehicle, where the skiers had planned to sleep, wouldn't be safe in the below-zero weather. Donna and Jim are just two examples of the "volunteer vibe": "There are ten million of those little stories of volunteers who have done those types of things for people," Donna said.[33]

Volunteers hand out race packets in Telemark's Red Arrow Room in 1980. By 1987, FIS official Lars Kindem praised volunteer leader Donna Hughes for her "flawless" registration operation. AMERICAN BIRKEBEINER SKI FOUNDATION ARCHIVES

A NEW BIRKEBEINER VOLUNTEER GROUP formed in 2018: the Birkie Ambassadors. It's a small group, about fifteen skiers, but with a noble mission. Wearing Ambassador bibs, these skiers provide support for racers and help ensure a positive experience, by offering words of encouragement, untangling pileups, or defusing tensions that might emerge between skiers on the trail. The program was started by Doug Peterson, the 1976 and 1980 Olympian from Minneapolis who trained at Telemark for his first Olympic team. When he returned for the Birkie many years later, Peterson didn't feel like he had anything to prove by racing but wanted to take part. He suggested the ambassador idea to the foundation's executive director, Ben Popp, who gave the go-ahead.

"It's been very rewarding for me to start the program and has helped me reconnect with a passion of mine," Peterson said. "Cross-country skiing is with you for life."[34]

One ambassador with Peterson has been Bruce Derauf, the St. Paul Academy teenager who competed in the 1973 race at his coach's urging despite not being old enough and has continued to come back. Derauf, now a radiologist in Duluth, has skied more than forty Birkies and has competed in Worldloppet races in Europe. He explained why the sport can feel so addictive:

> You can really appreciate the beauty of nature when cross-country skiing. There's nothing like a day when you're going through the woods and you see those afternoon shadows and a kind of blue light. It's just very special. It's fun to go fast on those 44-millimeter-wide skis, pretty thrilling actually. When you go down those big hills in the Birkebeiner, you can really fly. Cross-country skis are the wings of winter.[35]

Skiing through the deep-woods silence of winter while generating your own energy, maybe into a sunset or through falling snow, can border on a spiritual experience for some. "The first time I put on a pair of skis, the magic of the free-glide feeling was unreal, and I've never lost that," said longtime race entrant Steve Morales. "It's one of the most amazing things you can do as long as you're earthbound."[36]

Gliding *across the country* is the siren song of Nordic skiing. The Birkie adds a bib, a beguiling trail with thousands of people on it, and thirty-plus, grind-to-the-end miles. As skiers push into the woods and head south, with a tip of the stocking hat to Skadi and Ullr, the Norwegian goddess and god of skiing, Birkie Fever is at a fever pitch, a finish line the only cure.

1990 American Birkebeiner, with nearly 6,300 skiers
AMERICAN BIRKEBEINER SKI FOUNDATION ARCHIVES

EIGHT

1990–1999 REVERSING—AND STAYING—THE COURSE

THE BIRKEBEINER FOUNDATION had successfully muscled through the uncertainty of the previous decade as the 1990s began. The race's reputation remained strong and—with new legions of skate skiers—the race was growing. Plus, the foundation had amassed a surplus of $100,000 and bought its first trail-grooming machine, a sign that it was financially sound.[1]

By the early 1990s, the Birkebeiner had become entrenched as an American classic and an international phenomenon. As the *Chicago Tribune* reported in 1992, "There's little room for logic in a cross-country ski race that started in small town northern Wisconsin and is now an event of international proportions."[2] The 1990s proved to be yet another momentous decade for the Birkebeiner. Before the decade was done, the race would see entries rise by more than 13 percent, the first American winner in many years, the debut of a much-loved feature, multiple weather challenges, and the passing of its founder.

The decade started off cold. It was zero degrees at the start of the 1990 race, again sponsored by Curel. The low-snow winter that year resulted in the cancellation of the Mora Vasaloppet in Mora, Minnesota, in early February. But luckily it snowed a foot or more the week before the Birkebeiner. The 6,270 registered skiers enjoyed prime but frigid conditions on the push from Hayward to

Telemark. Founding skier Dave Landgraf finished with an icicle hanging from the chin of the face mask he wore to prevent frostbite.

Manfred Nagl, a police officer from Austria, won by a ski tip in 2:30, in a three-way photo finish with 1987 champion Konrad Hallenbarter and Markus Fandrich of Switzerland. Officials had put the laurel wreath over Hallenbarter's neck but after reviewing the videotape put it on Nagl's. Minnesotan Lynne Cecil, needing a replacement pole after breaking one in the start, rode a late surge to overcome friend and defending women's champion Betsy Youngman by eight seconds in 2:51. It was Cecil's first Birkebeiner win in five tries.[3]

A month after the 1990 race, another part of Tony Wise's business empire came down—this time literally. Over two weekends in late March, fire departments from Hayward and neighboring communities took part in a controlled-burn exercise in which they torched many of the buildings at Historyland.[4]

Lack of snow was an issue prior to the 1991 race too, resulting in another start in Rosie's Field and a shortened 46-kilometer route. Snow cover was thin that winter, and much of it disappeared during a mild stretch in February, leaving the trail a patchwork of bare spots and ice. Volunteers were organized to shovel snow onto the trail, and a snow gun was borrowed from a regional alpine hill to make more. Six inches of snow fell a few days before the race, but a warm Thursday melted much of it. It was nine degrees on race morning when it started snowing again, causing traffic jams, delays, and a slow track for the 6,269 skiers (one skier less than the year before). Eight inches would fall by the end of the race.

The new snow didn't bother Nagl, who won again, this time in 2:01—seven seconds ahead of countryman Wolfgang Ritzinger. Nagl had suffered a severe leg injury in a mountain bike race the previous August and had just spent fourteen days in the hospital in January with a virus. Yet he still managed to break away from a pack of about nine skiers with a kilometer to go. His secret weapon? An energy drink with coffee, served up to him at the last food stop by his hosts for the week, the Donald Peterson family. Amazingly, Canadian Pierre Harvey finished third, three seconds after Ritzinger, even though traffic delays had caused him to arrive two minutes late for the start. He passed an estimated 150 skiers on his way to the front and caught the leaders at 21 kilometers. Ingrid

Facing page: The parade at the 1992 opening ceremonies, honoring each state and nation represented in that year's race. 1973 champion Erik Ersson, lower left, carries the sign for Sweden. AMERICAN BIRKEBEINER SKI FOUNDATION ARCHIVES

Kansas
Iowa
Indiana
Illinois
rgia
necticut
Colorado
Arizona
Alabama
itzerland

Butts of Park City, Utah, took the women's title in 2:15, breaking away from a pack of three with 4 kilometers to go. "All I could think about toward the end was, 'I want that wreath,'" she said, referring to the champion's laurel wreath. Youngman was second again, forty-two seconds behind.[5]

AS THE 1992 BIRKEBEINER APPROACHED, the Olympics were happening in Albertville, France, but the Birkebeiner had its own celebration that year: the twentieth anniversary race. On Friday of race week, Governor Tommy Thompson lit an Olympic-style flame at a special opening ceremony, then a torch relay from Hayward to Telemark brought the flame to the lodge.

The event was billed as a Reunion of Friends, and none was more important than Tony Wise. The day before the event, he vowed that he still wanted nothing to do with the race. But, to the surprise of many, Wise showed up anyway, received a thirty-second standing ovation, offered a brusque statement to the crowd—"It's good seeing you all again. I hope you have a great race tomorrow"—and then sat down. It was his first official appearance at the race since he last managed it in 1984. The program included a tribute to Wise, who, by the end of the event, was greeting old friends and posing for pictures, including with original Birkebeiner champion Erik Ersson of Sweden.[6]

As part of the twentieth anniversary, the foundation board made a major change that would become such an iconic part of the race's identity that it begged the question why it hadn't been done sooner. After ten years of starting in Hayward, the racecourse was quietly reversed from north to south. The board wanted to try something special for the anniversary and bring the finish back to Hayward—and for the first time to Main Street.[7]

It was a conspicuous break with protocol. The 1984 legal agreement that gave the new foundation the rights to the race stipulated that it always finish at Telemark unless "further agreement is made." The original agreement also required Telemark to provide "in-kind" race support "in the form of employees, facilities, and related amenities," including a room for registration and bib pickup, space for the race finish, and use of the Colosseum for pre- and postrace events.[8]

However, Bill Papaik, owner of Telemark's parent company Lake Properties, was focused on selling time-share units in the resort and the new condominiums and wasn't necessarily endeared to the extra costs and issues associated with race week. By 1992, five years into Lake Properties' ownership of the resort, more financial cracks had started to appear. Bayfield County sought to foreclose on Lake Properties, which was $150,000 in arrears on a $729,000 block grant loan, and the Lac Courte Oreilles tribe had signed an option to buy the resort and open a casino next to it or in the Colosseum (a general idea Tony Wise also was promoting from 1992 through 1994 in an attempt to get the lodge back and possibly the race). Lake Properties' other newer investments, including the Chequamegon Hotel in Ashland, Wisconsin, and Fitger's on the Lake in Duluth, also were struggling.[9]

The proposal to move the finish to Main Street surfaced at an October 1991 foundation meeting, with board member Tom Duffy promoting the idea as a "grand display" of the sport. Director Linda Edgren was in favor, but several board members raised concerns about a projected $5,000 in extra security costs, not enough time to plan the change, skiers not returning to Telemark for postrace events, where to finish if the lake wasn't frozen, and the lack of a warm building to get finishers out of the cold. Also, one member noted that not one skier had ever asked for the race to finish on Main. The board sought Papaik's approval, and he gave it as long as the change was permanent. The board voted in November, and the finish on Main passed by the narrowest of margins in a 7-6 vote.[10]

Did the board know it would be an economic boon for downtown Hayward (with spectators and skiers in the central business district for most of the day), how weary skiers would be inspired by the cheers of thousands welcoming them home, and how the spectator gauntlet would visually set the race apart from others around the world?

If not, it did by the end of the race in 1992. Thousands of spectators lined the street—even Tony Wise came by to see it a decade after he watched the spectacular first start there—and witnessed the most unusual finish in race history. US Ski Team members Todd Boonstra of Minnesota and Audun Endestad of Alaska, a 1977–78 Telemark ski instructor, battled to the end. Endestad was leading, but when he passed a banner and red line in the snow with about two hundred yards to go, he thought he had won and raised his arms. Boonstra tried to point to Endestad that the finish still was ahead. They collided, Boonstra falling and snapping one of Endestad's poles. Boonstra recovered and pushed past the single-poling Endestad by two seconds. Hans Christian Udnaes of Norway closed on the pair, taking second. Although it appeared neither skier was at fault for the collision, Boonstra immediately went over to his friend and said, "I'm sorry, man." Boonstra's time was 2:15. Nina Skeime of Norway won the women's race in 2:26, four minutes ahead of Laura McCabe of Utah. Skeime took the lead after 5 kilometers and wasn't seriously challenged.[11]

Boonstra and Endestad had narrowly missed being named to the US Olympic team earlier in the year (Boonstra was on the 1984, 1988, and 1994 teams and Endestad, born in Norway, on the 1984 team). They had colds, and Boonstra had been battling a heart arrhythmia, but both were upset about not being chosen. They set their sights on the Birkebeiner, living in Seeley for six weeks with resident Gary Penman and training on the trail. Boonstra, who wore a US team suit—blue top and red-and-white-striped pants—was the first American to win a full race (excluding the rain-delayed, reduced-field 1981 event won by Tim Caldwell) in seventeen years, since Chris Haines of Alaska in 1975. "We really wanted an American to win," Boonstra said. Endestad had been close before in the Birkebeiner, including fifth in 1986 and third in 1988. At age thirty-nine, it would be his last good chance to add the Birkebeiner to his thirteen national and six Great American Ski Chase titles.[12]

Above: Todd Boonstra raises his arms in victory in the dramatic 1992 finish—the first finish on Main Street. Boonstra had collided with US teammate Audun Endestad, far right, breaking Endestad's left pole, after Endestad stopped because he thought he had crossed the finish line. *Facing page:* 1992 start at the twentieth annual race. AMERICAN BIRKEBEINER SKI FOUNDATION ARCHIVES

Heritage Bank
Heritage Bank
ActiBath
GTE Elite Sprints
PowerBar
SALOMON
DYNO
DYNO

Snow was plentiful, and the race start was a comfortable twenty-eight degrees. The twentieth event was the second largest Birkebeiner, with 6,373 skiers and a new long-term title sponsor, Dyno Overlays, a Norwegian-based company with a plant in Hayward that made paper overlays for paneling, plywood, and laminates. Writing in the *Birch Scroll*, Linda Edgren, the foundation's executive director, called it "the most successful in the history of the race," but added that she was stepping down after four years.[13]

THE MAIN STREET FINISH RETURNED IN 1993, and the Birkebeiner never looked back. Another exciting Main Street finish that year reinforced the value of the switch. At age twenty-nine, Manfred Nagl became the first skier to win three titles. Gliding down Main Street, he broke from a pack of ten skiers and outsprinted them to the finish in 2:05, with Hans Christian Udnaes a close runner-up again. Thousands of spectators watched the three-block sprint to the finish line and realized, if they hadn't already, that cross-country skiing really could be exciting.

Entries were down fifteen that year to 6,358, and the start temperature was a chilly ten degrees. Endestad got tangled up and fell again, this time early in the race, and finished nineteenth. Suzanne King, en route to the US Olympic teams in 1994 and 1998, took the women's title in 2:27 by less than a minute over fellow Minnesotan Jan Guenther. It was the first race for new foundation director Marilyn Schutz.[14]

In 1994, skier registration went up almost 300 to 6,632. It was five below at the start (which sounded balmy after an overnight low of negative twenty-two), a perfect day for an icicle beard and for Czech Republic skier Thomas Caslavsky, who won in 2:16, three seconds over Switzerland's Andre Jungen. Caslavsky had avenged his fourth-place loss in the 1993 sprint to the finish. Heike Wezel of Germany won the women's race by two minutes in 2:36 over Maria Theurl of Austria, giving Europeans their first sweep of the titles in a decade. Race week included 1,700 children in the Barnebirkie.[15]

The race even made national television. A Duluth, Minnesota, station, KDLH, was broadcasting live for the second time, covering the start and from Lake Hayward to the finish line. Unbeknownst to the KDLH producers, CBS was monitoring the station's satellite feed and picked up video. On the national network's coverage of the Olympics in Lillehammer, Norway, highlights of the American Birkebeiner aired.[16]

The 1994 runners-up Jungen and Theurl both won in 1995. Jungen pulled away after 45 kilometers "and then it was like flying," he said, finishing in 2:10 to win by thirty-eight seconds. Theurl was well rested after two weeks of battling a cold. She came out strong and never was challenged—admitting she liked the Birkebeiner hills because they reminded her of trails back home in Austria. Theurl posted 2:22 and won by nearly three minutes over Laura McCabe of Utah. The top American and Wisconsin finisher was Hayward's George Welk in tenth.[17]

Race day capped off a good week, ten years after the foundation took over. Entries remained steady in 1995 at 6,616, and the Barnebirkie drew a record of more than 1,700 children. Skiers enjoyed what some called perfect trail conditions and weather with a starting temperature of eighteen degrees, rising into the midtwenties with light snow. Snow had been scarce throughout the winter, but what did fall didn't melt. And the downtown finish line continued to prove popular, with spectators and skiers alike. Third-place finisher Gunnar Havel, of the Czech Republic, marveled at the festive finish. "We would wish all races to be so full of life," Havel said.[18]

TONY WISE TURNED SEVENTY-FOUR on March 15, 1995, and he celebrated at home with several children and grandchildren. With so many cars parked outside, at least one person thought Wise had died—but when a well-wisher called to offer condolences, Wise answered the phone. Still, he wasn't well, and when daughter Frances left the party, she worried it might be the last time she'd see him alive.[19]

Although Wise wanted to live to be one hundred like his cross-country skiing idol Herman "Jackrabbit" Smith-Johanssen, he had been battling dementia for about a year and other health issues for more than twenty-five years. In 1969, he was hospitalized after a heart attack while on a business trip to Ashland, Wisconsin. Wise recovered and dropped his weight from 218 to 196 pounds. In the early 1980s, he was severely beaten at Telemark by an angry condominium owner. He suffered a stroke in the attack and was flown to the Mayo Clinic in Rochester, Minnesota, where he had surgery to remove a blood clot and was hospitalized for several weeks. Then, in 1991, Wise had another heart attack while on business at a ski resort in Colorado and underwent quadruple bypass surgery in Denver.[20]

Soon after Wise's seventy-fourth birthday, he was taken to the Veterans Administration Medical Center in Minneapolis by his daughter Angeline Cloud and her husband, Kurt Kwakenat. Wise died there on April 6, about six weeks after the 1995 race. "He did live to be one hundred in words and action, just not physically," Frances said.[21]

Wise would have preferred to die in the bed in which he was born and where he slept his entire life at the family home near Main Street, the home where he also was married. Just as he wanted to still be in charge of his beloved Birkebeiner and Telemark. But in the end, most of what he created had survived him, validating his life's work beyond profit and loss. "If you keep score by counting money, Tony Wise lost," wrote Doug Grow of the *Minneapolis Star Tribune* a few days after Wise's death. "But if you keep score by tabulating dreams, creativity, and moxie, Tony Wise went out as a one-of-a-kind champ."[22]

Wise's legacy is complicated, but he led with such vigor and vision that in the decades after his death, the enduring positives have come to outshine the negatives. Today, Tony Wise is remembered as one of the first people in the United States to recognize and fully embrace the emergence of cross-country skiing. "His legacy is phenomenal from the Nordic perspective. It has changed that community," said Olympic skier Doug Peterson.[23]

Olympic medalist Bill Koch noted how Wise's vision "completely color[ed] the way the whole sport has gone, [so] even if maybe he lost it all, it wasn't really lost." Wise "saw things for the future of the sport that had never been done before," Koch said. "He had no limitations on what he thought was possible. . . . Look at what we still have because of him."[24]

Wise is also remembered for his ebullience and charm. He was the kind of person who "would never forget your name," said longtime skier Duncan McLean. And founding skier Rick Scott fondly recalled the many times he would arrive at Telemark to find Wise by the fireplace in his signature red sweater. "He'd come over and give you a hug," Scott said. "Telemark *was* Tony. He was happy we were all there enjoying what he created. And everybody wanted to be his friend."[25]

Former Telemark publicist Tom Kelly found Wise to be such a demanding and "crazy" boss that he quit once, before eventually coming back. Still, he called Wise "the most fascinating man I've ever met. . . . I learned about vision from him. There was nothing he felt he couldn't accomplish. He was eccentric, but boy was it fascinating."[26]

And Olympic skier, coach, and author John Caldwell said, "I have to hand it to him. He kept going, charging ahead. Everything a guy like Tony did, it was all for the good."[27]

Tony Wise was inducted into the US Ski and Snowboard Hall of Fame in 1988, four years after declaring bankruptcy and losing control of the race he started. COURTESY OF THE WISE FAMILY

That was a sentiment echoed by founding skier Ernie St. Germaine, who was mentored by Wise while being raised by his grandparents. St. Germaine later earned bachelor's, master's, and tribal law degrees; developed curriculum in tribal schools; and served for many years as a tribal judge. "You had to know Tony Wise and what an exceptional person he was," St. Germaine said. "[He was an] exceptional visionary who had what it takes to make dreams a reality. His dream was helping people live a better life. He was an incredible man." St. Germaine noted how he "grew closer to my own identity" by participating in the Native traditions that often were part of Telemark events.[28]

Frances Wise helped her dad run the race and lodge in the early years. "One key thing about my dad," she said, "is that he had an innate ability to bring people together—culturally, internationally, locally. He was one of those born leaders, and he enjoyed it."[29]

Wise's funeral on April 11, 1995, was a fitting final chapter of his life—in his hometown and with panache. Tom Kelly gave a eulogy on the lawn in front of an estimated 350 people after the pine coffin—donated by a local carpenter because there was no money to buy one—was carried out through a front window. A horse-drawn caisson slowly ushered the 150-person funeral procession up Main Street under a cloudy, damp spring sky. A Dixieland jazz band, including former Telemark musicians, followed behind, along with many members of Company B, 724th Engineer Battalion, Wisconsin National Guard, who marched in the rear. The entourage accompanied Tony more than a mile to Greenwood Cemetery on the south side of town. An Ojibwe pipe and drum ceremony was held graveside; a drum song was written by Edward Benton for the occasion, one of the tribe's highest honors for a warrior. After dirt was shoveled onto the coffin, Birkebeiner medals and other mementoes were spontaneously dropped in by mourners. A powwow and feast followed at the National Guard armory, the one Wise helped bring to Hayward—along with so much more. His flat gravestone reads, "Man of Vision."[30]

Fourteen months later, the family held an auction in Hayward, selling some of Wise's personal items to help raise money to pay his debts. The items included race memorabilia, the bed he was born and slept in his whole life, jazz records, and much more. "My father saved everything," Frances Wise said. "He did not value money, viewing it simply as a resource for moving dreams forward." Many of his personal papers now fill a collection at the Wisconsin Historical Society.[31]

"I wish I could shake his hand and say, 'Thank you,' again," said Karl Andresen, a race Founder with Norwegian roots who spent his honeymoon downhill skiing at Telemark and skied the first thirty Birkebeiners. "There's a special place in my heart for him. He's the only real founder of the Birkebeiner."[32]

Tony Wise and original Birkebeiner champion Erik Ersson in 1992 during an event celebrating the Birkebeiner's twentieth anniversary. It was Wise's last appearance at the race before his death in 1995.
AMERICAN BIRKEBEINER SKI FOUNDATION ARCHIVES

ANOTHER NEW ERA in Birkebeiner history began in 1996. The race joined the digital age with its first website, a now-defunct winona.com/birkie, sponsored by Winona Knits, a Minnesota company that made wool mittens and sweaters. "If you ski the Birkie, why not surf the net?" read the *Birch Scroll* headline announcing the news. Now, skiers could register for the race online; get weather, trail, and event information; and buy merchandise. Maybe online registration helped: for the first time since Tony Wise lost control of the race in 1984, entries topped 7,000, with 7,502, an increase of about 900, including some from overseas via the Internet. The 1996 race also marked the first time prize money was awarded to the top three men and women, $25,000 total, including $7,500 for first place (the same first-place prize awarded some twenty-five years later).[33]

And yet, some skiers likely wished they hadn't entered. Not counting the 1981 meltdown—when the elites raced in record warmth but the main race was delayed—the 1996 race was the warmest full race on record. The problem began in earnest Friday morning with rain, followed by heavy, wet snow that afternoon and evening. The snow piled up on the trail, which had a three-inch base with an icy crust, and the temperature dropped to only thirty overnight. Groomers worried their mechanical grooming machines would push through the soft new snow and break the crust below, making for hazardous trail conditions, especially on the early hills. So they made a decision that would prove highly controversial: they kept the big machines off most of the course and instead used a snowmobile to pull a drag down the center of the trail. This created a skate track that was fourteen feet wide—less than half the trail width.

Striders, meanwhile, had no tracks at all—groomers tried to set them, but the tracks collapsed. The first 4 and last 3 kilometers of the trail, which cut across flat areas, were properly groomed and held up well. But the vast majority of the course was a mess.

On race day, temperatures rose from thirty degrees at 9 a.m. to fifty-three degrees by 2:30 p.m. It made for a long day. Overheated skiers peeled off layers and drank the aid stations dry. When skiers finally reached Lake Hayward, they skied through water, and a warm south wind dried sweat into white salt on their faces. No icicle beards this year. A few men skied in shorts and went shirtless, and a few women skied in sports bras. Thus, it became known as the Bikinibeiner. Italian Silvano Barco, in 2:24, and Austrian Gudrun Pflueger, in 2:41, beat the heat and their fellow elite, winning by comfortable margins.

Skiers were livid about the lack of mechanical grooming, believing it would have firmed up the skate track and at least provided a trail wide enough for passing and some semblance of striding tracks. Groomers felt the heat long after the race. They wrote a letter to skiers in the *Birch Scroll* explaining their reasoning, which read, in part, "Mother Nature put us in a bad predicament." In April, foundation staff hosted a forum where skiers could vent their frustrations. Former Olympic coach Marty Hall, who helped design the trail in the 1970s and who returned to ski, couldn't understand the decision to not groom. "I feel Tony turning in his grave," he said in a letter to the foundation. If it were 1973, skiers likely wouldn't have complained, but the Birkebeiner had become a world-class event with skier expectations of world-class conditions.[34]

After the struggles in 1996, officials doubled down to make the twenty-fifth event in 1997 memorable for the right reasons. To head off another grooming disaster, they hired Kurt Proctor of Seeley to supervise winter grooming and summer trail maintenance. Proctor was a good choice; he had helped groom the trail since the 1980s with Gary "the Mayor of Seeley" Penman, and the two of them had started the Seeley Hills Classic race on the trail in 1992. Marilyn Schutz resigned in November 1996. Don Reinicke, a former school administrator, was named foundation interim director for the 1997 event.

For the silver anniversary race, the foundation board sought to begin healing a growing rift with striders. The increased popularity of skate skiing meant

Facing page: In the warm 1996 race, skate skiers in middle and later waves tried to stay close to the center of the path and avoided passing on either side, to keep from sinking into the ungroomed mess they called "mashed potatoes." AMERICAN BIRKEBEINER SKI FOUNDATION ARCHIVES

American Birkebeiner
5395
American Birkebeiner
8316

striders had been pushed to the edges of the trail—and, in their minds, almost out of the race. Even on the fringes, their tracks were often skate-mashed, especially during the first half of the race. The foundation purchased a new track setter to improve track quality, though officials acknowledged it would be up to the skaters, who made up the vast majority of Birkebeiner skiers, to be courteous and stay on their portion of the trail.

Officials also gave striders the option to register as such, resulting in their bibs stamped with "CL" for "classic" and a corresponding "C" in the list of race results. The first "C" skier in 1997, Ryan Finn of Madison, Wisconsin, was finisher number 309 in 2:31. He was more than thirty minutes faster and eight hundred places ahead of the next fastest strider—not only because he was that fast, but also because so few were following his tracks. Of the first two thousand male finishers, only twelve strided; of the first five hundred female finishers, it was nineteen. Overall, just 14.5 percent of finishers strided. The Birkebeiner would continue to list classic skiers in the results after 1997 but wouldn't have classic competition divisions for more than another decade.[35]

Mother Nature flipped the switch in 1997—from slow and painful race conditions the year before to lightning fast. A midweek warm spell followed by freezes firmed up the course, and skiers were cruising. The top five men finished in less than two hours. Mikhail Botwinov, a two-time Olympian born in Russia who had emigrated to Austria a year earlier, surged into the lead with about 5 kilometers to go and won by fifteen seconds in a record time of 1:57. (He would go on to win two Olympic medals for Austria in 2002 and 2006.) Pflueger comfortably repeated as women's champion in 2:19, shaving twenty-two minutes off her 1996 time. In fact, she was five minutes faster than the men's winning time from 1996. The 7,882 skiers started with temperatures in the midteens, reaching the low twenties by afternoon—for those who still were on the trail during the fastest day in Birkebeiner history.[36]

After the 1997 race, the Birkebeiner Foundation found a new home. It had been housed in a couple of rooms—with no bathroom—on the first floor of the Hayward Inn (on the corner of Main Street and Highway 63). The board paid $153,000 to purchase the former Western Auto Appliance Center building at 11 Main Street, on the east side of Highway 63, and staff moved in later that year. It was great timing—the Hayward Inn burned to the ground not long after.[37]

The fast, fun, celebratory 1997 race was an outlier in a string of bad weather races. So little snow had fallen during the winter of 1998—thirty-one inches,

The narrow, parallel tracks for classic striders near the edge of the trail could easily get mashed by skate skiers, as shown here in the 1993 race. AMERICAN BIRKEBEINER SKI FOUNDATION ARCHIVES

Patchy snow cover in 1998 resulted in the race being shortened to 25 kilometers. Some skiers chose to walk—not ski—down some of the hills. AMERICAN BIRKEBEINER SKI FOUNDATION PAPERS. NORWEGIAN AMERICAN HISTORICAL ASSOCIATION, NORTHFIELD, MINNESOTA

half as much as normal, coupled with dozens of days at or above freezing—that officials decided the race would not go across Lake Hayward or finish on Main Street. The route was cut to 25 kilometers with a Highway OO finish for both the main race and the Kortelopet.

Meanwhile, the financially troubled Lake Properties had decided to dismantle the Colosseum and sell its components for scrap, which meant the race needed a new start area—it was moved to a site next to the airport. The Barnebirkie became a fun run that year, and the elite sprint races on Main Street were held on roller skis. It was a challenging first year for Executive Director Gretchen Bercaw, who had taken over the previous June.[38]

The El Niño Birkie, as some called it, was a good year for Americans, however. Skiers were aided by temperatures in the low- to midthirties and cloudy skies, which helped preserve the snow on race day. Carl Swenson of Colorado (a 1994 Olympian), and Jennifer Douglas of Idaho (the 1997 Kortelopet women's champion who was competing in her first Birkebeiner), won in fifty and fifty-six minutes, respectively, on the shortened route. The wins were redeeming, as both Swenson and Douglas had missed qualifying for the US Olympic team in trials a few weeks earlier.[39]

THE 1990S ENDED, by one measure, the way they started, with Telemark once again in financial trouble. Lake Properties filed for Chapter 11 bankruptcy in July 1998, citing $1.5 million of debt. The downhill ski operation had been cut back, convention and restaurant business had declined, and a bad 1997–98 winter for snow sports hadn't helped. Condominium owners, through their Telemark Interval Owners Association, sought to save their investments in 1999 when they bought the complex for $2.9 million, staving off the resort's end for at least a few more years.

The resort was still closed during the 1999 Birkebeiner, so race headquarters moved to the Lac Courte Oreilles Casino east of Hayward, and the foundation decided the new start area, next to the airport, would be permanent. Entries dipped below 7,000, to 6,942, for the first time in three years. Still, entries were up more than 13 percent from a decade earlier, evidence that the Main Street finish, foundation leadership, and skate skiing popularity were making a difference.

Johann Muehlegg, of Germany, and Laura McCabe, of the state of Washington, won comfortably that year in 2:03 and 2:22, respectively, over the 52 kilometers. Muehlegg overcame tired legs and jet lag after winning the 76-kilometer Transjurassienne in France the previous weekend to wrap up the Worldloppet title with his Birkebeiner win. (Muehlegg was a three-time Olympian for Germany, but he was kicked off the team in 1998; he would join Spain's team and win two gold medals in 2002, only to lose them because of blood-doping accusations.) It was McCabe's first Birkebeiner title in five tries, including two second-place finishes. "I love this race, and I've always wanted to win this race," said the thirty-two-year-old McCabe, twice an Olympian. The ageless Marty Hall, at sixty-one, won his age class in the Kortelopet, skiing 1:26.[40]

The 1999 race also was warm, thirty-four degrees for most of the day, with rain, mist, and fog throughout the morning. The course held up until skiers hit Lake Hayward, where they slogged through standing water by afternoon. The ice still was plenty thick; core samples were taken on race morning to make sure the frozen lake could handle the weight of so many skiers.

It was the third time in four years that warm weather, lack of snow, or both had affected the race. Surely, the Birkebeiner's luck would change as it moved into the new decade, century, and millennium.

AMERICAN BIRKEBEINER
SKI FOUNDATION ARCHIVES

Second-wave Birkebeiner and Kortelopet skiers crowd the trail soon after the 2005 start. AMERICAN BIRKEBEINER SKI FOUNDATION, PHOTO BY BRETT MORGAN

NINE

2000–2013
A BETTER, THEN BIGGER, BIRKEBEINER

HEADING INTO 2000, much of the world was focused on a possible Y2K computer meltdown, but the Birkebeiner's biggest problem again would turn out to be a natural one. Weather woes that tripped up the race in the late 1990s only worsened, forcing the first cancellation in the Birkebeiner's twenty-eight-year history. However, by the fortieth race in 2013, reminiscent of the race's growth in the mid-1970s, it would become bigger, better, and more successful than ever.

In 2000, trail conditions were tenuous as race week began, because of the warm weather that followed a seven-to-ten-inch snowfall the week before. News releases from the Birkebeiner Foundation reaffirmed that some form of the race would be held. On Wednesday, officials announced that the race would end short of the lake in Duffy's Field at 46.5 kilometers. Then the route was pared down even farther, to 23 kilometers. But a hard rain on Friday wiped out snow on parts of the trail and melted snow in the woods that officials had planned to harvest overnight. Puddles were everywhere. Any snow on the trail had turned to slush. The foundation board quickly met and voted to cancel.[1]

Most of the 6,335 entrants were already in town when the announcement was made early Friday evening. The Telemark Lodge, now under the ownership of the condominium owners' association, had reopened, and inside the Red Arrow Room, the race's assistant director Shellie Milford climbed onto a table and announced the news to the crowd of skiers who were picking up their bibs. "There were hundreds of people," Milford said. "I remember being very emotional and very exhausted. Then people started to clap. That was an incredible experience. I think they all understood. It was a very sad day, but it gave me a sense of how meaningful the Birkie is to people." New executive director Cherie Morgan, a Wisconsin native and race office manager who had replaced Gretchen Bercaw, called it "very difficult and disappointing to all of us consumed with Birkie Fever." Orange buttons saying "Slush Sucks. Birkie 2000. Stop Global Warming!" soon began circulating among skiers.[2]

Other events during race week were held as planned, however, including the new Junior Birkebeiner, a competitive event (unlike the Barnebirkie) for ages ten to fifteen. Sixty-five skiers splashed through puddles at the start line on Friday and finished the 2.5-kilometer course midday before the heavy rain began to fall. Scott Wilson and Kevin Brochman cofounded and codirected the event. Wilson, of rural Hayward, was a veteran Birkebeiner skier and volunteer, coach, Central Cross Country (CXC) team cofounder, and FIS race technical delegate. Brochman, of Minnesota, was a 1984 and 1988 Olympian and coach for the 1998 US Olympic team.[3]

Unofficially, a Birkebeiner happened on Saturday, February 27, 2000. With temperatures rising to about fifty degrees, at least six skiers are known to have made it from the start to the finish line—using a combination of skiing, walking, and running. One of them was Jerrold Schneider of Rice Lake, Wisconsin. At the start, fifty-three-year-old Schneider expected to see more skiers but saw only a couple of curious European entrants who had walked down from Telemark and a photographer, who took Schneider's photo. The photo was published in newspapers across the country, and some of Schneider's friends saw it in California. "I guess I was Global Warming Boy," he said.[4]

The trail varied from skiable snow to dirt to puddles. Switching to running shoes when needed, Schneider ran about half of the way. When he started, he didn't know if he would try to finish but realized it was possible and figured

Facing page: The Junior Birkie debuted in 2000 and was one of the few events to be held that year because of rain and warm weather. Scott Wilson and Kevin Brochman cofounded the event after Brochman wondered why there wasn't a competitive event for pre-Kortelopet skiers. AMERICAN BIRKEBEINER SKI FOUNDATION ARCHIVES

JUNIOR
BIRKIE
18
TNT
Video
Wisconsin
State Fair Park

why not? "There's no way they could have held a race," he remarked later. "It was bad. It would have been suicide." He saw other skiers on the trail at about the midpoint, including Founder Dave Landgraf. Most downhills on the southern half, exposed to the sun, were bare. Of the six skiers who raced that day, five reached Duffy's Field then ran around the windswept Lake Hayward to the finish. But when Schneider reached the lake, he double poled across the bare ice. Then, he put on his running shoes and jogged up Main Street, also snowless, to the finish, where his wife was waiting.[5]

Executive Director Morgan was waiting too. Race officials had heard that someone was going the distance. Morgan invited Schneider to the foundation office, where a "Foodloppet" party featuring food station refreshments was being held for skiers. Morgan placed the winner's laurel wreath over Schneider's neck as fellow skiers cheered. (Many of them had worn their race bibs that day and ran, biked, walked, and roller-bladed around Hayward and Cable in a cross-country catharsis.) A Wisconsin skier finally had "won" the Birkebeiner, though there was no winner's check. Schneider had been an elite wave skier who had skied more than twenty Birkebeiners at the time, but because of the trail conditions it took him more than five hours to finish. "I was just doing it for myself," he said later. "It's the Birkie, and you've just got to do it." In 2001, Schneider, as an exemplar of the Birkebeiner spirit, was chosen to carry the torch in the opening ceremonies. More than twenty years later and now in his late seventies, Schneider was still skiing, with hopes of doing fifty Birkebeiners and with the 2000 laurel wreath still hanging in his house.[6]

It was the fourth weather-plagued race in five years. The foundation analyzed whether holding the race earlier would help. After reviewing weather data and considering other complications—including skier housing and the competing schedules of the Worldloppet and the Great American Ski Chase—the board concluded that rescheduling would "not offer assurance of increased snowfall, colder temperatures, or greater snow accumulation," Morgan said. The foundation offered discounts in 2001 to the Y2K entrants.[7]

A year later, snow was aplenty heading into the 2001 race. But it proved to be a little too much of a good thing. Snow began falling after midnight on race day and was whipping horizontally by daybreak. Eight inches had fallen by the race's end, making it a hard day's ski for all, despite the twenty-degree weather.

Facing page: Skiers on the 2001 course. AMERICAN BIRKEBEINER SKI FOUNDATION ARCHIVES

AMERICAN BIRKEBEINER
745
11030
720

After the previous year, however, few people were openly complaining. The 6,550 entrants had slow times, including winners Gianantonio Zanetel, of Italy, in 2:32 and Nadezhada Slessareva, of Russia, in 2:48 over the 51 beautiful but powdery kilometers.

The 2001 race also featured a new Kortelopet course, an effort led by Morgan, which eased congestion on the main trail and improved the short race experience. Instead of following the main route to finish at Highway OO, the new course cut away at kilometer 9 and looped back to Telemark, where it wound up the old Stormoen downhill run (the same hill that skiers descended at the Birkebeiner start in late 1970s) and finished downhill like the first Birkebeiners where the now-dismantled Colosseum had stood.[8] Telemark, for its part, was limping along, needing a $100,000 federal block grant loan that winter to help with renovations.[9]

The 2000s proved to be a decade of Italian *dominazione* at the Birkebeiner, as Zanetel's victory in 2001 began a string of six straight men's race wins by Italians. In 2002, Maurizio Pozzi won in 1:57; it was thirty degrees on race day that year, and the route was shortened to 46 kilometers because of inadequate snow cover.

Zanetel won again in 2003 in 2:10 and in 2004 in 2:11 by a whisker, becoming the second three-time winner in history, along with Austria's Manfred Nagl (1990, 1991, and 1993). Then, Italian Marco Cattaneo won in 2005 in 2:03, and again in 2006 in 2:08. Cattaneo was declared the 2006 winner by one-fourth of an inch after he and teammate Roberto DeZolt joined hands and tried to cross the finish line simultaneously.

Female winners included more Italians. Lara Peyrot achieved a historic three-peat, winning in 2003 in 2:24, 2004 in 2:23, and 2005 in 2:15, setting a women's course record. Peyrot came agonizingly close to becoming the first four-time winner in 2006, when she lost by one second to teammate Anna Santer, who finished in 2:24. The Italians also placed numerous skiers in the top ten during those years, before the Italian Winter Sports Federation stopped sending so many skiers to the US.

CORPORATE SPONSORSHIPS continued to thrive throughout the 2000s. From 2000 to 2003, the title sponsor of both the Birkebeiner and the Kortelopet was Johnson Bank (previously named Heritage Bank of Hayward), which was owned by S.C. Johnson Company, or Johnson Wax, the international conglomerate based in Racine, Wisconsin. Subaru was the title sponsor for the main race from 2004 to 2009, with Johnson Bank either sponsoring or cosponsoring the Kortelopet. Becker Law of Wisconsin became title sponsor from 2010 through 2013, and Marshfield Clinic's Hayward Center was the Kortelopet sponsor.

The Birkebeiner has had few financial supporters as loyal and as impactful as S.C. Johnson Co., fourth-generation leader Samuel Curtis Johnson Jr., his wife, Imogene, and their family. All told, Johnson family businesses sponsored more than a quarter of the first thirty-five Birkebeiners and nearly two-thirds of the Kortelopets. The company first sponsored both races in 1978 and 1979 via its Silva Company (makers of skis and related equipment). Its Curel lotion brand sponsored the main race from 1988 through 1990, and its Heritage Bank sponsored the Kortelopet from 1988 through 1997.

In 1984, Sam and Imogene Johnson were among the largest donors, giving $5,000, when the foundation formed during Telemark's bankruptcy. In 1987, when the foundation opened a shuttered Telemark to put on the race, a check for $25,000 appeared from the Johnsons without fanfare. The family, the global Johnson Financial Group, and the Johnson Family Foundation also have supported the Barnebirkie, the Tony Wise Museum, the purchase of land for a new race start area, and a new trail center at Highway OO.

The Johnsons' roots in the region go back many decades with a vacation compound on thirteen-hundred-acre Lake Owen near Cable, along with large tracts of forest land in Bayfield County. Sam, who was a pilot, would fly into the Cable Union Airport from the family's home in southeastern Wisconsin. Sam and Tony Wise knew each other for years—both were Harvard MBA grads, entrepreneurs, and interested in protecting the environment. Sam bought one of the first Valhalla townhouses at Telemark. By 2003, Sam was the nation's twenty-fifth richest man, worth $7.4 billion. He enjoyed socializing with the "up north" crowd at Metro's Ski Inn near the entrance to Telemark and would bring along executives during deer-hunting season. Sam's son, Fisk, who eventually became chairman and CEO, skied the Birkebeiner in the early years.

Sadly, Sam Johnson passed away in 2004. "We would not be where we are today without the support of Johnson Bank and the Johnson family," said Ben Popp, the foundation's executive director beginning in 2013. The Birkebeiner and the Johnson family's legacy "will forever be tied."[10]

AMERICAN
BIRKEBEINER
VII
TELEMARK U.S.A.
SILVA
HAYWARD
Lake Hayward
Highway 63
Phipps Flowage
Namekagon R.
SEELEY
Lake Paewawong
CABLE
Mosquito Brook Flowage
Airport
TELEMARK
February 24 1979
Mt. Telemark
storyland

26th Dyno American
Birkebeiner 52km
February 21, 1998
Cable to Hayward 52km
Dyno American Birkebeiner
Cable to Seeley 25km
Heritage Bank Kortelopet
DYNO
VOLVO

NORWEGIAN
AMERICAN
BIRKEBEINER IX
Telemark, Wisconsin USA
February 21, 1981
America's Greatest Ski Race
ALFA · ASNES · EPOKE
LIFA · NORMARK
SKILOM · SWIX · SXC
Products from NORWAY
Norwegian American Birkebeiner
55 kilometers
The Only American Race in the Prestigious World Loppet Series
The Biggest Race in the USSA Great American Ski Chase Series
Kortelopet
27.5 kilometers
February 21, 1981
Ski Pageantry
Races
Pre-Race Clinics
Training Camps
Exhibits
Nordic Film Festival
Sleigh Rides
Ice Sculptures
Hot Air Balloons

NORTH AMERICAN BIRKEBEINER
NORWAY
U.S.A.
1976
HAYWARD, WIS.

AMERICAN
BIRKEBEINER
TELEMARK
HAYWARD

AMERICAN VI BIRKEBEINER
TELEMARK-HAYWARD, WIS. U.S.A.

Race promotion and merch through the years include annual posters (1979, 1981, 1998, 2008, and 2013 posters shown here), patches, buttons, and bumper stickers. AMERICAN BIRKEBEINER SKI FOUNDATION ARCHIVES; BUTTONS AND BUMPER STICKER COURTESY OF THE AUTHOR

ALONG WITH SECURING VALUED SPONSORS and strengthening community relationships, the foundation moved forward in other ways early in the decade. In 2003, the first Birkebeiner Trail Run, initially held in the 1990s as a hike, was expanded with 5- and 15-kilometer events ending at Highway OO. The run would grow and become part of a larger race vision—a year-round commitment to a healthy lifestyle with the motto "Ski. Run. Bike. Live!" A new 12-kilometer Prince Haakon race began in 2005; it would become a long-term solution to providing a short, less competitive adult race—a starter Birkebeiner for less serious or less experienced skiers—after various similar races had been tried for many years. The same year, the Birkebeiner received the Putting Wisconsin on the Map award from Governor Jim Doyle, giving it a level of prestige comparable to great state attractions such as the Green Bay Packers. Wise, inspired to greatness by the "small-town" Packers, would have loved it.[11]

A new race director, Ned Zuelsdorff, took over in 2005, the third of the decade and the first male to lead the foundation full time, except for an interim director one year. Cherie Morgan had stepped down after 2002. Shirley Riedmann, a former American Express executive who had moved to the region, directed the race from 2003 to 2005 but left to pursue a doctoral degree. Zuelsdorff would bring long-term stability to the position over the next eight years, the longest tenure by far of a director since the foundation was formed in late 1984. He also was the first director who had been a veteran skier of the race, having done fourteen of them starting in 1987, plus many Kortelopets.

A run of four races with good conditions began in 2003 but ended in 2007, when the race for non-elites was shortened to an untimed, 25-kilometer open-track event because of an icy base and patchwork trail. The elite event was timed, and US skier Zack Simons won in 1:09 by three seconds as Americans swept the top three men's places. In part because of the conditions deterring elite international skiers, Americans also took all forty-eight elite women's places, led by Kate Whitcomb of Idaho in 1:18, winning by six seconds. It was fifteen degrees at the start.

American women continued their run of victories in 2008, when Evelyn Dong of Oregon won in 2:23, and in 2009, when Rebecca Dussault of Colorado won in 2:26 after thrusting a ski tip ahead of Alaska's Holly Brooks at the line for the victory. The men's winners, respectively, were Ivan Babikov of Canada in 2:07 and Matthew Liebsch of Minnesota in 2:11. Liebsch's lead was big enough

Above: Poor trail conditions in 2007 resulted in the race being shortened to 25 kilometers for the second time in nine years. AMERICAN BIRKEBEINER SKI FOUNDATION ARCHIVES, PHOTO BY MARK MILFORD

Right: Unofficially, two skiers did go the distance in 2007: Minnesota National Guardsmen Sgt. Bill Snellman (left) and Major Paul Peterson. Snellman and Peterson roller-skied 51 kilometers on race day while serving in southern Iraq. AMERICAN BIRKEBEINER SKI FOUNDATION ARCHIVES

that he could stop on Main Street and pick up his young son en route to the finish line. His win also was a triumph for the locally based CXC professional development team. His teammate Bryan Cook was runner-up. Plus, CXC skier Gus Kaeding won the classic race in a memorable duel over retired Olympic icon Bjorn Daehlie. The 2008 race began at eight degrees and the 2009 race at seventeen.

Winters with plenty of snow always boosted race enthusiasm, and the mostly good trail conditions helped the Birkebeiner rebound between 2000 and 2010. But the race didn't just rebound, it took off, with entries rising by nearly 23 percent in a decade, the most growth since the 1970s.

What happened? It started with something very old—classic skiing—and something new—a separate classic trail. In late 2005 or early 2006, trail committee chairman Dave Nelson, an avid skier and a forester for the Chequamegon-Nicolet National Forest Great Divide Ranger District, suggested the idea for a separate classic trail and offered to design it. Zuelsdorff pushed the classic trail idea to the board, which gave its okay, as did Bayfield and Sawyer Counties. Foundation officials quickly set about raising money for trail development and construction—they found so much enthusiasm for the idea that they raised $230,000 and had enough left over to buy another trail-grooming machine.

Nelson's lasting impacts on the race were many. He was on the foundation board for seven years, completed thirty-one Birkebeiners, and designed other ski and mountain bike trails in the area as well. In 2012, Nelson would receive the Tony Wise Spirit Award from the Birchleggings Club (the honor, which began in 2010, recognizes outstanding contributions to the race and sport), and he also worked with Zuelsdorff to design the 4.5-kilometer Birkie Ridge trailhead north of Seeley that connects to the main trail. That trailhead opened in 2014, thanks in part to 350 volunteers and donations of land and money. It was the same year Nelson died, at age seventy, with trail maps by his side, and a view from the top of a hill was dedicated as Dave's Overlook. "He was very soft-spoken," Zuelsdorff recalled later, "but [he] made so many positive changes to the Birkebeiner."[12]

In spring 2007, with funding secured for a separate classic trail, Nelson and his team got to work. He set out with Zuelsdorff and his wife, Kathy, as well as another dedicated volunteer, Jack Moin. They battled heat, ticks, and mosquitos as they marched through the deep woods to mark the trail—much like Sven Wiik, Marty Hall, Jim Bauer, and Bob Treland had done in the 1970s.[13]

The new, 27-kilometer race trail for striders would roughly parallel the main trail from the race start to Highway OO; striders would rejoin the main trail for the second half of the race. Trail construction began in 2007 and took three summers, with 9 kilometers of new trail ready for the 2007 race, 6 more for 2008, and the final 12 for the 2009 Birkebeiner.[14]

The classic skier, either returning or new, felt welcome for the first time in twenty years. The new trail added 4 kilometers to its total—54 (eventually 53) compared with 50 for skaters—but the striders had their sanctuary and weren't complaining, though some began referring to the skate race as Birkie Light. The new trail relieved congestion during the crowded first half of the race, improving skiability for everyone. A companion trail for classic skiers in a major marathon was believed to be unique in the world.

Recreational skiers and the sport's purists loved it. The Birkebeiner subsequently went from one in five entrants being a strider to one in three. Classic skiers now had their own wave starts and competitions. The first official Birkebeiner Classic champions were crowned in 2008 at the thirty-fifth anniversary race—Yuri Kozlov, of Russia, in 2:32, and Kelly Skillicorn, of Minnesota, in 3:00. For forty-four-year-old Skillicorn, it was a flashback of sorts—she was the women's champion twenty years earlier as Kelly Kimball, a young Olympic hopeful and, at that time, a skate skier.[15]

The new classic trail had another advantage: in theory, during low-snow winters, a 50-kilometer loop race for striders and skaters could be held on the two northern trails if conditions were poor south of Highway OO, where there's usually less snow and the south-facing hills are more exposed to the late winter sun.

RAISED IN WAUSAU, WISCONSIN, Ned Zuelsdorff took up cross-country as a way to help control his type I diabetes. With bachelor's degrees in biology and chemistry and a master's in entomology, he had worked for two years with the Environmental Protection Agency in Chicago, then twenty-seven years with the State of Wisconsin, including as director of the Bureau of Agrichemical Management, working on pesticide regulation, groundwater sampling, and more. He had worked in highly organized and productive environments and with up to $9 million budgets, about ten times that of the Birkebeiner. In 2005, he and Kathy were building a house near Cable with plans to move there, when the foundation began looking for its new director. Zuelsdorff, who had been a race

Classic tracks in 2005, before the separate classic trail was built
AMERICAN BIRKEBEINER SKI FOUNDATION ARCHIVES, PHOTO BY KELLY RANDOLPH

Classic tracks in 2014, on the new classic trail
AMERICAN BIRKEBEINER SKI FOUNDATION ARCHIVES, PHOTO BY BRETT MORGAN

director with Madnorski (the Madison Nordic Ski Club) in Madison, explained why he "just grabbed it" when he was offered the job:

> It was perfect for me at that time in my life. I remember the day I started, unlocking the door and going in, and it was a great feeling. I think maybe there was a status quo attitude. People thought, "It's fine the way it is" and "Let's just keep doing it." The skier numbers had been really flat for five or six years. I thought there has to be a possibility of improving this event, the numbers, which would mean more for the community in terms of economic benefit.[16]

Zuelsdorff was a fount of ideas and promoted good ones that came his way. In the late 2000s, Zuelsdorff put a cap on entries, which seemed counterintuitive to some but actually created growth. The cap meant skiers committed earlier than usual, afraid they might miss out, boosting entries to the desired goal; if met, the cap was raised in future years. By 2009, entries rose to 7,242, the second most in history. In 2010, the record was broken with 8,056 entrants, despite a cap of 7,500 skiers. The record was smashed yet again in 2011 with 8,836 entrants, despite the cap being raised that year to 8,400. And they hit 9,300 in 2012. As the number of race entrants grew, so did foundation net assets, from below $100,000 in the late 1990s to $990,000 by 2010.

Zuelsdorff oversaw many other race improvements, such as the building of new trail cabins at the Fire Tower and Mosquito Brook aid station sites, the latter funded by the Birchleggings Club. The Fat Tire Birkie on the trail each March was added, as was the Birkie Tour, an open-track event in January that grew to one thousand skiers. The Birkie Ridge trailhead was built. A tradition, dating to the early 1990s, of three skiers reenacting Prince Haakon's rescue was expanded. Two new events became part of race week: the smile-inducing Giant Ski team competition, where skiers compete on two extralong skis, and the Barkie Birkie, or skijoring with dogs. The Birkie Skiers for Cures fundraising effort helped bring in celebrity skiers and gave citizen skiers an altruistic reason to climb the hills; more than $300,000, for example, was raised from 2009 to 2012 for the National Multiple Sclerosis Society. "When people learned I was director of the Birkie, they were surprised to learn it was full time," Zuelsdorff said. "They don't generally understand what goes into holding an event like the Birkie."[17]

200
Barkie Birkie
3
Barkie Birkie
4

Dennis Kruse is a longtime foundation board member and president, race finisher, and a voice of live race coverage for many years. He has seen the race take major strides since the turn of the century. Serving as the Birkebeiner's Worldloppet representative and hosting many elite foreign skiers at his compound in Cable has given Kruse an informed, if somewhat biased, perspective on the race's international reputation. "I think the Birkebeiner is the best ski marathon in the world," he said, citing how well the race is organized, the unique terrain on the built-for-skiing trail, race week atmosphere, and more.[18]

The thirty-fifth race in 2008 not only introduced the new classic events, it also honored Tony Wise, with grandson Ryland Sabien lighting the Birkebeiner flame while wearing one of Tony's sweaters. The 2008 opening ceremonies included a prayer to the Great Spirit and victory dance by John "Little Bird" Anderson, Lac Courte Oreilles elder who once worked for Wise as a tour guide at Historyland. "I know a lot of you are thinking about Tony Wise today," Anderson said. "I sure am. Part of this ceremony was always inclusive to Native Americans. Tony was very good to Native Americans, and Native Americans were very good to him." Several skiers reenacted the old race start up Mount Telemark in Norwegian ski clothing and with wooden skis. Wise's idea for a grand ski race had drawn nearly 190,000 entrants over thirty-five years.[19]

BETWEEN 2000 AND 2013, the Birkebeiner witnessed the return of several race icons, the comeback of a world-class skier whose best days indeed were still ahead of him, the quiet arrival of a skier who would become a national sports hero, and the appearance of two Nordic ski legends. The Birkebeiner also said farewell to several race Founders, including one tragically.

In 2003, at the thirtieth annual race, Founder Karl Andresen of Eau Claire, Wisconsin, then age seventy-nine, skied his thirtieth and final Birkebeiner with his son, William, who had skied in the first short race in 1973. As darkness fell, several longtime friends joined Andresen as he skied across the lake and up Main Street, ending a nine-hour trek, against his doctor's advice. "I think it will be tougher to kiss this race goodbye than it is to finish it," he had said a decade earlier. "And it's pretty tough to finish."[20]

Facing page: Barkie Birkie competitors head down Main Street in the 2015 race.
AMERICAN BIRKEBEINER SKI FOUNDATION ARCHIVES, PHOTO BY BRETT MORGAN

After growing up in an orphanage in Drammen, Norway, Andresen emigrated to the US as an honorary fellow of the American Scandinavian Foundation. He became a political science professor at University of Wisconsin–Eau Claire, started the local Ski Striders club, and helped introduce soccer to the area. He remembers going to a ski shop in the city around 1960 but finding only alpine skis, not one pair for cross-country. So, he ordered some. He ended up teaching hundreds of people to ski (including fellow Founder Dave Landgraf) and inspired hundreds more. In the county forest east of Eau Claire, Andresen helped start the Tower Ridge ski trails and he skied there for decades; the trails were later named in his honor. He found peace in the rhythm of setting a pace and gliding through the woods. "It's a liberating feeling," he said.

Andresen defied odds by ever skiing the race at all. In 1967, a bad case of pneumonia damaged his right lung, and in 1980 the largest lobe of the lung was removed, leaving him with about half the oxygen intake as other skiers. "You've got to be either stupid or stubborn enough to do the Birkie, even though your rational self tells you not to," he said. "It's a tremendous feeling of satisfaction knowing that you've been able to endure." Andresen died in 2016 at age ninety-one. In 2019, William and two of Karl's grandchildren skied the race as the Birkebeiner warriors and Inga to honor Karl and their family heritage.[21]

While 2003 marked Andresen's race farewell, it was a competitive rebirth for Billy Demong. At age twenty-two, Demong was already a two-time Olympian and World Cup winner in Nordic combined (ski jumping and cross-country) when he suffered a fractured skull in August 2002 after diving into a hotel pool from a balcony. The 2003 Birkebeiner was Demong's first. He was using it as a training event but still finished an impressive fourteenth, and proudly wore his first-time finisher medal around his neck that night at the Round Lake hot spot Famous Dave's barbecue. This not only marked the beginning of Demong's comeback but also his rise to Nordic stardom. In 2010, Demong skied to a historic US Nordic first, a gold medal in Nordic combined in the Olympics in Vancouver, along with a US team silver medal in the relay. Many more World Cup gold medals would hang around his neck before the five-time Olympian's career ended in 2015.

In 2005, Sven Wiik was the honorary starter. He was one of the instigators of the race, 1973 runner-up, original trail designer, former US Olympic coach, and national ski hall of fame member. After sending skiers on their way, the eighty-four-year-old Swede from Colorado took off with the field—excited to skate the race. Wiik finished in 7:24, third in the eighty-plus age class. He

Founding skier Karl Andresen at the 1989 race
AMERICAN BIRKEBEINER SKI FOUNDATION ARCHIVES, PHOTO BY BRETT MORGAN

would return for the fortieth annual celebration in 2013 before dying in 2016 at age ninety-five. "He was very proud and honored to help make Tony Wise's dream come true," said Birgitta Wiik Lindgren, his daughter.[22]

In 2008 and 2009, a new star appeared—a teenager from Afton, Minnesota, who won back-to-back women's Kortelopet skate titles at ages sixteen and seventeen. The Kortelopet is a highly competitive proving ground and a coveted title that often goes to well-trained high school racers who aren't yet eighteen and able to enter the Birkebeiner. The teen, Jessie Diggins, was already somewhat of a phenom, with two state titles. She competed at Stillwater Area High School and had watched her father, Clay, compete at the Birkebeiner. By 2011, Diggins was on the US team. In 2018 she and relay partner Kikkan Randall won an Olympic gold, the first in US history in the sport. She would go on to win two more Olympic medals, individual silver and bronze, by 2022, star on the World Cup circuit, and bring attention to the sport in the US unlike any other skier since Bill Koch in 1976. Both Diggins and Koch could trace the arc of their careers to Telemark and the Birkebeiner.

In 2009 and 2012, the Birkebeiner hosted two of the most accomplished skiers in history. Bjorn Daehlie, then forty-one and an eight-time Olympic gold medalist, appeared at the 2009 Birkebeiner, followed in 2012 by Vegard Ulvang, then forty-eight, a three-time Olympic gold winner who had become FIS Nordic executive director. The two Norwegian legends each skied in the classic marathon, and both lost by an eyelash to skiers about half their age. As retired champions, Daehlie and Ulvang were competing in the race to raise money for multiple sclerosis research (Daehlie's mother had the disease). Ulvang was used to skiing in the mountains of Norway and called the notorious Birkebeiner hills "nice and small" while still admitting to very tired legs at the finish.[23]

Daehlie and Ulvang discovered that their popularity seemed even greater in the US than in Norway. They signed dozens if not hundreds of autographs and gave public remarks at various race week events, and Daehlie was featured on the cover of the *Birch Scroll* results issue (wearing his signature line of ski clothing) along with other lead striders. Ulvang gave a race-week presentation on his 800-mile ski expedition to the South Pole three months earlier to mark the one hundredth anniversary of countryman Roald Amundsen's feat.

During a prerace news conference, Ulvang, who also had retraced Norwegian explorer Fridtjof Nansen's route across Greenland, addressed a point of Norwegian pride. The Birkebeiner races in Hayward, Norway, and Canada

A teenage Jessie Diggins en route to winning the Kortelopet in 2008, ten years before her history-making Olympic gold medal. AMERICAN BIRKEBEINER SKI FOUNDATION ARCHIVES, PHOTO BY KELLY RANDOLPH

Legendary Norwegian skier Vegard Ulvang at the 2012 Birkebeiner
AMERICAN BIRKEBEINER SKI FOUNDATION ARCHIVES, PHOTO BY DARLENE PROIS

are patterned after the rescue of baby Prince Haakon—who later would reign as king for forty-six years—by two Birkebeiner warriors during a civil war in 1206. Ulvang, however, disputed the popular legend, saying it didn't happen as commonly believed, if at all. "It's a myth, of course," Ulvang said, adding that it was embellished by a young nation a long time ago. At best, the soldiers would have walked, he argued, likening the story to modern-day "marketing."[24]

Soon after King Haakon's death in 1263, Icelandic historian Sturla Poroarson wrote *The Saga of Haakon Haakonarson*, a biography that included a chronicle of Haakon's dramatic rescue. Indeed, the biography describes a rescue effort much larger and more complicated than the popular story of two warrior skiers. As Poroarson recounts, numerous Birkebeiner warriors were involved in a multiple-day rescue of the one-year-old illegitimate prince and his mother, Inga, soon after Christmas. At one point, two elite warriors, Torstein Skevla and Skjervald Skrukka, were sent with the prince ahead of the group. Skevla and Skrukka are described as "ski runners," which seems to indicate they skied at least part of the way, although skiing isn't directly mentioned in the text (it does mention the two men breaking through deep snow with spear handles, walking, and using roads and horses). Erik Opsahl, professor of Medieval

Josie Nelson of Medicine Lake, Minnesota, skis down the trail dressed as Inga during the 2010 race, with baby Karl on her back representing the infant prince. AMERICAN BIRKEBEINER SKI FOUNDATION ARCHIVES

history at Norwegian University of Science and Technology in Trondheim, Norway, believes the rescue did happen based on Poroarson's account. "One assumes that the events described in the saga are relatively reliable," Opsahl said, "although details may be omitted or incorrect."[25]

The American Birkebeiner, like Norway, had celebrated the eight hundredth anniversary of the prince's rescue in 2006. Whether the legend is true or partially true, the prince was real, and one of his descendants skied the Birkebeiner that year. He was Ken Furst, of Appleton, Wisconsin. Furst's mother is full-blooded Norwegian, and when she studied her genealogy, going back twenty-five generations, the lines traced directly to Haakon, who is considered one of the great leaders in the nation's history.[26]

Though Ulvang brought star power to the Birkebeiner in 2012, a figurative cloud hung over the race that year because of the absence of one person. Dave Landgraf was one of three remaining skiers who had done every race. In August 2011, after Dave and his wife, Laurie, had worked all day on a home they were building, Dave went out for an evening bicycle ride. He didn't get far before he was hit by a distracted driver on Highway 27 near Stone Lake, Wisconsin. Laurie heard the sirens and thought they were going to a fire. Dave died three days later in a Duluth hospital.[27]

Six months later, at the 2012 Birkebeiner, Dave was missed by many. Laurie lit the Birkebeiner flame and spoke at the opening ceremonies, encouraging skiers to enjoy the experience. Their son and daughter, Cole and Emalea, wore his red Founder bibs and took their dad's start place in the elite wave. Dave had become a top-notch competitor and at age sixty-one was second in his age class in 2:43. However, he wasn't among the top two hundred finishers, which had been his goal, and before his death he'd been training hard to redeem himself in 2012. Laurie, who caught Birkie Fever from Dave, had done twenty Birkebeiners but at first didn't plan to enter in 2012. In the end, though, she decided to ski to honor him, and she and their children carried some of his ashes to the finish line. "It was one of my best races. I felt like he was carrying me," Laurie said. "I'd get to the top of a hill and I'd be crying; all of a sudden I'd get this burst of energy."[28]

Facing page: Founding skier Dave Landgraf competes in the elite wave in his thirty-sixth Birkebeiner in 2009. Landgraf died in 2011 after a traffic accident while riding his bicycle.
AMERICAN BIRKEBEINER SKI FOUNDATION ARCHIVES, PHOTO BY KELLY RANDOLPH

BeckerLaw
American
Birkebeiner
38
BIRCHLEGGINGS CLUB
Cable - Hayward
USA
BIKES
-N-
BOARDS
FISH
nordic
SALOMON

Others honored Dave, too. Twenty-five of Dave's friends skied with leather pouches containing some of his ashes. "He was a symbol of the Birkie," said close friend Dick Gladitsch, who believed that Dave's true legacy was integrity and inspiring others to improve mind, body, and spirit. Dave lived in Bloomer, Wisconsin, about seventy-five miles south of Hayward, and taught hundreds of kids to ski in middle school phys ed classes, including at the nearby Hickory Ridge forest trails that he helped start and loved because they simulated the Birkebeiner. He also coached the high school track team. An estimated one thousand people attended his memorial service at the middle school where he had impacted thousands of young lives.

Another skier carrying Landgraf's ashes during the 2012 Birkebeiner was Founder Ernie St. Germaine, and he continued to carry them through the fiftieth race. Ernie and Dave were childhood friends who had suffered through the first Birkebeiner together and were each other's best man in their weddings. When Dave became the faster skier, he always returned to the finish line to wait for Ernie, who called Dave's death "the hardest loss I've ever gone through."[29]

Laurie honored Dave again with a small metal sculpture of a skate skier at the top of the final hill—his favorite place on the trail—engraved with the words, "A View to the Finish: Dave Landgraf, Birkie Founder, 1973–2011." She spread some of his ashes there, and when she passed the sculpture in future races, she'd always stop and say hello to him. St. Germaine has done the same. "I always stop at the marker during the race and thank him," St. Germaine said. "It's emotional. I tell him, 'You should be here [in the race], not me.' As I go down the hill, tears are flowing. Then I get to the bottom and I'm empowered. I double pole the rest of the way. Every year, nobody passes me on the lake."[30]

Like Ernie, Dave had hoped to ski the first fifty races. "I have to do it," he once said. "It's become part of me." He thrived on physical challenges—roller skiing, running, biking, canoeing. Although low-key about it, he was proud of maintaining his elite wave status for many years against skiers half his age and winning several national master's titles. "The pinnacle of the year was doing the Birkie," Laurie said. "Every ounce of energy he had, he left on the course. He was going to give it his all."[31]

Another farewell in 2012 was for another ski-loving, intense competitor, George Hovland, whose knowledge about the growing sport factored into Tony

Wise's decision to start the race. He won twelve age class titles, including his thirty-third and final Birkebeiner in 2012, when he was the only entrant in the eighty-five-and-older classic division. Hovland's time that year was 8:25; he skied across the lake at sunset. It was a challenge beyond his age: he skied much of the race with his heart in atrial fibrillation, or out of rhythm, causing energy loss and numerous stops. Hovland died at age ninety-four in 2021, three years after winning his age group at a different national race.[32]

In 2013, Founder John Kotar bid farewell to the race, leaving just St. Germaine as the first to do forty races and beyond. Kotar, then seventy-three, was skiing with his wife, Nina Albanese-Kotar, who was doing her twenty-first Birkebeiner. But he dropped out about three-fourths of the way because of leg numbness related to back surgery three years earlier. "You only quit the Birkie for a good reason," Kotar said. "You go down and then they scrape you off—and that's what they did. I knew my mission was totally accomplished. This is a great way to go."[33]

Also making a final appearance in 2013 was a "friend" to anyone who had ever been part of the race: the cavernous yet cozy Telemark Lodge. It closed for good in March 2013. The decline had been long, slow, and painful, with no one ultimately able to recapture its heyday from the 1970s and early 1980s.

The Telemark condominium owners' association, which bought the lodge after Lake Properties declared bankruptcy, ran it from 2001 to 2011. But the group struggled with negative cash flow and eventually accumulated $1.25 million in debt. The lodge "just got worse and more run down," said Gary Crandall, former association member and president. In 2011, Telemark was saved from demolition when Telemark Partners (led by Paul Eckerline, a Wausau Paper Co. executive who worked at the lodge in 1975) bought it for an estimated $2 million, with plans to invest $20 million and turn it into an Olympic training venue.[34]

Those plans fell apart, as did plans for another potential buyer, Telemark Hospitality, in 2012. Things were so bad at the lodge that it was featured in 2012 on the television reality show *Hotel Impossible*. After closing in spring 2013, the lodge was sold at a Bayfield County sheriff's auction (fifty miles away in a courthouse foyer in Washburn) for $926,000. The buyers were Clifton Louis, a landowner at nearby Lake Owen who was part of the S.C. Johnson family through marriage, and his sister, Carrie Hulburd, who, in turn, endeavored to resell it.[35]

Wisely, Zuelsdorff and the foundation board had begun to separate race operations from the resort. Registration and bib pickup were held inside the Red Arrow Room for the last time in 2010, after which they moved to Hayward Middle School and then the high school. Other race functions and activities eventually moved to Hayward as well. The foundation faced additional challenges around that time. A short distance from the start, the Birkebeiner trail crossed six parcels of private property, requiring annual easements. In 2010, a landowner threatened to hold up the race by requesting $100,000, before eventually settling for $25,000. Other easement issues prompted the foundation to begin looking for alternative start areas. This led to the creation of the Birkie Ridge trailhead, which ended up being used for additional trail access and parking on race day.[36]

Losing Telemark was the end of an era for the Birkebeiner and northwestern Wisconsin. The race was conceived at the lodge, which had hosted the start or finish for forty years. It housed skiers and was where entrants, dropped by school bus on race mornings, camped out in the hallways until heading to the start line. It was the scene of opening and Birkiefest awards ceremonies, the birth of the Worldloppet, news conferences, waxing clinics, prerace spaghetti feeds, skier fashion shows, postrace parties, tens of thousands of reunions of friends and families, and so much more.

AFTER STEALING THE SPOTLIGHT from 2001 to 2006, the Italians returned to the winner's circle in 2010. Fabio Santus set a record in 1:56:58, defeating Tad Elliott of Colorado by eight seconds. Rebecca Dussault of Colorado repeated as women's champion, in 2:16, winning by thirty-one seconds. The fast times were partly because of ideal weather—starting at ten degrees and rising to the midthirties by the afternoon—and trail conditions.

In 2011, the start was twenty degrees colder, ten below, setting up a frigid and fast race on a firm trail. The temperature reached only single digits during the day, causing frostbite and hypothermia as skiers fought off dangerous windchills on the fast downhills. Veteran international skier and law student Tore Gundersen of Norway tore through the trail in 1:59:57 to top the men, and Caitlin Compton of Minnesota nearly set a record to win her first Birkebeiner. The race featured the return of three-time champion Manfred Nagl, then forty-seven, of Austria. Wearing bib No. 1, he finished with ice covering his trademark mustache and an impressive seventy-eighth in 2:16, two decades after winning his second Birkebeiner.

In 2012, Caitlin (Compton) Gregg (having married fellow elite skier Brian Gregg) almost made it two in a row, but her former Olympic teammate and bridesmaid Holly Brooks of Alaska edged her by a half second in 2:18 for her first win. Brooks herself had suffered a similar close loss in the 2009 Birkebeiner. Tad Elliott also avenged a close runner-up finish in 2010, catching the leaders at 35 kilometers, breaking away about 5 kilometers later on Bitch Hill, and taking the men's title in 2:04. Trail conditions were nearly perfect again and the temperature too, with a start at ten degrees rising to the midtwenties.[37]

In 2013, another Italian topped the podium. Sergio Bonaldi took the title in 2:09, edging fellow Milan resident Santus in a photo finish (the third- and fourth-place finishers were Italians as well). Caitlin Gregg's half-second loss the year before prevented her from three straight titles when she won the 2013 women's title in 2:28, collapsing to the ground with a smile. After eight inches of snow the day before, skiers enjoyed a mild day—twenty to thirty degrees—as did the thousands of spectators, who by now had made Main Street the place to be, especially for the elite sprint-to-the-finish duels.

Caitlin Gregg, with her husband (and fellow elite skier), Brian Gregg, after her 2013 win
AMERICAN BIRKEBEINER SKI FOUNDATION ARCHIVES, PHOTO BY LENORA LUDZACK

The 2013 race marked the Birkebeiner's fortieth anniversary, and its fortunes were on the upswing. It was a time to celebrate the event's recent successes and its history. The race included five people who were in the first Birkebeiner: St. Germaine, Kotar, Jacque Lindskoog, Bruce Derauf, and original champion Erik Ersson—along with original Kortelopet skier and Birkebeiner regular Duncan McLean. Lindskoog, the women's winner in the first two events because she was the only woman when they technically weren't allowed, was a winner again. She topped the seventy-to-seventy-four age class despite having had two knee replacements several years earlier. Derauf, who also wasn't supposed to ski the 1973 race because he was underage at seventeen, skied the fortieth on the same wooden skis he had used forty years earlier. Also returning was Colorado's Don Quinn, the speedy 1974 runner-up to his twin brother, Dave.[38]

Skiers Chris Lawn, Tom Lawn, and Lori House represent prince Haakon's rescuers during the 2013 race—the 40th annual—followed by three of the Founders (left to right): Ernie St. Germaine, Jacque Lindskoog, and John Kotar. AMERICAN BIRKEBEINER SKI FOUNDATION ARCHIVES, PHOTO BY DARLENE PROIS

After his win in 1973, Ersson returned to his native Sweden, where he directed recreation and tourism in Åsele, taught Nordic and alpine skiing, and built village youth soccer programs for the national federation. In 2013, Ersson lit the Birkebeiner flame during opening ceremonies on Main Street and, accompanied by Lindskoog and the retired Andresen, led the Parade of Nations. "It's a big, big race now. I could not dream of this in 1973," Ersson said. "This is one of the greatest things in my life, to see how it has grown." He skied his fourth Birkebeiner that year, at age seventy-five, in 4:53, winning his age class by nearly thirty minutes. His wife, Elena, wasn't far behind him, finishing in 5:15. In 2024, a few days after the fiftieth Birkebeiner, Ersson died in Sweden. He was eighty-six.[39]

BY YEAR FORTY, the number of people entering Birkebeiner week events had topped ten thousand. Entries in the two main races actually dipped during the anniversary event by about 1,200 to 8,111, but it was an aberration as numbers climbed in the ensuing years. Skiers from forty-five or more states and twenty or more countries were participating. The Junior Birkie, which began in the puddles of the 2000 meltdown, lived up to codirector Scott Wilson's predictions, drawing more than three hundred skiers by the end of the decade, and would continue to grow.

The popularity of youth events during race week was a positive sign for the future of the Birkebeiner. Participants in the Barnebirkie and Junior Birkie included Alayna Sonnesyn of Minnesota, who would win the Kortelopet and multiple Birkebeiners; brothers Bryan and Chris Cook of Rhinelander, Wisconsin, who would become top-flight Birkebeiner and national competitors (and Chris a 2010 Olympian); and brothers Adam and Ben Loomis of Eau Claire, Wisconsin, who would make the US Nordic Combined team (and Ben a 2018 and 2022 Olympian).

One of the youth event skiers in the 1980s and 1990s was Ben Popp. He became an elite skier too, taking forty-third in 2013. Soon, Popp would be on his way back to Hayward, but not to ski.

A wave of skiers breaks from the start line in 2022, in a welcome return of on-site races after COVID limited events in 2021. AMERICAN BIRKEBEINER SKI FOUNDATION ARCHIVES, PHOTO BY BOB PEARL

TEN

2014–2024
TWO SKIS FORWARD, ONE GLANCE BACK

WHEN BEN POPP FINISHED the fortieth American Birkebeiner in 2013, he already knew he could soon be returning as executive director of the Birkebeiner Foundation. Popp had applied for the position—Ned Zuelsdorf had announced his retirement in January—and was a finalist.[1]

Popp, then thirty-eight, loved the race, which he had done fifteen times. A son of teachers, he developed an early love for the outdoors while growing up in Phillips, Wisconsin, about seventy miles southeast of Hayward. Popp skied for the first time at age three, did his first Kortelopet in 1987 at thirteen, and skied competitively in high school. His mom, Toni, skied twenty-five Birkebeiners. His dad, Tim, oversaw the Bill Koch Ski League in Phillips, and Popp met Koch at the weather-impacted 1981 Birkebeiner at Telemark. After earning a biology degree and master's in education from Minnesota colleges, he coached two Minnesota college ski teams, taught at a charter school in St. Paul, and started an athletics endurance company. Then, for six years, he led the SISU Nordic Ski Foundation in Minneapolis–St. Paul, where he helped to quadruple participation in a dozen silent-sport events. He believed his life had pointed toward the Birkebeiner. "I feel passionate about a sport that totally shaped my life," Popp said.[2]

In early May 2013, the foundation board named Popp its next executive director. Moving back to the area with his wife, Megan, and their two young sons, Popp was excited to get to work on June 1, 2013. He didn't arrive with an agenda; but, like Ned Zuelsdorff and Tony Wise, he was a long-term, big-picture thinker. He quickly surmised that money was the key to elevating the mission and impact of the race. Amazingly, skiers and tourists during Birkebeiner week already accounted for nearly a quarter of the $110 million spent in a year by visitors to Sawyer County. However, after achieving financial stability under Zuelsdorff, the foundation was skeptical of undertaking major changes—such as new facilities, equipment, or adding to the mere handful of full-time employees.[3]

Ben Popp speaking at the weather-challenged 2014 race, his first as director of the Birkebeiner Foundation. AMERICAN BIRKEBEINER SKI FOUNDATION ARCHIVES, PHOTO BY DARLENE PROIS

Two of Popp's earliest requests of the board were ways to create more revenue. One was to raise the entry fee, which was about $100 at the time for early registration, by $15 per person. This was the first of many similar increases over the next decade, none of which seemed to adversely impact entries. Popp correctly believed skiers would pay more for a better experience, and his intent was to use the extra revenue for that purpose. He also instituted a user fee on the trail for the skiers, hikers, and bikers who used it throughout the year, a first in its thirty-seven-year history. The fee met some opposition from the Sawyer County Board because the trail was public land, but ultimately it was approved. Within months, first-ever trail manager Chris Campbell was hired. "Our greatest asset is that trail," said board president Sue Scheer, "and we need someone's eyes on it full time." Year-round trail maintenance and winter grooming began to improve; skiers noticed, and trail revenue grew.[4]

On one hand, chock full of ideas, Popp sounded a lot like Tony Wise. On the other, he represented a new, more prudent era in race growth. Unlike Wise's autocratic operation, Popp reported to a board that largely controlled the finances. And he understood that major projects had to be funded mostly through sponsorships and donations, reducing risk through capital planning.

High energy, goal oriented, and outgoing, Popp quickly became the face of the race. He often went to the finish line and helped tired skiers take off their skis. He felt their fatigue and shared their sense of accomplishment. He was one of them. He took to social media, even while skiing down the trail with a smartphone in one hand, to provide video updates to skiers when the first snow of the winter fell, during race week, and more. The Birkebeiner, keeping up with the times, now had an active online presence, and its Facebook followers grew by the thousands.[5] With disarming friendliness and the infectious belief that after forty years the Birkebeiner's best years were ahead, Popp took charge. "Ben is the visionary that no one expected," said Scott Wilson, a longtime skier, race official, and volunteer.[6]

Popp's mettle as director was tested during his first race week in 2014 when a blizzard dumped up to eighteen inches of snow Thursday into Friday, requiring thirty-six hours of skid steers, snowplows, and dump trucks to clear roads and parking lots and reach the remote food stations. Then, the temperature dropped and the wind picked up, collapsing a start area skier tent Friday night. It was a long night for the groomers, who also had to deal with fallen trees and branches. The weather wasn't much better on race morning with temperatures below zero and a dangerous windchill with gusts of twenty to thirty miles per hour. The race started on time, however, with swirling snow and a brisk headwind for the record 10,280 skiers—the first time the two main events topped 10,000. A courthouse conference room was heated to eighty-two degrees to warm chilly finishers, and one skier said he wouldn't have finished without battery-operated socks that kept his feet from freezing.[7]

The 2014 start followed an 18-inch snowfall the day before. The race featured new bibs and more than 10,000 skiers. AMERICAN BIRKEBEINER SKI FOUNDATION ARCHIVES, PHOTO BY DARLENE PROIS

For most skiers that year, it was a long haul to Hayward. Tom Reichelt, of Germany, a 2010 Olympian who was winding down an eleven-year World Cup career, won in 2:14 in a photo-finish, four-person sprint to the line. Caitlin Gregg, also a 2010 Olympian, finished in 2:40 for her second straight win and record-tying third title overall. Swix Sport USA, which had steadfastly supported the race since 1973 with wax stations and more, was the new title sponsor, contributing $130,000 over two years.[8]

One change Popp made that year seemed minor but signaled the beginning of a new era. Gone were the cloth bibs—white for Birkebeiner skiers and yellow for Kortelopet—with strings that tied the front to the back. The bibs of 2014 were thinner and lighter, and stretched sleek and snug over skiers' torsos. Plus, each wave had a separate bib color, turning the trail and Main Street into a sliding rainbow. Skiers could quickly gauge their performance during the race based on what colors were around them: Did you catch the wave ahead of you or fall into the one behind?

Popp's next idea was a race changer. Ever since the finish came to Main Street in 1992, skiers had to ski across Highway 63. North-south traffic through downtown was detoured around Main Street, along roads that were already jammed. The detour created backups and potentially dangerous situations for emergency vehicles. How could it be improved? In 2014, the foundation asked civil engineering/transportation systems students at the Georgia Institute of Technology in Atlanta to study the situation, and their answer was, ideally, don't interrupt Highway 63 traffic flow. So Popp suggested a radical idea, one that some people thought couldn't be done: send the race *over* Highway 63. Despite the skeptics, the foundation received approval from the state Department of Transportation, the city, and the county to build a bridge that would be installed over the highway before each race and taken down afterward. No longer would highway traffic need to be interrupted; after crossing the lake, skiers would go a block south on Railroad Street, turn right onto Main, go another block, then climb the bridge and return to Main Street on the other side.[9]

The pieces of the project came together over the fall and winter of 2014–15. The foundation announced a $650,000 fundraising campaign to cover the cost of the bridge ($170,000) and the purchase of land for a new race start area and multipurpose building. Hayward architect Terry Penman designed the bridge—a fifteen-section wooden structure in the shape of a giant trapezoid—and Trussworks, a local company that builds trusses for the housing industry—created it.

A sampling of Birkebeiner bibs through the years: (top row) 1973, 1976, (center) 1983, (bottom row) 1997 and 2014
AMERICAN BIRKEBEINER SKI FOUNDATION ARCHIVES, PHOTOS BY JAMES NETZ

The bridge debuted in 2015 and was an instant hit with motorists, emergency officials, skiers, and spectators. It was 198 feet long and required a 17-foot climb—providing clearance for semitrucks on the highway below—with a 10 percent grade on the ascent for weary legs that rewarded skiers with an exhilarating view of the scene on Main Street they were about to enjoy. A 20 percent grade on the descent offered a quick slide down, creating a slingshot to the finish. "You are looking over the whole downtown, and it's glorious," was the first impression of skier Ben Cooper from Minnesota. The bridge initially allowed two lanes of traffic on Highway 63 and was later lengthened to allow two lanes in each direction. Adorned with flags representing the skiers from various nations and dedicated to Wise, it was named the International Bridge in honor of a similar bridge used in the 1970s that helped set up dramatic finishes at Telemark.[10]

Skiers ascend the International Bridge during the 2016 race.
AMERICAN BIRKEBEINER SKI FOUNDATION ARCHIVES, PHOTO BY BOB PEARL

The 2015 race, with 9,936 skiers starting and the temperature at fifteen degrees, featured a second title for Sergio Bonaldi of Italy, who won by less than a second in 2:12. Olympian Holly Brooks of Alaska also won her second title—to go along with 2012—by about thirty seconds in 2:34. Several inches of snow fell during the race, and spectators watched four male skiers crest the International Bridge almost simultaneously before barreling to the line—the electrifying Main Street finish now was even better.[11]

The 2015 race was a bridge to retirement for longtime employee Shellie Milford, who received the first Shellie Milford Spirit of the Birkie Award that year and was the honorary starter. Milford's behind-the-scenes, year-round efforts had kept the race on track during her twenty-eight-year tenure, including serving as director of race operations since 2000. "We've had tens of thousands of volunteers, more than thirty board members, nine executive directors, and one Shellie Milford," said board president Sue Scheer. When bib pickup and registration was still held in the Red Arrow Room at Telemark, Milford usually slept there on Friday nights. Once, while in her pajamas at 4 a.m., she used her body as a shield to prevent garbage haulers from towing away a motor home that held the race computers, potentially saving the race.[12]

A former Telemark Lodge recreation director who taught kids to downhill ski, Milford started at the foundation part-time in 1987 and became the glue that held the race together, Popp said. She put out the *Birch Scroll*, determined wave seeding, ordered bibs and pins, coordinated volunteers, and took calls any time of day or night. One year, she doggedly solved the mystery of how a fourth-wave skier took fiftieth place in the race: he'd taken a bus a good part of the way. She would put in sixteen hours on race day, beginning at 5:30 a.m. at the start line. "There are always issues, almost every year something major, but I never felt things were falling apart," said Milford, a longtime Cable resident. "I liked multitasking and particularly liked seeing happy skiers."[13] The award in Milford's name has been given out annually since 2015.

IN 2016, AFTER TWO YEARS WITH SWIX as title sponsor, Slumberland Furniture of Minnesota took over with a three-year agreement. Slumberland became the first company to sponsor the entire event lineup—the Birkebeiner, Kortelopet, and other events year-round—in race history. The company, which previously supported the race and had a store in Hayward, also was a lead sponsor for

Olympian Jessie Diggins (her father, Clay, was an executive with the company and a veteran Birkebeiner skier himself). Popp was one of Jessie's many coaches while she was growing up. His connections to the thriving Minnesota skiing scene were reaping dividends for the Birkebeiner.[14]

The 10,102 skiers in 2016 enjoyed an expertly groomed, fast course despite temperatures steady in the low thirties. Among them was Caitlin Gregg, the 2010 Olympian, who made Birkebeiner history to become the first skier—female or male—to score a fourth victory. After winning in 2011, 2013, and 2014, Gregg won again, finishing in 2:22, despite skiing with a broken toe. "This is a special race," she said. David Norris of Alaska, a 25-year-old mountain running champion and skier on the rise, took the men's title in 2:05:35 in his first Birkebeiner, edging two French skiers by one second and four other international skiers on their tails. "Winning the Birkie is like no other win," Norris said.[15]

A few months later, the foundation honored race history when it opened the Tony Wise Museum of the American Birkebeiner at its remodeled offices down-

Skiers double pole to start the race in 2016.
AMERICAN BIRKEBEINER SKI FOUNDATION ARCHIVES, PHOTO BY BOB PEARL

town. Members of the Wise family attended the August 2016 dedication. The museum featured a 3D landscape model of the trail, the medal Wise received from Norway's King Olav V, early race equipment and videos, and other displays and memorabilia.[16]

Other big changes were in the works. The foundation bought forty acres from the new Telemark owners, Clifton Louis and Carrie Hulburd, to provide a permanent trail easement and allow for a new Birkebeiner start area. A major overhaul was underway for the Kortelopet as well. Kortelopet entries had grown 40 percent in the previous decade, and Popp was looking to provide a better race experience and ease congestion on Saturday. The Kortelopet was moved to Friday, with a new and longer course that would start at Highway OO and go south to Main Street, instead of the loop course back to Telemark.

Thanks to these changes, 2017 was shaping up to be a big year. However, for only the second time in its history, the race was canceled. Warm weather and rain the previous week severely eroded snow cover on the trail, and a last-chance snowstorm never materialized. Instead, a "BirkieStock" was held at the new start area with food and music. Several thousand disappointed entrants skied a loop or two for fun on a crowded 5-kilometer course that groomers had patched together.[17]

A few weeks before the 2018 race, the International Bridge attracted national attention when it was featured in Super Bowl LII festivities in Minneapolis. The bridge was so large that it took twelve semis to transport it to Minneapolis. It was assembled on Nicollet Mall over Ninth Street and used for skiing demonstrations leading up to the big game between Philadelphia and New England at US Bank Stadium.

Luckily the weather cooperated in 2018, and the Birkebeiner and Kortelopet changes came together. Eight inches of snow fell Thursday night, slowing conditions for the first Friday Kortelopet. The new Kortelopet start featured a guest appearance by Clay Diggins, representing Slumberland. A few days earlier, his daughter Jessie Diggins, with sprint relay teammate Kikkan Randall, had won an Olympic gold medal, America's first in cross-country, in South Korea. Clay Diggins told skiers that Jessie's dreams began to come true as a teen when she won the 2008 and 2009 Kortelopets. It was where she learned to love the sport, Clay said. Fired-up skiers chanted "Jessie! Jessie!" It was reminiscent of the 1976 Birkebeiner when bicentennial pride swelled for Bill Koch after he won America's first Nordic medal soon after training at Telemark.[18]

On Saturday morning, skiers gathered in the heated Derksen Family Great Hall, part of the new start area stadium—a much-improved venue for hanging out before the race. The 9,512 skiers enjoyed a start temperature around seventeen, rising to thirty-three.[19]

The new start shortened the route to the Power Line Hills. About a kilometer had to be added elsewhere to get the Birkebeiner back to 50K; most of it came from eliminating the straight shot through Rosie's Field near kilometer 43 and adding a U-turn into the Fish Hatchery Creek bottoms—as well as moving the final aid station there. The stop was followed by a gradual 130-foot climb out of the bottoms on a new trail section around a ridge south of Rosie's Field, then a long glide down to the Highway 77 crossing.[20]

Caitlin Gregg, now thirty-seven, broke her own record in 2018, winning her fifth title, in 2:23. She was officially the most successful skier in Birkebeiner history. "I'm trying to set the bar pretty high for the next person," Gregg said. The men's winner was thirty-one-year-old Anders Gløersen of Norway in 2:02. Gløersen was a 2014 Olympian with five World Cup wins and fifteen World Cup podiums to his credit.[21]

BY 2018, THE FOUNDATION STAFF had tripled to fourteen, and a $1.85 million capital campaign continued to fuel the race revolution. Initially, about $250,000 was used to develop a start area snowmaking system. Snowmaking—in which well water is pumped into snow guns, flash frozen, and blown out as snow—was growing in popularity in the Upper Midwest and was considered all the more important with the previous year's race cancellation. Could snowmaking save the race in some form in years when snow was scarce? With seven hundred people donating $70,000 to purchase two snow guns, snowmaking began in November 2018 on a 2.5-kilometer loop. Mother Nature no longer was the sole source of trail snow. Tony Wise had done it once before, too, installing an alpine snowmaking system at Telemark after the nearly snowless winter in 1960–61.[22]

Race and trail infrastructure also improved with the construction of three more cabins used for food stops and skier rest breaks. The cabins, placed at Gravel Pit, Boedecker Road, and Timber Trail, had running water, electricity, and solar-generated heat. Previously, water was trucked in on milk tanks early on race morning and heated with propane; water and food couldn't be delivered

Caitlin Gregg, shown here after her 2014 win, when she became the first skier with four Birkebeiner titles. Four years later, she would win yet again. AMERICAN BIRKEBEINER SKI FOUNDATION ARCHIVES, PHOTO BY DARLENE PROIS

the day before or they would freeze. The modern cabins eased setup, greatly reducing the volunteer burden.[23]

In October 2018 another structure was added to the trail, the Key Log Rolling Crossing bridge, with major sponsors Judy and Jay Hoeschler, over Highway OO. The steel bridge was 14 feet wide, 112 feet long, and 16½ feet tall—amounting to another small hill to climb for the racers and high enough to let logging trucks roll through underneath. The aesthetically pleasing arch improved the trail experience on race days and year-round and eliminated the danger of trail users crossing the road.

Six weeks after the bridge was installed, and just a few double poles north of it, a new four-thousand-square-foot Samuel C. Johnson Family Outdoor Center opened November 20, 2018. The equivalent of a year-round Birkebeiner Trail chalet, the center was conceived as a place where skiers, hikers, and cyclists could change clothes, gather with friends, hold meetings, wax skis, repair a bike, and get something to eat or drink, while also doubling as a food station on race days. The $700,000 facility—also funded through the capital campaign with a lead gift from the Johnson Family Foundation—was a major upgrade from the rustic cabin on the south side of Highway OO that was heated with firewood and lacked indoor plumbing. The Scandinavian-style center, with mostly south-facing windows to capture natural light, was designed by architect Terry Penman, who also designed the International Bridge, the start area's Great Hall, and the new trail cabins.[24]

The winter of 2019 was cold but not snowy in Wisconsin—until February, when it started snowing and didn't stop. The record-setting month saw fifty-plus inches in many places. By race day, the trail had a twenty-inch base, with three more inches falling on race morning (followed by eight inches and a blizzard the night after the race).

It was a dream Birkebeiner for women's winner Alayna Sonnesyn of Minnesota, a former Kortelopet winner who had grown up coming to the race each year with her family and admiring the fast skiers who sprinted to victories on Main Street. "I never thought I could be one of them," said Sonnesyn, who won in 2:34. Men's winner Akeo Maifield-Carucci, a Montana native and ex-Harvard skier, outsprinted Brian Gregg by one second to win in 2:12.[25]

The 2019 race, with a steady temperature around thirty, drew a record 10,342 skiers. One of them was Kikkan Randall, who had summarily retired from professional racing after her 2018 Olympic win then four months later was diagnosed with breast cancer. It was a victory to be competing again, let alone her first 50-kilometer event, taking twelfth and inspiring many with her resilience and energy. She would become a Birkebeiner regular over the next six years.

The many changes between 2014 and 2018—as many as the race had seen in a short span since the mid-1970s—were but a warm-up for the biggest move yet. In summer 2019, the Birkebeiner Foundation signed a two-year lease with the option to purchase the Telemark Resort property. The resort had been closed since 2013, after Louis and Hulburd bought it at a sheriff's auction. They had found a potential buyer in late 2017, a Florida-based hospitality management company whose $47 million investment plans included reopening the downhill skiing, adding a second golf course, demolishing the hotel units, and building 250 new rooms. But those plans, like the others, died too.[26]

In stepped the foundation, which saw opportunity. The lease initially provided access to 30 kilometers of the historic trail system for events at the new trailhead. The property also had wells needed for the foundation's new snowmaking operation. After so many had tried—and failed—over the past thirty years to revive the property, could the foundation succeed?[27]

GOOD KARMA APPEARED TO BE IN THE AIR in February 2020, when skiers and spectators enjoyed something akin to Nordic nirvana: perfect trail conditions, temperatures in the midtwenties at the start and rising to the midthirties by the afternoon, sunshine, and a huge crowd on Main Street. It was another record-setting year with 10,825 skiers. "You could not ask for better skiing. It was gorgeous out there," said Jessica Yeaton, of Australia, a 2018 Olympian and World Cup veteran who finished in 2:13 and won the 2020 women's race by about a minute. Norway's Niklas Dyrhaug, also a 2018 Olympian and World Cup racer, won the men's race in 1:59, two seconds ahead of runner-up Ian Torchia, of Minnesota. "They talk about Birkie Fever, and [you think] it's kind of a joke," Torchia said. "Then you get here, and it's real. You get so stoked."[28]

The good vibes from the 2020 race didn't last long, unfortunately. The COVID-19 pandemic was officially declared a couple of weeks later, making the 2020 Birkebeiner one of the nation's last mass participatory events for well over a year. The foundation began planning for a 2021 race that might be different from any previous Birkebeiner.

Popp eliminated another highway race detour in October 2020 with the construction of a $300,000 steel bridge called the Becker Law Link—136 feet long, 12 feet wide, and 19 feet high—over Highway 77, at about the 44-kilometer mark in the race.[29] Neither the bridge nor the full Birkebeiner trail would be used in the 2021 race, however, as the COVID-19 pandemic continued to grip the country. The foundation was committed to having a Birkebeiner of some kind while minimizing the risk of becoming a virus superspreader. The solution was three events: a traditional competition for the elite waves (minus international skiers) on a 43-kilometer loop on the skate and classic trails (skate Saturday, classic Sunday); a series of open-track events for the other waves from Wednesday to Sunday, about one thousand people a day, alternating classic and skate; and the option to ski a virtual race anywhere (other sports included, such as running or swimming, with equivalent distances determined) and self-report the result.

Entries fell by nearly 3,000 to 7,994 and were evenly split between in-person and virtual participation. For those who skied in person, safety protocols included drive-up bib pickup, no busing, no spectators, face masks and distancing in the start area, no food stops, and a push-pedal water bottle refill station. Packages containing race bibs, finisher medals and pins, and stocking caps were mailed out to the thousands who participated virtually. The skiers who made the podium wore face masks, including winners Johnny Hagenbuch, of Idaho, in 1:54 and Alayna Sonnesyn, winning her second title, in 2:06. The foundation's efforts at preventing a regional spike in COVID-19 cases seemed to have worked, with only minor increases reported in Sawyer County the first few weeks after the race.[30]

A silver lining during the pandemic was that more people than usual used the trail, where social distancing was easy, boosting trail revenue by 19 percent. The foundation balanced a 20 percent loss of entry revenue by cutting expenses 22 percent and with a federal COVID relief grant of nearly $550,000.[31]

The pandemic didn't shut down the foundation's progress. In spring 2021, the foundation announced its purchase of the entire Telemark property. The total cost, $2.16 million, included demolishing the historic lodge, which had been emptied the year before when the previous owners auctioned off furnishings and even portions of the structure, like the cedar beams. It was official: Telemark Lodge was history.

The big, vacant lodge likely was the millstone that sank other redevelopment plans over the years. In 2020, when former lodge owners' association president Gary Crandall said the beloved building needed to disappear before Telemark could truly move forward, residents at a community hearing applauded. Telemark without Telemark Lodge at one time seemed unthinkable. But the foundation had no need for a hotel and wanted no part of expensive renovations. Demolishing the building was "one of those hard decisions," Popp said, "but we celebrate [the lodge] for what it was."[32]

The opportunity to buy Telemark forced the foundation to examine its long-term goals and whether the purchase would support them. Certainly, creating more opportunities for people to live an active lifestyle by reviving Telemark's trails and building a permanent race headquarters near the race start that could serve as a base for other events, including for the Cable community, made sense. "It's an immense project, and it's what my dad originally imagined Telemark to be: a community," Frances Wise wrote in a letter to Birchleggers.[33] The diverse partner- and donor-supported plan, with an initial fundraising campaign of $1.43 million, was named Mt. Telemark Village. The plan eventually grew to $10.2 million over five years and was heralded in promotional materials as "the biggest thing the American Birkebeiner has ever done."[34] The heart of the race was coming back to its birthplace. "It's almost like it was meant to be," Popp said.[35]

The first step, demolishing the lodge, started in spring 2021, although thirty-foot-high concrete walls from elevator shafts and the entryway were preserved for future use, including as climbing walls. The stones from the famous lobby fireplace were saved for a new fireplace at Mt. Telemark Village. Other parts of the lodge and property were repurposed, such as red poles from the ski lifts, which were used in new starting gate arches for the Birkebeiner and Kortelopet. Of the seven-hundred-plus acres that came with the purchase, more than five hundred were set aside for conservation purposes: the Landmark Conservancy purchased 218 acres for the Telemark Forest Preserve, and another 286 acres went into the new Mt. Telemark Conservancy. The land was protected from development but included easements for the Birkebeiner Trail.[36]

Planning began for other village features. The focal point was a planned twelve-thousand-square-foot central Base Camp building on the site of the old Colosseum. It would house the Tony Wise Museum, coffee shop, taproom, bike and ski rental shops, showers, meeting space, and a great room for socializing. Facing the ski hill with a mono-pitch roof, the building resembled Tony Wise's original ski chalet in design and purpose. Work also began on the trails: Jim Sokup, director of facilities and operations, led the effort to clear and reopen old Telemark ski trails; new mountain bike trails were developed in partnership with the Wisconsin-based Trek Bicycle Corporation; and a 5-kilometer trail (named after skier George Hovland) for roller-skiers, hikers, and bikers was paved. Other plans included an outdoor plaza, a biathlon range, a skating pond, a sledding hill, a fitness park, an observation tower atop the old ski hill, and a small, private hotel. In 2022, the project received major boosts from a $762,750 state tourism capital investment grant announced by Governor Tony Evers, part of the federal American Rescue Plan Act, and a $1.2 million federal loan from the Small Business Administration (Tony Wise secured a similar loan sixty years earlier to buy his snowmaking equipment).[37]

THE COVID-19 PRECAUTIONS IN 2021 had meant no Main Street finish—but the Birkebeiner returned to Main Street in 2022 with plenty of snow, including fourteen inches to start the week. The lead skiers didn't disappoint the crowd that had once again assembled. Gerard Agnellet of France—who called the downtown finish the best in the distance-skiing world—pushed a ski tip ahead of Alaskan David Norris at the line, winning in 2:07 in a photo finish. Alayna Sonnesyn took a "silly" fall at the bottom of the last hill before crossing the lake. She quickly recovered, caught up, crested the International Bridge in the lead, and sprinted home—her forte—as she won her third title in four years in 2:22, by two seconds ahead of Vermont skier Caitlin Patterson.

It was a cold start in the single digits but warmed to the thirties under sunny skies. Entries rebounded from the previous year to 9,993, but the skiing was slow with new snow. Race week also featured the new Open Track Birkebeiner and Kortelopet on Wednesday—a less competitive alternative that allows skiers to complete the course without the pressure of crowds or racing for a time or place.[38]

Gerard Agnellet of France, left, edges a lunging David Norris, of Alaska, to win in 2022.
AMERICAN BIRKEBEINER SKI FOUNDATION ARCHIVES

At a 2022 prerace reception in Hayward, Clay Diggins announced that Slumberland's sponsorship would continue at least through 2024, or nine years, one of the longest in race history. Four days earlier, Jessie Diggins became the most decorated US Olympian ever in cross-country skiing, adding silver and bronze medals in Beijing, China.

In 2023, the Birkebeiner marked its forty-ninth race (the cancellations in 2000 and 2017 meant the race's fiftieth anniversary wouldn't be celebrated until the following year). For the 10,232 skiers, the start temperature was about eight degrees. Light snow covered a firm base, resulting in more injuries and more skiers taken to the hospital than usual. Tragically, a skier in the Kortelopet died near the start from a heart issue; another in that race collapsed near the finish, also with a heart issue, but survived.[39]

Sonnesyn returned to win the women's race in 2:27, by seven seconds over Jessica Yeaton and six seconds over Caitlin Gregg. It was Sonnesyn's fourth title, making her the second-most decorated skier in race history, behind the five titles won by Gregg. Norris, the 2016 winner, won his second title, in 2:05, avenging his close loss to Agnellet in 2022, this time with Agnellet a distant second. Sonnesyn and Norris each won $10,000—$7,500 for first and $2,500 for the Tony Wise Award given to American winners.[40]

David Norris celebrates his second win, a dominating performance, at the 2023 finish line.
AMERICAN BIRKEBEINER SKI FOUNDATION ARCHIVES, PHOTO BY JAMES NETZ

One of the Birkebeiner's very first finishers returned for the first time. In 1973 Bob Levin was just fifteen—one of the trio of St. Paul Academy teens whose coach advocated for them despite not meeting the minimum age of twenty. Levin was the youngest skier in the inaugural race. In 2023, at age sixty-five, he finished again and was just twenty-six minutes slower than his debut.[41]

BY FALL 2023, MT. TELEMARK VILLAGE was starting to take shape. The paved recreation loop and private hotel tucked into the trees were done, as were some of the new Trek mountain bike trails. Construction was underway on the Base Camp building. And perched atop the ski hill was a new beacon for the redevelopment—the observation tower. It was far from the twenty-story, round glass hotel tower Tony Wise envisioned building there in the mid-1960s, but this cylindrical structure, thirty-five feet high, was significant in its own right. It was named Kawabaming ("a place to look out from") by major donors Pat and Sue Quinn, of Cable and Eau Claire, to honor the Ojibwes' ancient name for the site and Ernie St. Germaine's Birkebeiner legacy.

St. Germaine explained the significance of the tower and its placement for the Anishinaabe people and their ancestors, whose cultures are deeply rooted in the Great Lakes region of what we now call the United States and Canada:

> Important locations always had a marker tree, which was made by bending and tying a sapling that grew into a larger tree, often with a loop in it. No doubt, near the top of Mount Telemark, there at one time stood such a marker tree. It is fitting that today stands a tower from which many will remember their past and see what might be possible in their future. When we take the time to look all around, we can see not only those places where we've already been, but also the dreams of where we have yet to be. We follow the footsteps of those who came before us, and we make new paths for those who are yet to be.[42]

The tower's name also honored Wise's original vision to include the Ojibwe people in Telemark's growth, said Pat Quinn, who skied thirty Birkebeiners, some of his first races climbing the same Morgedal slope on which the tower stood.[43]

At the dedication ceremony on October 1, 2023, St. Germaine snipped a red ribbon atop the brown tower on the warm afternoon with fall colors just beginning. It was a day for the ages, the North Woods' canopy spreading to a blue horizon. About seventy people attended, many of them walking up the steep hill on a new trail, including Frances Wise. Her dad had made the same trek on snowshoes in late 1946 when he first saw the undeveloped property. History had been recycled: about 90 percent of the tower's building materials had come from Telemark's old alpine ski lift mechanisms. Tower designer Pat Hover and his crew from Spooner, Wisconsin, had reclaimed and reshaped them into a functional symbol of the new Telemark.

HEADING INTO THE FIFTIETH ANNIVERSARY RACE IN 2024, the foundation hoped to bring back a World Cup event. After all, the first one in the world was held at Telemark, depending on opinions, either in 1976 or 1978. Unfortunately, the major sponsorships totaling $2.8 million to secure the world's best skiers didn't materialize. But the Birkebeiner wasn't shut out. A cadre of the world's best, including Jessie Diggins, came on a weekend when no World Cup event was scheduled, adding a new level of excitement.

The golden Birkebeiner was indeed a fiftieth to remember, even without two of the race's key features—natural snow and a Main Street finish. Race week and the fiftieth anniversary celebration had to be reinvented because of a nearly snowless winter up north. The mild El Niño winter in the Upper Midwest that year meant a brown Christmas and golf courses open in January and February in Wisconsin. By mid-January, it became clear that the full race was in doubt. But Popp and the foundation were fully committed to holding some kind of race to mark the fiftieth. Luckily, they had an ace to play: artificial snow. If the foundation hadn't invested six years earlier in a snowmaking system near the start, there would have been no 2024 race, just like 2000 and 2017.

Ten days before the race, thousands of skiers watched the livestream on Facebook and YouTube where Popp and event director Kristy Maki announced their plan B. A 4-kilometer loop near the start stadium, which had been maintained all winter, would be expanded to 10 kilometers to hold the race. Officials had stockpiled huge mounds of artificial snow—more than could fill a football field. That snow would be harvested, dumped onto bare ground, and groomed into a trail. The massive, race-saving effort would mean working twelve hours a day for ten days to move thirty thousand cubic feet of snow in one thousand loads. The undertaking was coordinated by facilities director Jim Sokup, with the help of local drivers and volunteers—like a groomer from the Milwaukee area known only as Beattle—who wanted to help the skiers who collectively had paid upward of $2 million in entry fees, trained, and booked rooms and flights. Trail workers created a kind of figure-eight, twenty-five-foot-wide, twisting trail made of packed snow about two feet high. It wound through the woods and on parts of the old Telemark golf course, which had been sold in 2023 by the private owners for a new housing development.[44]

Skiers would begin at the start stadium and follow the main trail for nearly 2 kilometers to the edge of the Power Line Hills, then return to the start area via the Classic Trail before heading out toward the site of the old lodge and golf course. Skiers would loop back on sections of old Telemark Lodge trails that recently had been reopened, including the World Cup Trail (last used in 1978), Nordmor, Mount Bauer, and the infamous Elevator Shaft drop (for elite skiers only). After multiple laps around the trail, skiers would finish back at the start.[45]

The ski gods, in a Tony Wise twist of fate, had brought the Birkebeiner back home for the fiftieth anniversary. It wasn't just the snowmaking capability that made the 2024 Birkebeiner possible, but the fact that the foundation had bought the entire Telemark complex. The improvised race trail became an unexpected opportunity for skiers to see what the new Mt. Telemark Village was all about. For many, this meant it was a Birkebeiner *and* Telemark homecoming. A nostalgic Doug Peterson, race ambassador on the course, pointed to the old cement elevator shafts, as skiers glided by a few feet away, and said, "That's where I learned that I made my first Olympic team [in 1976]."[46] Don Quinn, the 1974 runner-up, returned in 2024 at age seventy-five to win his age class in the Sunday classic race. Duncan McLean and others from 1973 were back, too.

The 2024 Birkebeiner happened as well because of the massive logistical pivot by the foundation staff and volunteers. Most race infrastructure—including for the food stations, clothing bag pickup, the Birkebeiner souvenir shop, changing tents, finisher medals, finish timing, fencing, portable toilets, and more—was trucked north for four full days of replanned skiing. The regular open track on Wednesday was followed on Thursday by an alternative open track that drew more than two thousand skiers, who were allowed to switch

A looping, 10-kilometer path of artificial snow meant the course in 2024 looked significantly different than in any previous year. AMERICAN BIRKEBEINER SKI FOUNDATION ARCHIVES, PHOTO BY KELLY RANDOLPH1

in the last week to alleviate congestion on other race days; the Kortelopet on Friday; skate races on Saturday; and the classic on Sunday. Birkebeiner elite skiers went the traditional 50 kilometers, but everyone else was held to 30 and Kortelopet skiers to 20 to keep it all flowing. To get everyone through the course, race days were segmented; on Saturday, for example, waves one and two skied from 7 to 10 a.m., elites from 10 a.m. to 1 p.m., and waves three through ten from 1 to 6 p.m.

The weather during race week was mild, as it had been all winter, with three days above forty degrees, and a sunny Saturday with elite wave starts at sixteen degrees. The more durable artificial snow held up through the sun and repeated pounding by skiers. Most skiers were delighted to be skiing at all, praising the efforts of race officials to build a ski trail on six miles of brown ground. With a poor winter to train, more than a few skiers didn't mind the shorter, less hilly race. Unsurprisingly, it was a record-smashing year for entries—by nearly 2,000—with 12,700 in the Birkebeiner and Kortelopet. The race was 235 times larger than when it began.

Part of the 2024 trail went through the old lobby and past what remains of Telemark Lodge, which was torn down in 2021. AMERICAN BIRKEBEINER SKI FOUNDATION ARCHIVES, PHOTO BY BEN HAMILTON

The 2024 Birkebeiner didn't include the festive atmosphere of Main Street, but the five-lap course for elite skiers offered even more skiing action for spectators: multiple sightings of the leaders and a chance to follow the race more closely. The most watched skier that week was Jessie Diggins, whose popularity and positive energy had turned her into something akin to the Taylor Swift of American Nordic skiing. One of the nation's most recognized Olympians, the thirty-two-year-old Diggins was leading the women's World Cup standings and having one of the best seasons in US Nordic history.

Diggins appeared at two prerace fundraisers, and on race day she received a special, glittery gold bib with her name on it (a second, autographed bib was auctioned for $1,000 at a Birchleggings Club breakfast the next morning). Fans—some wearing glitter on their cheeks the way she did—rang cowbells as they clustered near the start stadium and spread out along the course to see one of America's best Nordic skiers ever at the peak of her career. Diggins's success and willingness to become the face of Nordic skiing in the US had spurred new interest in the sport and had a ripple effect on the rising US teams. "I give Jessie a lot of credit for raising the whole level of American women's Nordic skiing, all the way down to high school kids," said former Olympian Kevin Brochman, who helped coach Diggins for a time in high school.[47]

Diggins wasn't the only US star in the field. Twenty-three-year-old Gus Schumacher, a Madison, Wisconsin, native who grew up and was living in Alaska, headed the men's race. The week before, Schumacher had won the 10-kilometer race at the long-awaited Stifel World Cup in Minneapolis (the 2020 race was canceled because of COVID-19), his first triumph on a world stage. The large Twin Cities crowds also witnessed Diggins's US debut as a professional skier. She took a third and a fourth in the World Cup event, where artificial snow also was needed but was supplemented a few days before the race with six inches of natural snow (in a storm that missed northern Wisconsin). Diggins was the star World Cup fans came to see; Schumacher became the star they weren't expecting.

The duo didn't disappoint at the Birkebeiner, which *FasterSkier* described that year as "America's most loved, most famous, and most traditional cross-country ski race."[48] Prior to the elite race starts, US Navy veteran Stephanie St. Germaine, Ernie's daughter, sang the national anthem and three Black Hawk military helicopters performed a ceremonial flyover. Then, Diggins and Schumacher were on the hunt for Birkebeiner gold. In less than one lap, Diggins and fellow World Cup veteran and 2022 Olympian Flora Dolci of France broke from the pack and made it a two-person race the rest of the way. On the final lap, Diggins powered away on the last hill with about 2 kilometers to go and cruised to a 26-second victory, in 2:10. Defending champion Sonnesyn was another four minutes back.

Schumacher was in a large men's lead pack that thinned after each lap. He, too, dug deep on the homestretch and won by seven seconds in 1:58. Schumacher originally came to the Birkebeiner to cheer on his mom, who had entered; then he entered, too, when he realized the course wouldn't be too taxing. Sam Hendry, of Utah, edged defending champion David Norris, an Alaskan living in Colorado, for second.

The elite women started fifteen minutes before the elite men, which meant Schumacher finished just three minutes later than Diggins, thrilling the thousands of fans who ringed the start/finish area and witnessed back-to-back American triumphs. Laurel wreaths, a Birkebeiner tradition since Erik Ersson's win in 1973, were draped over their shoulders. Together, Diggins and

Schumacher posed for photos under the start gate in a Birkebeiner moment for the ages—American star champions at the quintessential American ski marathon. Three weeks later in Europe, Diggins's legend would grow when she won the final race of the 2023–24 World Cup, securing her second season-long championship. At the event, she also received Norway's prestigious Holmenkollen medal, awarded by Crown Prince Haakon for achievements in skiing, the first American honored in the medal's 129-year history.[49]

After the elite race, as skiers in later skate waves whizzed past, Popp led a ceremony marking the race's fiftieth anniversary, near where the original Telemark ski chalet once stood. Dignitaries like Ernie St. Germaine, Frances Wise, Kikkan Randall, Caitlin Gregg, and others were introduced. Both Diggins and Schumacher addressed the crowd, praising the course and the enthusiastic fans. "I feel like until I did the Birkebeiner, I was really missing something big. Now I can finally say I'm a true Midwesterner," Diggins said, as the crowd erupted in cheers.[50]

Skiers complete another loop around the spectator-lined 2024 course, where races were held over five days for a record 12,700 entrants. AMERICAN BIRKEBEINER SKI FOUNDATION ARCHIVES, PHOTO BY JAMES NETZ

US team members Gus Schumacher and Jessie Diggins celebrate after winning the elite skate races during the fiftieth annual event in 2024. AMERICAN BIRKEBEINER SKI FOUNDATION ARCHIVES, PHOTO BY JAMES NETZ

Sharing the spotlight with Diggins was St. Germaine, the seventy-six-year-old who didn't ski nearly as fast and didn't wear glitter but was a household name among the Birkebeiner faithful. Fittingly, St. Germaine was the first to finish in 2024. He received permission to ski on Tuesday, finishing his fiftieth—and what he said would be his last—Birkebeiner, without much fanfare. He carried pouches with ashes from fellow founding skiers Dave Landgraf and Wayne Lindskoog and kept his usual, steady classic pace around the property where he had worked for Tony Wise.

St. Germaine skied the race early because he had other plans for the rest of the week. From Wednesday through Friday, he hiked the length of the official 53-kilometer classic trail—his own full Birkebeiner—from the start to the Lumberjack Bowl, where the first race began. The Lumberjack Bowl Pancake House log cabin, used for 1973 registration but now the River Deck restaurant used for lumberjack shows, still was there, the start pond frozen but snowless. Joining him on the trek were his daughter, Stephanie; Frances Wise; and other family and friends that varied by day.

Ernie St. Germaine at the 2024 race, where he was presented with custom-made skis and a custom bib in honor of his fiftieth American Birkebeiner. AMERICAN BIRKEBEINER SKI FOUNDATION ARCHIVES, PHOTO BY KELLY RANDOLPH

Slender and agile, St. Germaine inspires skiers a quarter his age, despite type 1 diabetes that forced him to monitor his blood sugar throughout most of his fifty races and as he trained. More than once his streak was almost broken, but he never seriously considered missing a race. He awoke one race morning sick and with a fever of 103 degrees. His wife, Lori, asked him what he was going to do. "I'm going to ski," he told her, and by the end of the race, his fever was gone. "I can't say the Birkie cured me," he said later, "but there are so many spiritual things that go on." Another year he was caught in a multiskier pileup early in the race and dislocated a shoulder. He grabbed hold of a small tree, yanked on the arm, and popped the shoulder back into place to relieve the pain, then skied the rest of the race poling with one arm. "It never entered my mind to stop," he said. "No one ever taught me to quit."[51]

But in 2022, his forty-eighth race when he skied the new open-track event, St. Germaine had doubts about whether he'd be able to finish. He had surgery for a ruptured Achilles tendon the previous summer, and then, in November, he fell off a ladder in his garage and broke five ribs. By 2 kilometers into the race, he felt fine and knew he could make it. His daughter met him at each food stop for additional support. In Ojibwe, St. Germaine is revered as Ogitchidaa, or warrior. Wisconsin has never had a male winner of its own race. St. Germaine is that champion.[52]

St. Germaine, who is both soft-spoken and resolute, explained his key to finishing: "You have to find that spiritual strength inside of you." He found that strength time and again on the Birkebeiner trail, which became a personal sanctuary. The trail, he said, is the only place in his life where he hasn't experienced racism.

The fiftieth race awards ceremony ended with St. Germaine receiving a proclamation from the Lac Courte Oreilles Band near where he crossed the finish line of his first race. The award was presented by Michelle Beaudin of the Tribal Governing Board, for St. Germaine's "lifetime commitment" to "promoting an active, healthy, and positive lifestyle, while demonstrating cultural identity." The presentation concluded with a traditional honor dance by tribal members, adults and children alike, in full regalia.[53]

St. Germaine wishes for more Native participation—and more diversity in general—in both the sport and the race. That is a goal of Birkie One, an inclusion initiative aimed at expanding the race's majority white male base and helping people of all cultures and backgrounds enjoy the sport. Birkie One

slumberland
BIRKIE
Ski. Run. Bike. Live!
Ernie St. Germaine
93
American Birkebeiner

backed a new event for women, Ski de She; supported Hayward High School athlete Brooke Zen Dorman-Defoe in the 2023 North American Indigenous Games; held the ParaBirkie for athletes with disabilities; and renovated a forty-year-old, 3-kilometer trail called Zhooshoomemiikaanis, which means "sliding on the snow on a little trail," near the Lac Courte Oreilles Ojibwe School, Lac Courte Oreilles University, and Tribal Government Center southeast of Hayward. St. Germaine helped build the original trail, and he helped rebuild it with Birkie One volunteers. He hopes to see it flourish again as it did in the early 1980s, when a learn-to-ski program drew forty Lac Courte Oreilles schoolchildren, who earned points toward ski equipment when they helped maintain the trail. As his race days wound down, he pushed toward a brighter future for the Birkebeiner, including as a youth ski coach. One of those youths was his grandson, Benjamin. "This is what it's really all about. This is Valhalla," St. Germaine said of inspiring children to ski.[54]

Imprinted with the fire of Diggins and the inspiration of St. Germaine, the state of the American Birkebeiner at fifty included record numbers of skiers, major improvements to race infrastructure, and the future promise of Mt. Telemark Village. The twelve-thousand-square-foot main building opened in August 2024. The foundation was larger (with a staff of about thirty and a budget upward of $7 million), more financially sound, and more event-diverse than ever before—going back in some respects to the year-round Tony Wise business model. "I think this is the best race in the world," said founding skier John Kotar. "We have really built something. Let's keep it going."[55]

WHAT COULD STOP BIRKEBEINER MOMENTUM? In the early 1980s, the biggest hurdle was financial. By the early 2020s—forty years after Telemark first went bankrupt—the largest threat seemed to be natural. The first twenty-seven races were mostly held without major interruption—but in the next twenty-three, a lack of snow and mild weather caused two cancellations and would have wiped out a third if not for the foundation's ability to make snow.

Tony Wise and Hobart Hewett built Telemark in 1947 because snow and cold were so reliable. Winters have changed since then. Between 1950 and

Facing page: Ernie St. Germaine on the Birkebeiner Trail in 2024
AMERICAN BIRKEBEINER SKI FOUNDATION ARCHIVES, PHOTO BY KELLY RANDOLPH

2020, Wisconsin's average daytime winter temperature warmed by three to four degrees; the average winter night warmed by four to seven degrees. Scientific projections indicate the pace of warming will be even greater through 2050. Although average annual snowfall in northwest Wisconsin increased slightly to more than sixty-one inches from 1991 to 2020 compared to the previous two decades (and increased in Wisconsin overall), warmer winters are starting to cause more of that snow to melt. By the end of the century, total snowfall across Wisconsin is projected to decrease by twenty inches a year. Wisconsin climatologist Steve Vavrus said in 2023 that all seasons in Wisconsin are getting warmer "but winters are warming faster than any other season since the middle of the twentieth century," especially in northern Wisconsin.[56]

Two inches of snow fell in Hayward in November and December of 2023, the least amount of snow since 1972. Only about a foot total fell during the meteorological winter (December through February), all of which melted soon after falling. The 2023–2024 winter was the warmest winter on record in Wisconsin and the first virtually all-brown winter in race history.[57] Cold and snow haven't disappeared—the winter of 2022–23 in Wisconsin was like old times—but warmer winters have become far more frequent. For three-quarters of the United States, warming trends since 1970 have been the most significant in winter. This has been particularly pronounced in the Upper Midwest and Northeast, where average temperatures have climbed as much as seven degrees higher.[58]

The problem is global. February 2024 was the warmest February recorded on Earth and the ninth straight warmest month; 2023 was the warmest year recorded on Earth going back 174 years and the tenth straight record-setting year for heat.[59] In 2024, Worldloppet races were canceled because of warm weather and lack of snow in the Czech Republic, France, Germany, and Poland. In 2023, nearly three hundred professional skiers, concerned that climate change was endangering the future of their sports, called on the FIS to more forcefully address the issue with lawmakers. In a related effort, Diggins, Schumacher, and other US athletes were among the many outdoor sports enthusiasts who joined the global organization POW—Protect Our Winters—to advocate for progressive climate policies that encourage outdoor enthusiasts to vote, protect public lands, and promote education about the issue.[60]

The Birkebeiner Foundation began a Birkie Green initiative after the 2017 race cancellation. Birkie Green addressed climate change through common-sense reforms, such as replacing skiers' plastic clothing bags with reusable backpacks and using skier bibs made from recycled plastic bottles. Charging stations for electric vehicles were added at the Highway OO trailhead. The foundation committed to becoming a carbon-neutral operation by 2026, including the use of sustainable energy in all its buildings. "We have a responsibility to influence people," Popp said.[61]

Constrained by climate, cross-country skiing will always be a niche American sport. Mild winters will further melt its natural footprint. If people can't ski on their local trails, will they continue to ski at all? Beyond Hayward and Cable, the increasing absence of snow dampens skiers' enthusiasm for the sport and their ability to train. A sports shop in southern Wisconsin stopped selling cross-country skis in 2019 because of too many snowless winters. The foundation hopes to expand its snowmaking efforts, but a point-to-point full race on artificial snow may never happen because of cost, increasing the chances that races in future years will be abbreviated like in 2024.[62]

A path of artificial snow cuts through the woods as part of the 2024 course.
AMERICAN BIRKEBEINER SKI FOUNDATION ARCHIVES, PHOTO BY KELLY RANDOLPH

More than five million people in the US cross-country ski each year, about ten times more than in 1973. The number hasn't grown appreciably since 1987, however, despite the US population increasing by one hundred million in that span. In general, finding groomed snow on mostly low-altitude landscapes isn't easy. Snowmaking helps in places but isn't a viable solution for the masses who want a convenient location to enjoy the sport. Accessibility is one of the reasons the sport took off in the 1960s—you didn't have to travel to an alpine hill sixty or one hundred miles away but could ski in the local forest.[63]

Ultimately, natural snow is key to ensuring the future survival of the sport and preserving the Birkebeiner's hard-earned identity as America's ski marathon. Cross-country skiers are dedicated: in the US, 77.6 percent of them skied more than once in 2022–2023 and 25 percent skied seven or more times. Cognizant of how their lives, let alone the environment, will be impacted without natural snow, citizen skiers have an opportunity, much like emissaries Diggins and Schumacher, to help lead efforts that protect and preserve our winters for future generations.[64]

THE AMERICAN BIRKEBEINER is a powerful reason to fight for our winters. Its growth over more than half a century has brought together tens of thousands of people from all over the state, region, country, and world; boosted the economy of northwest Wisconsin; inspired countless participants to get fit and stay fit and find out what they're capable of; and generated midwinter heat and joy amid the celebration of snow and cold and forests and small-town America.

Tony Wise's vision, thankfully, didn't dissolve in 1984 along with his company. The race was rescued amid a legal tug-of-war, rushed to safety like a figurative Prince Haakon. It matured from the solid foundation Wise and his team built, and over the ensuing forty years has enhanced its legacy as the king of ski marathons in North America.

Logically, it shouldn't exist, this race that releases thousands of people into the frozen North at a time of year when the vast majority of people prefer to stay indoors. Staging it on the shoulders of volunteers and the foundation staff in two Wisconsin hamlets 25 miles apart via a remote, twisting trail is an annual

Facing page: Skiers in 2023 fly down the International Bridge to the scenic Main Street finish. AMERICAN BIRKEBEINER SKI FOUNDATION ARCHIVES, PHOTO BY LENORA LUDZACK

minimiracle. Skiers and the region embrace the palpable energy of race week events. Cowbells ring in February in Hayward.

For all its pageantry and good vibes, skiing the Birkebeiner is a punishing task, self-induced though the pain may be. It involves hours of sweating and extreme fatigue, often with cold and sometimes frozen body parts, ice beards, muscle cramps, crashes, broken equipment, periods of self-doubt, long climbs in loose snow, and treacherous downhills. It forces you to find the will to persevere, when at times the entire escapade seems pointless. But then you reach a food stop, where you find a much-needed break from the glacial moraine, a little burst of energy from a chunk of banana, and a word of encouragement from a volunteer or fellow skier. Stride by stride, glide by glide, you ski another kilometer, closing in on a winterlong, yearlong, or lifetime goal, a downtown reunion with family and friends, a triumphant moment when you can say that you finished the American Birkebeiner, the nation's greatest ski marathon—or, even better, finished it again.

Bjorn Arvnes of Norway kicks and glides his way to the 1977 Birkebeiner title on the new Birkebeiner Trail, during the year of the "Norwegian Invasion."
AMERICAN BIRKEBEINER SKI FOUNDATION ARCHIVES

AMERICAN BIRKEBEINER FACTS AT A GLANCE

1973–2024

Entry figures reflect the combined number of registered marathon and half-marathon skiers.

YEAR	LENGTH	ENTRIES	CHAMPIONS	START TEMPERATURE
1973	48K, Hayward to Cable (Lumberjack Bowl to Mt. Telemark chalet)	54	Erik Samuel Ersson, Sweden, 2:48; Jacque Lindskoog, Minnesota, 4:33	10°
1974	48K, Hayward to Cable (Lumberjack Bowl to Mt. Telemark chalet)	98	Dave Quinn, Minnesota, 2:59; Jacque Lindskoog, Minnesota, 4:53	−13°
1975	55K, Hayward to Cable (Lake Hayward near Historyland to Mt. Telemark chalet)	324	Chris Haines, Alaska, 3:00; Vigdis Snekkevik, Wisconsin, 5:00	19°
1976	53K, Cable to Hayward (Mt. Telemark golf course to Lumberjack Bowl) First start up Mt. Telemark	993	Audun Kolstad, Norway, 2:40; Jana Hlavaty, Illinois, 3:05	21°
1977 (5th annual)	55K, Cable to Hayward (Mt. Telemark golf course to Lumberjack Bowl) Debut of American Birkebeiner Trail	2,206	Bjorn Arvnes, Norway, 3:00; Berit Mørdre-Lammedal, Norway, 3:29	16°
1978	55K, Cable to Hayward (Mt. Telemark golf course to Lumberjack Bowl)	2,717	Alfred Kaelin, Switzerland, 3:10; Valborg Ostberg, Norway, 3:41	21°
1979	55K, Cable to Hayward (Mt. Telemark golf course to Historyland) Last start up Mt. Telemark	4,459	Arnt Haarstad, Norway, 2:47; Judy Rabinowitz, Alaska, 3:10	9°
1980	53K, Cable to Hayward (Mt. Telemark golf course to Historyland)	4,387	Per Knotten, Norway, 2:24; Gry Oftedal, Norway, 2:53	22°

YEAR	LENGTH	ENTRIES	CHAMPIONS	START TEMPERATURE
1981	A-48K, B-42K, C-42K, D-55K, Cable (Telemark to Telemark) for the first three weather-adjusted courses; Cable to Hayward (Telemark to Historyland) for main event postponed until March 7	6,356	A) Jean-Paul Pierrat, France, 3:09; Marianne Hadler, Vermont, 3:57; D) Tim Caldwell, Vermont, 2:34; Muriel Gilman, Minnesota, 3:22	40°, 48°, 45°, 10°
1982 (10th annual)	55K, Hayward to Cable (west of Main Street to Telemark Colosseum) First start using Main Street	6,348	Ola Hassis, Sweden, 2:42; Gry Oftedal, Norway, 3:04	24°
1983	50K, Hayward to Cable (Duffy's Field to Telemark Colosseum)	6,800	Rudi Kapeller, Austria, 2:14; Jennifer Caldwell, Vermont, 2:39	20°
1984	48K, Hayward to Cable (Duffy's Field to Telemark Colosseum)	7,150	Bengt Hassis, Sweden, 2:02; Vigdis Roenning, Norway, 2:27	22°
1985	48K, Hayward to Cable (Rosie's Field to Telemark Colosseum) First race organized by American Birkebeiner Ski Foundation	5,464	Oddvar Braa, Norway, 2:07; Muffy Ritz, Minnesota, 2:40	28°
1986	55K, Hayward to Cable (west of Main Street to Telemark Colosseum)	5,500	Anders Blomquist, Sweden, 2:53; Muffy Ritz, Minnesota, 3:26	12°
1987	44K, Hayward to Cable (Rosie's Field to Telemark Colosseum)	5,769	Konrad Hallenbarter, Switzerland, 1:54; Ellen Justina "E.J." Holcomb, Idaho, 2:20	28°
1988	55K, Hayward to Cable (west of Main Street to Telemark Colosseum)	5,621	Orjan Blomquist, Sweden, 2:20; Kelly Kimball, Minnesota, 2:52	1°
1989	55K, Hayward to Cable (west of Main Street to Telemark Colosseum)	6,108	Orjan Blomquist, Sweden, 2:19; Betsy Youngman, Ohio, 2:35	33°
1990	55K, Hayward to Cable (west of Main Street to Telemark Colosseum)	6,270	Manfred Nagl, Austria, 2:30; Lynne Cecil, Minnesota, 2:51	0°

YEAR	LENGTH	ENTRIES	CHAMPIONS	START TEMPERATURE
1991	46K, Hayward to Cable (Rosie's Field to Telemark Colosseum)	6,269	Manfred Nagl, Austria, 2:01; Ingrid Butts, Utah, 2:15	9°
1992 (20th annual)	55K, Cable to Hayward (Telemark golf course to Main Street) First finish on Main Street	6,373	Todd Boonstra, Minnesota, 2:15; Nina Skeime, Norway, 2:26	28°
1993	55K, Cable to Hayward (Telemark golf course to Main Street)	6,358	Manfred Nagl, Austria, 2:05; Suzanne King, Minnesota, 2:27	10°
1994	52K, Cable to Hayward (Telemark golf course to Main Street)	6,632	Thomas Caslavsky, Czech Republic, 2:16; Heike Wezel, Germany, 2:36	−5°
1995	52K, Cable to Hayward (Telemark golf course to Main Street)	6,616	Andre Jungen, Switzerland, 2:10; Maria Theurl, Austria, 2:22	18°
1996	52K, Cable to Hayward (Telemark golf course to Main Street)	7,502	Silvano Barco, Italy, 2:24; Gudrun Pflueger, Austria, 2:41	30°
1997 (25th annual)	52K, Cable to Hayward (Telemark golf course to Main Street)	7,882	Mikhail Botwinov, Austria, 1:57; Gudrun Pflueger, Austria, 2:19	15°
1998	25K, Cable to Seeley (Cable airport to Highway OO) Race shortened because of trail conditions	7,097	Carl Swenson, Colorado, 50 minutes; Jennifer Douglas, Idaho, 56 minutes	32°
1999	52K, Cable to Hayward (Cable airport to Main Street)	6,942	Johann Muehlegg, Germany, 2:03; Laura McCabe, state of Washington, 2:22	34°
2000	Race canceled—lack of snow	6,335		
2001	51K, Cable to Hayward (Cable airport to Main Street)	6,550	Gianantonio Zanetel, Italy, 2:32; Nadezhada Slessareva, Russia, 2:48	20°
2002	46.7K, Cable to Hayward (Cable airport to Duffy's Field, east of Lake Hayward)	5,903	Maurizio Pozzi, Italy, 1:57; Jeannie Wall, Montana, 2:24	30°

YEAR	LENGTH	ENTRIES	CHAMPIONS	START TEMPERATURE
2003 (30th annual)	51K, Cable to Hayward (Cable airport to Main Street)	5,625	Gianantonio Zanetel, Italy, 2:10; Lara Peyrot, Italy, 2:24	10°
2004	51K, Cable to Hayward (Cable airport to Main Street)	6,047	Gianantonio Zanetel, Italy, 2:11; Lara Peyrot, Italy, 2:23	25°
2005	51K, Cable to Hayward (Cable airport to Main Street)	6,398	Marco Cattaneo, Italy, 2:03; Lara Peyrot, Italy, 2:15	–4°
2006	51K, Cable to Hayward (Cable airport to Main Street)	6,780	Marco Cattaneo, Italy, 2:08; Anna Santer, Italy, 2:24	2°
2007	25K, Cable to Seeley (Cable airport to Highway OO) Race shortened because of trail conditions; only elite skiers timed	6,600	Zack Simons, Utah, 1:09; Kate Whitcomb, Idaho, 1:18	15°
2008 (35th annual)	50K freestyle, 53K classic Cable to Hayward (Cable airport to Main Street) First year of Birkebeiner Classic races on new classic trail	6,709	Freestyle, Ivan Babikov, Canada, 2:07; Evelyn Dong, Oregon, 2:23; Classic, Yuri Kozlov, Russia, 2:32; Kelly Skillicorn, Minnesota, 3:00	8°
2009	50K freestyle, 54K classic Cable to Hayward (Cable airport to Main Street)	7,193	Freestyle, Matthew Liebsch, Minnesota, 2:11; Rebecca Dussault, Colorado, 2:26; Classic, Gus Kaeding, Michigan, 3:00; Martina Stursova, Czech Republic, 3:26	17°
2010	50K freestyle, 54K classic Cable to Hayward (Cable airport to Main Street)	8,056	Freestyle, Fabio Santus, Italy, 1:56; Rebecca Dussault, Colorado, 2:16; Classic, Juergen Uhl, Vermont, 2:28; Audrey Weber, Minnesota, 2:51	10°
2011	50K freestyle, 54K classic Cable to Hayward (Cable airport to Main Street)	8,836	Freestyle, Tore Gundersen, Norway, 2:00; Caitlin Compton, Minnesota, 2:16; Classic, Juergen Uhl, Vermont, 2:28; Jennie Bender, Minnesota, 2:50	–10°

YEAR	LENGTH	ENTRIES	CHAMPIONS	START TEMPERATURE
2012	50K freestyle, 54K classic Cable to Hayward (Cable airport to Main Street)	9,300	Freestyle, Tad Elliott, Colorado, 2:04; Holly Brooks, Alaska, 2:18; Classic, David Chamberlain, Minnesota, 2:51; Carolyn Ocariz, Wisconsin, 3:03	10°
2013 (40th annual)	50K freestyle, 54K classic Cable to Hayward (Cable airport to Main Street)	8,111	Freestyle, Sergio Bonaldi, Italy, 2:09; Caitlin (Compton) Gregg, Minnesota, 2:28; Classic, Doug Debold, Minnesota, 2:50; Ingrid Saupstad, Norway, 3:17	25°
2014	50K freestyle, 54K classic Cable to Hayward (Cable airport to Main Street)	10,280	Freestyle, Tom Reichelt, Germany, 2:14; Classic, Caitlin Gregg, Minnesota, 2:40; Classic, Santiago Ocariz, Wisconsin, 3:01; Natalja Naryshkina, Wisconsin, 3:26	−10°
2015	51K freestyle, 55K classic Cable to Hayward (Cable airport to Main Street)	9,936	Freestyle, Sergio Bonaldi, Italy, 2:12; Holly Brooks, Alaska, 2:34; Classic, Ole Christian Mork, Norway, 2:54; Natalja Naryshkina, Wisconsin, 3:13	15°
2016	51K freestyle, 54K classic Cable to Hayward (Cable airport to Main Street)	10,102	Freestyle, David Norris, Alaska, 2:05; Caitlin Gregg, Minnesota, 2:22; Classic, Welly Ramsey, Maine, 2:48; Deedra Irwin, Wisconsin, 3:11	32°
2017	Race canceled—lack of snow			
2018	51K freestyle, 55K classic Cable to Hayward (Birkebeiner stadium to Main Street)	9,512	Freestyle, Anders Gloersen, Norway, 2:02; Caitlin Gregg, Minnesota, 2:23; Classic, Benjamin Saxton, Vermont, 2:47; Felicia Gesior, Wisconsin, 3:08	17°
2019 (45th annual)	50K freestyle, 55K classic Cable to Hayward (Birkebeiner stadium to Main Street)	10,342	Freestyle, Akeo Maifeld-Carucci, Montana, 2:12; Alayna Sonnesyn, Minnesota, 2:34; Classic, Peter Holmes, Minnesota, 3:04; Cate Brams, Massachusetts, 3:21	30°

YEAR	LENGTH	ENTRIES	CHAMPIONS	START TEMPERATURE
2020	50K freestyle, 55K classic Cable to Hayward (Birkebeiner stadium to Main Street)	10,825	Freestyle, Niklas Dyrhaug, Norway, 1:59; Jessica Yeaton, Australia, 2:13; Classic, Peter Holmes, Minnesota, 2:26; Nichole Bathe, England, 2:49	25°
2021	43K freestyle (Saturday) and classic (Sunday) for elite skiers; open track days for citizen skiers; virtual options because of COVID-19 pandemic	7,994	Freestyle, Johnny Hagenbuch, Idaho, 1:54; Alayna Sonnesyn, Minnesota, 2:06; Classic, Ian Torchia, Minnesota, 2:39; Rosie Frankowski, Alaska, 2:51	0°
2022	50K freestyle, 55K classic Cable to Hayward (Birkebeiner stadium to Main Street)	9,993	Freestyle, Gerard Agnellet, France, 2:07; Alayna Sonnesyn, Minnesota, 2:22; Classic, Leo Hipp, Minnesota, 2:51; Delaney FitzPatrick, Wisconsin, 3:23	7°
2023	50K freestyle, 53K classic Cable to Hayward (Birkebeiner stadium to Main Street)	10,232	Freestyle, David Norris, Colorado, 2:05; Alayna Sonnesyn, Minnesota, 2:27; Classic, Scott Hill, Canada, 2:52; Julie Ensrud, Minnesota, 3:14	8°
2024 (50th annual)	50K freestyle (Saturday) and 30K classic (Sunday) for elite skiers, 30K for citizen skiers on weekend race days and for weekday open track options, Birkebeiner stadium to Birkebeiner stadium on 10K loop with artificial snow	12,700	Freestyle, Gus Schumacher, Alaska, 1:58; Jessie Diggins, Minnesota, 2:10; Classic, Reid Goble, Montana, 1:11; Hannah Rudd, Montana, 1:26	16° (elite skate race, Saturday)

ACKNOWLEDGMENTS

THANKS TO the Wisconsin Historical Society Press and to Birkebeiner Foundation Executive Director Ben Popp and his dedicated staff for helping make this book possible, including for unrestricted access to archival material and photos. It also couldn't have been done without initial support from WHS Acquisitions Editor Kate Thompson, the special talents and patience of manuscript editor Carrie Kilman, and other WHS experts. Likewise: WHS archives in Madison; archivist Kristina Warner with the Norwegian American Historical Association in Northfield, Minnesota, including access to archival photos and information; legendary Ernie St. Germaine, for his encyclopedic knowledge of the race and Ojibwe history; General Manager/Editor Rich Jackson and his staff at the *Sawyer County Record*, which has covered the Birkebeiner like no other news source, year-round, for half a century; Wisconsin public

Above: Audun Kolstad of Norway strides to victory in the 1976 Birkebeiner, becoming the first Norwegian to win the American version of his country's namesake ski marathon.
AMERICAN BIRKEBEINER SKI FOUNDATION ARCHIVES

libraries in Eau Claire, Hayward, and Menomonie; archivists Heather Stecklein at University of Wisconsin–Stout and Greg Kocken at University of Wisconsin–Eau Claire; Hennepin County Library in Minnesota; Professor Erik Opsahl, Norwegian University of Science and Technology; the intrepid race week photographers from James Netz Photography; Epp Paal, Worldloppet CEO; dozens of people like St. Germaine, Frances Wise, Janie Wise, Jerry Berard, and the Treland brothers who sat for interviews that sometimes lasted for hours; 1973 winner and longtime race entrant Duncan McLean; my wife, Lynn, who has waited patiently for me to finish many Birkebeiners and this book; and the support of my sons, Jerad and Matthew, nearly Birchlegger Birkebeiner veterans themselves (on the trail, we're triple Poling). Another thanks to WHS for donating a portion of book proceeds to the nonprofit race foundation to support this one-of-a-kind Wisconsin and national tradition. During the writing of this book, several key figures in race history passed on. They include Jim Bauer, Jerry Berard, Carol Duffy, Erik Ersson, Marty Hall, and Bob Woodward. They will be missed by many.

Elite skiers, including eventual fourth-place finisher Florian Kostner (bib number 4) of Italy, crest a hill during the 2014 race. AMERICAN BIRKEBEINER SKI FOUNDATION, PHOTO BY BRETT MORGAN

NOTES

CHAPTER 1

1. Kurt Proctor, interview by the author, April 18, 2022.
2. "There's no Birkie, Korte, or Prince Haakon without those buses," *Silent Sports*, February 2023, 44–46; Eric Maki, interview by the author, January 2, 2024.
3. Dave Johnson, interview by the author, March 8, 2023.
4. James Krueger, interview by the author, March 17, 2023; Allan Serrano, interview by the author, October 14, 2022. A portable spectrometer that can immediately analyze PFAS molecules on skis debuted at the 2025 Birkebeiner. Skiers are encouraged to follow the non-fluoro policy year-round on the Birkebeiner Trail, part of the Birkie Green initiative.
5. Bill McKibben, *Long Distance* (New York: Rodale, 2010), 204.
6. Jerome and Karen Malmquist, interview by the author, April 1, 2023; Erik Hansen, interview by the author, April 4, 2023; Rachel Frydenlund, interview by the author, April 14, 2023; Chris Draganowski, interview by the author, December 29, 2023.
7. Dave Tworek, interview by the author, April 14, 2023.

CHAPTER 2

1. Donald A. Bluhm, "Risk taking spurred Tony Wise," *Milwaukee Journal*, February 14, 1988.
2. Tony Wise biographical sketch, unpublished, Wise family records; Jay Weiner, "Tony Wise builds skiing empire in Wisconsin," *Minneapolis Tribune*, March 11, 1979.
3. Wise biographical sketch; Tony Wise oral history I, Side A, Side B, American Birkebeiner Ski Foundation archives, Hayward, WI (hereafter cited as Birkebeiner archives).
4. Wayne Christensen, "Cross Country Frenzy!" 63–65, 99–101, *Corporate Report*, March 1979, reprinted in *Telemark Memories*, 183–88, by Deb Malesevich, Telemark Educational Foundation (Hayward, WI: Advance Printing, 2007), 233; Peter Maller, "Past motivates Telemark mastermind," *St. Paul Pioneer Press*, March 15, 1981, reprinted in *Telemark Memories*, 207; Wise oral history I, Side A; Peter Maller, "Past motivates Telemark mastermind," *Pioneer Press*, March 15, 1981.
5. "Stage set for the big Winter Carnival," *Sawyer County Record*, February 11, 1937; "Hayward's bid for winter sports mecca," *Sawyer County Record*, December 9, 1937; "Big carnival starts tonight," *Sawyer County Record*, February 17, 1938; John Dettloff, *Trail Blazer Magazine*, "Hayward's first winter sports carnival," 15–18, February 2, 1998.
6. "Win third place in basketball tourney," *Sawyer County Record*, March 17, 1938.
7. Meg Jones, "March Madness: It was a former UW–Madison basketball legend's idea," *Milwaukee Journal Sentinel*, March 21, 2018.

8. Frances Wise, interview by the author, April 9, 2022.
9. Ohio State University basketball records, Men's Basketball All-Time Box Scores, https://ohiostatebuckeyes.com/sports/2018/7/5/mens-basketball-all-time-box-scores; Wise oral history I, Side A.
10. Anthony Wise Army records, Anthony Wise Collection, box 1, folder 2, Wisconsin Historical Society, Madison, WI (hereafter cited as Wise Collection); Wise oral history I, Side A.
11. Joseph Carter, *History of the 14th Armored Division* (Atlanta, GA: Albert Love Enterprises, 1945), 67; https://14thad.org/history/history_of_the_14th.pdf.
12. The 14th Armored Division and the Liberation of Stalag VIIA, Army Historical Foundation, https://armyhistory.org/the-14th-armored-division-and-the-liberation-of-stalag-viia/; Wise oral history I, sides A, B.
13. Wise letter to mother, April 1945, Wise Collection.
14. Capt. Frank Wallace Jr., ed., *History of the 125th Armored Engineer Battalion* (Diessen, Germany: Art Printing Establishment, 1945), 66–67.
15. Wallace, *History of the 125th*, 77; Presentation to Lt. Col. Anthony Wise, 25th Annual Convention of Wis. National Guard Association, Telemark Lodge, April 26, 1975, Birkebeiner archives; Wise oral history II–III, Side A, Side B.
16. The Winter Games included appearances by Adolf Hitler and a German military presence but did not have the level of anti-Jewish propaganda and ensuing backlash as the Summer Games that year in Berlin.
17. Wise biographical sketch; Wise oral history II–III, Side A.
18. Wise oral history I, Side A; Wayne Christensen, *Corporate Report*, March 1979.
19. Wise oral history II–III, Side B; "Punce is just as tall," *Sawyer County Record*, December 16, 1937.
20. Wise, oral history II–III, Side A; Jay Weiner, *Minneapolis Tribune*, March 11, 1979.
21. Wise biographical sketch.
22. Wise biographical sketch; Frances Wise interview.
23. Telemark business records, box 1, folder 1; box 6, folder 3, Wise Collection.
24. Anthony Wise, "To the citizens of the Hayward–Cable recreation area," *Sawyer County Record and Hayward Republican*, July 31, 1947.
25. "Winter Tourist Trade in Wisconsin," box 6, folder 2, Wise Collection.
26. Mount Telemark pamphlet, box 10, folder 2, Wise Collection.
27. Mount Telemark pamphlet.
28. Wise biographical sketch.
29. "Mt. Telemark ski instructor arrives from Norway," *Ashland Daily Press*, December 8, 1947; "700 attend opening of Mt. Telemark," December 15, 1947; "New ski area will open at Hayward, Wis.," *Ski Sport*, December 9, 1947.
30. "Vets build new skiers' paradise," *Minneapolis Star*, November 20, 1947.
31. Frank Elkins, "Berg, Norwegian skiing star, captures Eastern Downhill skiing title," *New York Times Archives*, February 18, 1946.
32. Malesevich, *Telemark Memories*, 233.

33. *The Mid-West 1946–47 Skier's Guide*, box 6, folder 2, Wise Collection.
34. 4 Wise oral history II–III, Side B.
35. Wise oral history II–III, Side B; Wise biographical sketch.
36. Janie Wise, interview by the author, May 13, 2022; Jayden Erie, "Expanded features turn Mont du Lac into year-round attraction," Perfect Duluth Day website, July 26, 2022, www.perfectduluthday.com/2022/07/26/expanded-features-turn-mont-du-lac-into-year-round-attraction; Jerry Berard, interview by the author, May 13, 2022; Wise oral history 8–19, Side B, II–III, Side B.
37. "Mary Sheila Maline, Anthony Wise marry," *Sawyer County Record*, May 31, 1951.
38. Historyland promotional materials, box 13, folders 40 and 44, Wise Collection; Fred Vortanz interview; Treland interview.
39. Wise biographical sketch.
40. Berard interview; Wise oral history I, Side B.
41. "Lumberjack days return to city in form of promotion," *Sawyer County Record*, July 14, 1960; "World's Championship log rollers to vie in Hayward tournament this Saturday–Sunday," August 4, 1960.
42. Wise oral history I, Side B; Gene Divine, "Hayward: Where the action is," *Milwaukee Sentinel*, November 22, 1965.
43. Marc Michaelson, "Largest snow making machine used at Wisconsin's Mt. Telemark," *Chicago's American*, January 11, 1962; "Snow and fun: Grade A in Dairyland," *Sports Illustrated*, February 17, 1958; *Ski Magazine* cited by Ralph Thornton, "Ski pals cross paths in Telemark's 25th," *Minneapolis Star*, January 11, 1973.
44. Bankruptcy court records, 1984, box 14, folder 3, Wise Collection; Wise oral history II–III, Side A.
45. Fred Vortanz interview; Wise oral history II–III, Side B.
46. Frances Wise interview.
47. Wise biographical sketch; Jim Carr, "Telemark's Wise man of skiing," *Nordic World*, March 1979.
48. Michael Strauss, "Skiing problem solved by seven miles of pipe," *New York Times*, January 19, 1962; "Snowmaking machines inspire white Thanksgiving at Telemark," *Milwaukee Sentinel*, Nov. 22, 1961; various news articles, box 10, folders 1 and 3, Wise Collection; Wise biographical sketch.
49. Gene Devine, "Hayward: Where action is," *Milwaukee Sentinel*, November 22, 1965; "Monkees discover Old Hayward Saturday," *North Wisconsin News*, August 4, 1967.
50. "Telemark breaks one-day skier records with 2206," *Sawyer County Record*, January 7, 1965.
51. Terrell Boettcher, "Telemark, Historyland and Company B: Jerry Berard remembers them all," *Sawyer County Record*, August 3, 2018; Wise biographical sketch.
52. Wise biographical sketch.
53. Frances Wise interview.
54. Ben Kern, "Tony Wise may be his own Paul Bunyan," *Minneapolis Tribune*, February 21, 1965.

55. Telmark promotional materials, circa 1971, Birkebeiner archives.
56. Ralph Thornton, "Ski pals cross paths in Telemark's 25th," *Minneapolis Star*, January 11, 1973, box 6, folder 34, Wise Collection; Wise biographical sketch.
57. "Editorial: Why Telemark has the world's most beautiful lodge," *North Wisconsin News*, January 9, 1973; Malesevich, *Telemark Memories*, 61–65; Telemark promotional materials, box 6, folder 34, Wise Collection.
58. "Telemark hails double-barreled achievement," *Central Skiland*, January 9, 1973.
59. Scott Wilson, "Superlodge," *Ski Magazine*, November 1977, reprinted in *Telemark Memories*, 103–104.
60. Donald A. Bluhm, "Telemark Lodge bouncing back from bankruptcy," *Milwaukee Journal*, February 14, 1988.
61. Keith Thomsen, "Midwest is good for skiing," Duluth News Tribune, Jan. 10, 1973.
62. Wise oral history 8–19, Side B.
63. Malesevich, *Telemark Memories*, 4–5.
64. "Where the Indians make the snow," *Ski Magazine*, March 1964.
65. Chelsey Lewis, "Once a hopping ski resort, Telemark Lodge is nearing its end. But it could be busy again soon," *Journal Sentinel*, May 13, 2021; Ernie St. Germaine, interviews by the author, February 25 and May 16, 2024.
66. Janie Wise interview; Frances Wise interview; Fred Vortanz interview.
67. Berard interview; St. Germaine interview, February 25, 2024.
68. Janie Wise interview.
69. St. Germaine interview, February 25, 2024.
70. Janie Wise interview; Frances Wise interview.
71. Angeline Cloud, interview by the author, April 6, 2024.
72. Janie Wise interview; Jeanette Vortanz, interview by the author, April 14, 2023.
73. Jeanette Vortanz interview.

CHAPTER 3

1. Telemark silver anniversary edition, *North Wisconsin News*, January 9, 1973; Ralph Thornton, "Ski pals cross paths in Telemark's 25th," *Minneapolis Star*, January 11, 1973.
2. Jeff Leich, "A Selective Chronology of Nordic Skiing," New England Ski Museum, 2009, https://newenglandskimuseum.org/wp-content/uploads/2012/06/nordic_timeline.pdf.
3. "The Wapack Trail's Place in the History of Skiing in the US," Friends of the Wapack, https://wapack.org/the-wapack-trails-place-in-the-history-of-skiing-in-the-us/, October 22, 2021; Central US Ski Association annual report, 1939, Adrian Watt private collection, Duluth, Minnesota.
4. Caroline Eubanks, "The US Ski Resorts Built by WWII Soldiers," *British Broadcasting Corp.*, January 6, 2023, www.bbc.com/travel/article/20230105-the-us-ski-resorts-built-by-ww2-soldiers.
5. *Birch Scroll*, December 1975.
6. John F. Kennedy, "The Soft American," *Sports Illustrated*, December 26, 1960; Arthur J. Snider, "The Fitness Craze," *1974 Year Book* (Chicago: World Book, 1974), 106–19.

7. Kenneth Miller, "The Lure of Touring," *Skiing Magazine*, February, 1965, 30, 76–82.
8. Wayne Lindskoog, North Star Ski Touring Club, Club History, 1967–77, https://north-stars.org.
9. Berard interview; Rick Scott, interview by the author, June 13, 2022.
10. Seth Masia, "Featured ISHA Member: George Hovland," 2017, International Skiing History Association, www.skiinghistory.org/news/featured-isha-member-george-hovland; Jane Hovland, interview by the author, June 11, 2022.
11. Scott interview.
12. *Ski Magazine,* November 1973; Bob Woodward, interview by the author, December 27, 2023.
13. "The new cross-country gear; touring equipment," *Ski*, January 1974.
14. *Ski*, August 1972, November 1972; Sven Wiik and David Sumner, *Regenery Guide to Ski Touring* (Chicago: H. Regenery, 1974), 181–86.
15. Wayne Christensen, "Cross-country Frenzy!" *Corporate Report*, 63–65, 99–101, March 1979; also in *Telemark Memories*, 183–88.
16. John Henry Auran, "Update on Telemark," *Skiing*, October 1979.
17. Berard interview; Jim Bauer, interview by the author, June 3, 2022.
18. Wiik ski touring school, *North Wisconsin News*, September 1972, box 10, folder 8, Wise Collection; Wiik and Sumner, *Regenery Guide*, 184–85.
19. Bauer interview; *Skiing*, October 1979.
20. Berard interview; transcribed Tony Wise interview, undated, Birkebeiner archives.
21. Wise biographical sketch.
22. Tom Kelly, *Birkie Fever* (Osceola, WI: Specialty Press, 1982), 10.
23. Kelly, *Birkie Fever*, 10.
24. "Norwegians in Wisconsin," Wisconsin Historical Society, www.wisconsinhistory.org/Records/Article/CS1854, accessed November 14, 2024; City of Hayward, About the City, 2024, https://cityofhaywardwi.gov/about-the-city/.
25. Berard interview.
26. Sven Wiik comment, Birkebeiner archives.
27. Jeanette Vortanz interview; Janie Wise interview.
28. Wise oral history, with Phil Van Valkenberg, September 21, 1991, Birkebeiner archives.
29. "50 racers enter Rabbit Ears sprint," *Steamboat Pilot*, May 11, 1972; Shirley Johnson, "Steamboat Village Voice," *Steamboat Pilot*, April 26, 1973; "Sun Shone on Rabbit Ears," *Steamboat Pilot*, May 2, 1974; Tom Gibbons, "Fort Klamath to Crater Lake Ski Race, 1927–1938," www.oregonencyclopedia.org/articles/fort_klamath_to_crater_lake_race/; "Donner Trail Memorial Ski Marathon," Emigrant Gap Lodge, History 1950–2008, https://emigrantgaplodge.blogspot.com/p/history-of-emigrant-gap-1950-now.html.
30. *Birch Scroll*, Race Issue 1976, February 1977; John Caldwell, interview by the author, September 5, 2022; Bill Koch, interview by the author, September 20, 2022; Marty Hall, interview by the author, April 24, 2022; John Kotar, interview by the author, December 8, 2022.
31. Bob Treland, interview by the author, May 28, 2022.

32. Treland interview; Bauer interview.
33. Ward Williamson, interview by the author, October 16, 2023; Treland interview.
34. Williamson interview.
35. Berard interview.
36. Treland interview
37. Williamson interview; Steve Maznio, interview by the author, March 12, 2023.
38. Rick Eliot with John Caldwell, "Faster, Easier, Better: Evolution of XC Track Setting," *International Skiing History Association* 33, no. 3 (May–June 2021).
39. Kotar, "A Founder Remembers," *Trail Blazer*, February 3, 1997, 4–5, 8–10; Kotar interview; *Birch Scroll,* Pre-race 2002, 17.
40. Kelly, *Birkie Fever*, 12.
41. Bauer interview.
42. Tony Wise, description of racecourse, Birkebeiner archives.
43. Kelly, *Birkie Fever,* 12; Lovisa Ersson, interview by the author, December 14, 2023.
44. Kelly, *Birkie Fever*, 12; Ersson interview.
45. Ersson interview; Kelly, *Birkie Fever*, 12; Kotar interview.
46. Ersson interview.
47. Kelly, *Birkie Fever*, 12.
48. Kotar interview.
49. Ersson interview; Kelly, *Birkie Fever*, 12; Kotar interview.
50. Kotar interview; Kotar, "A Founder Remembers."
51. Kelly, *Birkie Fever*, 14.
52. St. Germaine interview, February 25, 2024.
53. St. Germaine interview, February 25, 2024; Kelly, *Birkie Fever*, 13–14.
54. Joe Knight, "Favorite not sitting on the pole," *Eau Claire Leader-Telegram*, February 16, 1997; St. Germaine interview, February 25, 2024.
55. *Birch Scroll,* Pre-race issue 2012, 8–9.
56. Karl Andresen, interview by the author, April 4, 2000.
57. Jim Backus, "Fond memories of the first two Birkebeiners," Birkebeiner Preview, *Sawyer County Record*, February 20, 2019.
58. *Birch Scroll*, Fall 1996, 8–13.
59. *Birch Scroll*, Pre-race 1997, 10–14.
60. Jacque Lindskoog, interview by the author, April 25, 2022; Treland interview; Jeanette Vortanz interview; Race Results 1973, Birkebeiner archives.
61. Lindskoog interview.
62. Bruce Derauf, interview by the author, January 7, 2023.
63. Duncan McLean, interview by the author, September 30, 2022.
64. Maznio interview.
65. McLean interview; *Birch Scroll*, 2008 Pre-race issue, 11–12.
66. *Birch Scroll*, Pre-race 1995, 19; Kelly, *Birkie Fever*, 18.
67. Treland interview; Jeanette Vortanz interview.
68. Jerry Poling, "Ghost Birkie: Crash kept man from finishing first Birkebeiner," *Leader-Telegram*, February 27, 2005.

CHAPTER 4

1. Kelly, *Birkie Fever*, 23.
2. Karl Andresen race notes, Birkebeiner archives.
3. Don Quinn, interview by the author, June 13, 2022.
4. "50 Racers enter Rabbit Ears sprint," *Steamboat Pilot*, May 11, 1972.
5. Quinn interview; Kelly, *Birkie Fever*, 20–25.
6. "Sun Shone on Rabbit Ears race," *Steamboat Pilot*, May 2, 1974.
7. *Birkie Fever* records, Birkebeiner archives; John Gannett feature, Birkebeiner Foundation news release, December 9, 2004.
8. Gregg Wong, "Skiing," *St. Paul Dispatch*, February 28, 1974.
9. Lindskoog interview.
10. McLean interview.
11. Kelly, *Birkie Fever*, 29
12. Kelly, *Birkie Fever*, 28.
13. *Birch Scroll*, December 1975.
14. Kelly, *Birkie Fever*, 39–42; Hall interview.
15. Hall interview; Doug Peterson, interview by the author, June 28, 2022.
16. Kelly, *Birkie Fever*, 40.
17. Hall interview.
18. Hall interview.
19. Koch interview.
20. Kelly, *Birkie Fever*, 40–42; "Olympic destiny for some determined at Telemark," *Telemarks,* Telemark Owners' News, January 12, 1976; *Birch Scroll*, December 1975.
21. Peterson interview.
22. Kelly, *Birkie Fever*, 36–37
23. Kelly, *Birkie Fever*, 42.
24. *Birch Scroll*, March 1976.
25. *Birch Scroll*, March 1976.
26. Thornton, "Telemark turns to touring," *Minneapolis Star*, undated, reprinted in *Birch Scroll*, March 1976.
27. *Birch Scroll*, October 1976.
28. William Oscar Johnson, "A Wise man and his gift," *Sports Illustrated*, January 3, 1977.
29. Peterson interview.
30. Johnson, *Sports Illustrated*, January 3, 1977; Wise letter to ski industry, New Clippings 1980 folder, Birkebeiner archives; *Birch Scroll*, February 1977; Hall interview.
31. St. Germaine interview, February 25, 2024.
32. Frances Wise interview; Kelly, *Birkie Fever*, 48, says it was Haakon Randar, a Norwegian immigrant from Elm Grove, Wisconsin, who created the name using the same deduction.
33. Sten Fjeldheim, interview by the author, January 20, 2024; Kelly, *Birkie Fever*, 49; Jacqui Banaszynski, "2,200 race in Birkebeiner," *Duluth News Tribune*, February 27, 1977.
34. Fjeldheim interview; Kelly, *Birkie Fever*, 49.

35. Harold Treland, interview by the author, June 13, 2022.
36. *Birch Scroll*, spring 1977; spring 1983.
37. Kelly, *Birkie Fever*, 55–59; Wise oral history, with Van Valkenberg.
38. Kelly, *Birkie Fever*, 55; *Sawyer County Record*, March 2, 1977.
39. *Ski*, November 1977.
40. Treland interview.
41. Treland interview.
42. Berard interview.
43. *Birch Scroll*, March 1977
44. *Birch Scroll*, March 1977.
45. *Birch Scroll*, March 1977; October 1977.
46. *Birch Scroll/Telemarks* combined issue, December 1977.
47. *Birch Scroll*, December 1977; February 1978.
48. Quinn interview; *Birch Scroll*, February 1977, reprint of *Denver Post* article by Charlie Meyers.
49. "Foreigners win Birkebeiner," *Milwaukee Journal*, February 26, 1978.
50. Epp Paal and Angelo Corradini, *Worldloppet: 30 Years of Skiing Around the World* (Estonia: Puffet Invest, 2007), 18–21.
51. Peter Graves, host, "Tom Kelly's 50-Year Cross-country Legacy," *Cross Country Skier*, February 25, 2021, www.crosscountryskier.com/podcast.
52. Worldloppet, 2023, www.worlloppet.com; Epp Paal, interview by the author, November 12, 2023.
53. Frances Wise interview.
54. *Birch Scroll*, spring 1978.
55. *Birch Scroll*, Pre-race 2008, 19–20.
56. Bill Nelson, "55 kilometers of glorious agony," *Milwaukee Journal Insight*, February 20, 1977; Karl Andresen memories, Birkebeiner archives.
57. Adrian Watt, interview by the author, June 12, 2022.
58. *Birch Scroll*, Fall 1978.
59. *Birch Scroll,* February 1979; *Sports Illustrated*, January 8, 1979; Hall interview.
60. Peterson interview; Koch interview; Allison Slavick, "Full Circle," February 2021, www.birkie.com/wp-content/uploads/2021/02/XCS-40-Full-Circle.pdf.
61. Kelly, *Birkie Fever*, 74–89.
62. *Birch Scroll*, Spring 1979.
63. *Birch Scroll*, Spring 1979.
64. *Birch Scroll*, Spring 1979; "The Keepers of the Moosalamoo," *Vermont Sports Magazine*, September 27, 2021, https://vtsports.com/the-keepers-of-the-moosalamoo/.
65. *Birch Scroll*, February 1980; *Nordic World*, February 1980; Woodward interview.
66. Berard interview.
67. Telemark records, box 2, folder 17, Wise Collection.
68. Berard interview; profit and loss statement, 1978 Birkebeiner, Birkebeiner archives; Wise letter to ski industry, New Clippings 1980 folder, Birkebeiner archives.
69. Fred Vortanz interview.

70. Carr, *Nordic World*, March 1979.
71. Mailgram, March 7, 1979, box 2, folder 17, Wise Collection.

CHAPTER 5

1. *Birch Scroll,* April 1, 1975; Kelly, *Birkie Fever*, 28.
2. Treland interview.
3. *Birch Scroll*, May 12, 1975.
4. *Birch Scroll*, May 12, 1975.
5. *Birch Scroll*, October 1976.
6. Hall interview; Kelly, *Birkie Fever*, 37–38.
7. Hall interview; *Birch Scroll*, May, 1975, May–June 1976.
8. *Birch Scroll*, May–June 1976; October 1976.
9. Kelly, *Birkie Fever*, 51–52; Treland interview; Hall interview.
10. *Birch Scroll*, March 1977; Kelly, *Birkie Fever*, 52; City of Haward Resolution, February 15, 1977, Birkebeiner archives.
11. John Kotar, "A Founder remembers: Bringing up Birkie," Birkebeiner Souvenir Program, 15th Anniversary, February 21, 1987, 4–5; Bruce Adomeit, "Birkebeiner V: Skis, poles, growing pains," *Minneapolis Tribune Picture Magazine*, April 3, 1977; Bernie Peterson and Tom Running, "Hill and Trail," *Appleton Post-Crescent*, March 6, 1977.
12. *Birch Scroll*, March 1977.
13. *Birch Scroll*, Spring 1979.
14. *Birch Scroll*, Fall 1979; Kelly, *Birkie Fever*, 95–97.
15. *Birch Scroll*, February 1980.
16. *Birch Scroll*, Fall 1979; Spring 1980.
17. John Morton, "America's greatest ski race," *Birch Scroll*, Pre-race 1993, 30–31, excerpt from *Don't Look Back* (Harrisburg, Pa: Stackpole Books, 1992).
18. *Birch Scroll*, Spring 1983; Fall 1985.
19. *Sawyer County Record*, March 1, 15, 22, 1995; *Sawyer County Record*, Birkebeiner Results, February 23, 1997; "Timber Management and Protection of the Birkebeiner Trail," Sawyer County Conservation Committee, Birkebeiner archives.
20. Kotar interview.
21. *Birch Scroll*, February 1988.
22. Hall interview; Hall letter, August 14, 1980, Birkebeiner archives.
23. Koch, "Birkie Reflections," *Birch Scroll*, 1992, 16; Peterson interview.
24. Ron Bergin, interview by the author, April 25, 2022.
25. Serrano interview.
26. Serrano interview.
27. Koch interview.
28. FIS trail data provided by Allan Serrano, FIS official; Serrano interview.
29. Serrano interview.
30. Treland interview.
31. Eldon Marple, "Birkebeiner Country," *Visitor Magazine*, January 26, 1977.
32. Ernie St. Germaine, written correspondence with author, October 28, 2024.

33. Birkebeiner Trail proposal, Trail folder, Birkebeiner archives.
34. *Ski Magazine*, November 1977.
35. Proctor interview; untitled Telemark news release draft, November 22, 1976, Birkebeiner archives; Malesevich, *Telemark Memories*, 146.
36. American Birkebeiner Ski Foundation to Sawyer County, June 3, 1985, Trail folder, Birkebeiner archives; Proctor interview.
37. *Birch Scroll*, Fall 1987; February 1989; Birkie Trail Maintenance Expenditures, May 1988 to March, 1989, Birkebeiner archives.
38. Proctor interview.
39. Anna Kurth, "County passes Birkie trail fees on split vote," *Sawyer County Record*, December 26, 2013; "New Birkie ski pass system in place," *FasterSkier*, December 26, 2013, https://fasterskier.com/2013/12/new-birkie-ski-pass-system-in-place/; Foundation Annual Report, 2017–18.
40. Proctor interview.
41. Proctor interview.

CHAPTER 6

1. *Birch Scroll*, February 1980; Kelly, *Birkie Fever*, 100.
2. *Birch Scroll*, Spring 1980.
3. Minutes of Third Meeting of the World Loppet League, June 7–9, 1979; Tom Kelly, "Worldwide citizens' ski league heads into second season," World Loppet League news release, November 1979, Birkebeiner archives; *Birch Scroll*, February, 1980.
4. Kelly, *Birkie Fever*, 100.
5. Toby Markowitz, interview by the author, March 6, 2033; *Birch Scroll*, February 1980.
6. "Telemark Colosseum opens with a full slate of happenings," "Tim Gullikson tips brother in exhibition," *Sawyer County Record*, December 10, 1980.
7. *Birch Scroll*, February 1981.
8. Tom Kelly, "Olympic medalist Bill Koch designs new cross country ski trail at Telemark," Telemark Lodge news release, fall 1980, reprinted in *Telemark Memories*, 193–95; Koch interview.
9. *Birch Scroll*, Fall 1981.
10. Fred Vortanz interview.
11. *Birch Scroll*, Fall 1981; Fred Vortanz interview.
12. Fred Vortanz interview.
13. Jay Weiner, "Tony Wise builds skiing empire in Wisconsin," *Minneapolis Tribune*, March 11, 1979.
14. Bob Treland interview; Gary Crandall, interview by the author, December 9, 2023.
15. Maller, *Pioneer Press*, March 15, 1981; Crandall interview; "Success story: An entrepreneur become Vacationland Restaurateur of the Year, Telemark news release, box 1, folder 2, Wise Collection.
16. *Birch Scroll*, Fall 1981; January 1982; February 1982.
17. Kelly, *Birkie Fever*, 137–40.
18. Kelly, *Birkie Fever*, 151–52.

19. Kelly, *Birkie Fever*, 144–51; *Birch Scroll*, Fall 1982.
20. Erik Bengt Bengtsson, "Cross-Country Skating: How It Started," cxcacademy .wordpress.com, Nov. 23, 2016
21. Wiik and Sumner, *Regenery Guide*, 66.
22. Koch interview.
23. Bengtsson, "Cross-Country Skating: How It Started"; McLean interview.
24. *Birch Scroll*, Spring 1983.
25. *Birch Scroll*, January 1983; Spring 1983; Crandall interview.
26. Frank Riley, "Winter wonders in Wisconsin," Los Angeles Times, Jan. 23, 1983; various news clippings, Birkebeiner archives.
27. Janet Krokson, "Birkebeiner XII is 'best ever'; some records fall," *Sawyer County Record*, February 27, 1984.
28. *Telemarks*, March 1, 1984, Birkebeiner archives.
29. "Telemark gets a loan," *Sawyer County Record*, December 4, 1985.
30. Fred Vortanz interview.
31. Janet Krokson, "Temporary manager is appointed at Telemark," *Sawyer County Record*, May 29, 1984.
32. David Shaffer, "Court-run Telemark seeking fiscal lift," *Pioneer Press*, May 27, 1984; Weiner, *Minneapolis Tribune*, March 11, 1979.
33. In Re Telemark Management Co, Inc. (Bankr W.D. Wis. 1984), CaseMine, www .casemine.com/judgement/us/5914c314add7b049347c3bca; *Journal Sentinel*, May 19, 1984; Shaffer, *Pioneer Press*, May 27, 1984.
34. "Judge rules on Telemark rights," *St. Paul Dispatch/Associated Press*, October 4, 1984; Todd C. Schuman, "Wise is banned from Telemark," *Sawyer County Record*, July 18, 1984.
35. *St. Paul Dispatch/Associated Press*, October 4, 1984.
36. *Birch Log*, Fall 1984, Birkebeiner archives.
37. "Birkebeiner's future brighter," *Sawyer County Record*, November 14, 1984; Doug Grow, "Slush may be big winner in Birkebeiner war," *Star and Tribune*, February 23, 1985.
38. Tom Duffy, interview by the author, May 13, 2022.
39. Duffy interview; Grow, February 23, 1985, *Star and Tribune*.
40. Kelly, Telemark news release, November 5, 1984, Birkebeiner archives.
41. "Birkebeiner's future brighter," *Sawyer County Record*, November 14, 1984.
42. "Birkebeiner 'alive and well,'" Tony Wise goes out of state," "Birkie fund started," (photo), *Sawyer County Record*, December 5, 1984; *Birch Scroll*, Winter 1984.
43. Krokson, "Birkebeiner's future brighter," *Sawyer County Record*, November 14, 1984; "Agreement," February 1, 1985, between Lawrence J. Kaiser (Trustee), Telemark Enterprises, and the American Birkebeiner Ski Foundation Inc., agreement folder, Birkebeiner archives.
44. "Birkie '85 wins the sanction; financial support is building," *Sawyer County Record*, December 12, 1984; *Duluth News Tribune & Herald*, December 8, 1984; Lawrence Kaiser and Eugen Peter letters, box 11, folder 11, Wise Collection.

45. "Birkebeiner's future bright," *Sawyer County Record*, November 14, 1984; Lea Justice letter to Eugen Peter, November 14, 1984, Birkebeiner archives; Frances Wise interview.
46. Bernard Radloff, Town of Cable chairman, letter to Foundation, December 6, 1984, Foundation folders, Birkebeiner archives.
47. Foundation folders, Birkebeiner archives.
48. Foundation advertisement, *Sawyer County Record*, December 5, 1984.
49. Terrell Boettcher, "From 1964 to 1984: Dilworth recalls Olympics," Sawyer County Record, January 25, 1984; *Birch Scroll*, Fall, 1985; Foundation Board of Directors meeting, Aug. 12, 1985, Foundation folders, Birkebeiner archives.
50. *Birch Scroll*, Special Issue, Winter 1984.
51. "Birkebeiner 'alive and well,'" *Sawyer County Record*, December 5, 1984; Steve Morales, interview by the author, October 7, 2023.
52. *Birch Scroll*, Special Issue, Winter 1984; Articles of Incorporation, Foundation folders, Birkebeiner archives; "Birkebeiner Foundation donors are announced," *Sawyer County Record*, January 16; "Birkebeiner planners 'comfortable,'" *Sawyer County Record*, January 30; "All is 'go' for American Birkebeiner," *Sawyer County Record*, February 20, 1985.
53. *Pioneer Press*, March 13, 1985.
54. Joe Chisholm, "The way I see it," *Four Seasons News*, February 18, 1986.
55. *Grow,* "Slush may be big winner in Birkebeiner war," *Star and Tribune*, February 23, 1985, February 23, 1985; *Birch Scroll*, Special Issue, Winter 1984.
56. Curt Brown, "Waxless skier skates to women's title," *Pioneer Press*, February 24, 1985.
57. Brown, *Pioneer Press*, February 24, 1985; *Birch Scroll,* Results, 1985.
58. *Birch Scroll*, Fall 1985; Foundation board meeting minutes, August 12, 1985, and Founders letter, 1985, Birkebeiner archives.
59. St. Germaine interview, February 25, 2024; Frances Wise interview; Bob Treland interview; Berard interview.
60. *Birch Scroll*, Fall 1985; Kevin Brochman, interview by the author, January 25, 2024; Bengtsson, "Cross-Country Skating"; Peter Ashley with Hennie Kashiwa, "Birth of Skating: Flipping the Switch," *Boulder Nordic Sport*, 2019.
61. *Birch Scroll*, February 22, 1986; Morales interview; Ralph Thornton, "Ski-skating is reaching the Sunday crowd," *Star and Tribune*, February 6, 1986.
62. *Birch Scroll*, Results, 1986; "New era dawns, Birkie 'tremendous success,'" *Sawyer County Record*, February 27, 1985; Doug Grow, "He had the stars on the run," *Star and Tribune*, February 23, 1986.
63. John Dettloff, interview by the author, October 24, 2023.
64. Hal Lancaster and Roger Lowenstein, "Nation's businesses are scrambling to sponsor the nation's pastimes," "What worked in Olympics may not work in baseball," *Wall Street Journal*, June 25, 1986; Jody Homer, "Getting a run for its money," *Chicago Tribune*, October 19, 1984.

65. "Birkie 1986 to be a 'Whopper race,'" *South County Journal*, October 24, 1985; Foundation board meeting minutes, August 12, 1985, Birkebeiner archives; *Birch Scroll*, February 22, 1986; Doug Grow, "The noble Birkie gets commercial," *Star and Tribune*, January 15, 1986.
66. "Birkie ski foundation annual meeting held," *Sawyer County Record*, July 16, 1986; *Birch Scroll*, February 1987.
67. Fred Vortanz interview
68. Court records, box 14, folder 15, Wise Collection; Fred Vortanz interview.
69. Bob Treland interview.
70. Janie Wise interview.
71. Lars Kindem, Technical Delegate report, 1987, Birkebeiner archives.
72. *Birch Scroll*, February 1987; Ralph Thornton, "Swiss wins Birkebeiner at wire," *Star and Tribune*, February 22, 1987.
73. *Birch Scroll*, Update, December 1986.
74. Gary Johnson, "Telemark brings top bid of $1.35 million," *Leader-Telegram*, September 16, 1987; Ingrid Sunstrom, "Telemark's buyer anxious to reopen slopes," *Star Tribune*, September 18, 1987; Sunstrom, "Telemark bid loser making noise about it," Star Tribune, September 29, 1987.
75. Dianne Klump, "Historyland offer is accepted," *South County Journal*, October 29, 1987.
76. Bill Gardner, "Telemark's new owners mean business in Cable," *St. Paul Pioneer Press and Dispatch*, December 13, 1987.
77. S.C. Johnson Co. letter to Race Director Marty Eckhardt, 1988, and Sponsor/Payment Schedule, 1988 Birkebeiner, Birkebeiner archives.
78. Gregg Wong, "Blomquist beats cold, fellow Swede to win Birkebeiner," *Pioneer Press*, February 21, 1988; *Birch Scroll*, February 1988; *Birch Scroll*, Results 1988; *Birch Scroll*, Spring 1983.
79. Gregg Wong, "Blunder puts Kortelopet leader in wrong race at wrong tine," *Pioneer Press*, February 21, 1988; Alex Kochon, "USSA's Bodensteiner recalls his Korte DQ," *FasterSkier*, February 29, 2012, https://fasterskier.com/2012/02/ussas-bodensteiner-remembers-his-korte-dq/.
80. Gregg Wong, "Blomquist wins fierce Birkie duel," *Pioneer Press*, February 26, 1989.
81. *Birch Scroll*, fall 1986; Gregg Wong, "Ideal conditions expected for Saturday's Birkebeiner," *Pioneer Press*, February 24, 1989; Ralph Thornton, "Lack of fees will hurt cross country trails," *Star and Tribune*, January 8, 1987; Patrick Murphy, "Treating the wounded and the weary at a large cross-country ski marathon," *The Physician and Sports Medicine*, February 1987, 170–174, 183.
82. James Lileks, "Snow job," *Pioneer Press*, February 24, 1989.
83. Ingrid Sunstrom, "Telemark condo owners win lawsuit," *Star Tribune*, February 2, 1989, 2D.
84. Barbara Lloyd, "Boston Marathon of skiing," *New York Times*, February 13, 1989.

CHAPTER 7

1. Harvey Duck, "Telemark race tough assignment," *Chicago Daily News*, undated, reprinted in in *Birch Scroll*, March, 1976; Michael Strauss, "Ski touring is becoming more popular," *New York Times*, February 22, 1976.
2. Kelly, preface to *Birkie Fever,* 3; Woodward interview; *Birch Scroll*, February, 1978.
3. Kotar, "A Founder Remembers," *Trail Blazer*, February 3, 1997, 4–5, 8–10.
4. *Birch Scroll*, Pre-race 1993, 30–31.
5. Jim Quinn, "Everybody's a celebrity: Merely finishing Birkebeiner ski marathon makes you a hero," *Akron Beacon Journal*, March 24, 1991.
6. John Arntzen, interview by the author, January 15, 2024; *Birch Scroll*, Results 2003; Adomeit, "Birkebeiner V: Skis, poles, growing pains," *Minneapolis Tribune, Picture Magazine*, April 3, 1977.
7. Nelson, "55 kilometers of glorious agony," *Milwaukee Journal Insight*, February 20, 1977.
8. Sam Anderson, "What Cross-Country Skiing Reveals about the Human Condition," *New York Times Magazine*, Olympics issue, March 6, 2018.
9. *Birch Scroll*, Spring 1978, 5.
10. *Birch Scroll*, Results 1993; Michelle Drolet, interview by the author, February 15, 1993; John Flinn, "Disabled skiers plow their way across Sierra Nevada," *San Francisco Examiner*, April 15, 1993.
11. Leslie Hamp, "Brotherly love on the Birkie trail," *Sawyer County Record*, Birkebeiner Special, February 8 and 11, 2006.
12. Jerry Poling, "Cancer-free Tenorio finishes Birkie," *Leader-Telegram*, March 2, 2012.
13. Terrell Boettcher, "A flotilla of friends guides retired kindergarten teacher Barb Klippel to her 19th Birkie finish," *Sawyer County Record*, February 27, 2008; *Leader-Telegram*, March 1, 2012.
14. Bob Britz, interview by the author, December 5, 2023; Poling, "Comeback trail," *Leader-Telegram*, February 23, 2017; Morales interview; Scott interview.
15. "A veil, a bow tie & Birkie bibs," *Birch Scroll,* 2019–20 Annual, 31.
16. Darrell Thompson, interview by the author, July 17, 2023.
17. Julian Emerson, "Pastor gets taste of original Birkie," *Leader-Telegram*, February 27, 1997.
18. *Birch Scroll*, Results, 1997, 13–14; Ron Bergin, "Elmer Hassett: Vintage skier," *Trail Blazer*, February 21, 1995, 10; Lissa Radke, "Those crazy first Birkies: Elmer Hassett, Cable," February 3, 1997, 33.
19. Leslie Hamp, "Arts council funds Birkie song," Birkebeiner news release, February 5, 2001, www.skinnyski.com/notices/archives/Birkie-6.html.
20. Fjeldheim interview.
21. Paul J. Anderson, Ralph S. Bovard, Mohammad Hassan Murad, Timothy J. Beebe, Zhen Wang, "Health Status and Health Behaviors among Citizen Endurance Nordic Skiers in the United States," July 24, 2017, https://pmc.ncbi.nlm.nih.gov/articles/PMC5525345/.
22. *Birch Scroll*, Pre-race, 1997.

23. *Birch Scroll*, Results, 1993, 2023; "Bjorn to Ski," Minnesota Nordic Ski Association, March 1, 2001, mnnordicski.org.
24. "Birchleggings established," *The County Journal*, February 25, 1993; Birchleggings Club, www.birchleggingsclub.com; Kotar interview.
25. Birchleggings Club.
26. Steve Carmazon, interview by the author, October 6, 2023.
27. Serrano interview.
28. Ronda Tworek, interview by the author, August 10, 2023.
29. James Krueger, interview by the author, March 17, 2023; Johnson interview.
30. Erik Hansen, interview by the author, April 24, 2023.
31. Dave Tworek, interview by the author, April 14, 2023.
32. Donna Hughes, interview by the author, October 9, 2023.
33. Hughes interview.
34. Peterson interview.
35. Derauf interview.
36. Morales interview; "Marathon Snow Skiing in Cable, Wisc.," *American Profile*, January 27, 2002.

CHAPTER 8

1. *Birch Scroll*, Fall 1989.
2. K.C. Johnson, "Why do they do it? Because it's there: Birkebeiner's 'Founders' relish in its 20th running," *Chicago Tribune*, February 23, 1992.
3. Jim Ferstle, "Nagl wins Birkie by a ski tip," "Birkie was a cold one," *Pioneer Press Dispatch*, February 25, 1990.
4. "Historyland buildings used for firefighter, police training," *Sawyer County Record*, March 28, 1990.
5. Nolan Zavoral, "Nagl, Butts glide to victory in Birkie," *Star Tribune*, February 24, 1991; Ferstle, "Nagl, Butts win Birkie with a little help from friends," "Austrian Nagl wins his 2nd Birkebeiner," "Women's champ gets quicker start," *Pioneer Press*, February 24, 1991.
6. Zavoral, "Birkebeiner is all or nothing for Wise," *Star Tribune*, February 21, 1992; Zavoral, "Wise returns for Birkie festivities," *Star Tribune*, February 22, 1992; Wise oral history, Side A.
7. Dennis Kruse, interview by the author, December 5, 2023; Linda Edgren, interview by Kruse, Dec. 8, 2023, reported to the author.
8. "Agreement" document, Foundation Birkie Agreement and Tax Info folder, Birkebeiner archives.
9. Zavoral, "Officials confident despite doubts about Birkebeiner," *Star Tribune*, December 12, 1991; "Papaik projects are struggling financially, but he is confident," *Pioneer Press*, September 2, 1990; Karl J. Karlson, "Telemark orders foreclosure on Telemark lodge," *Pioneer Press*, April 23, 1992.
10. Foundation board meeting minutes, October 28, 1991, November 11, 1991, December 9, 1991, American Birkebeiner Ski Foundation records, 1973–2011, box 9, folders 2–3, Norwegian American Historical Association, Northfield, Minn.

11. Zavoral, "Boonstra wins men's race after unusual collision," "Oslo woman takes early lead, keeps it," *Star Tribune*, February 23, 1992; Ferstle, "Boonstra survives wild Birkie finish," "Two skiers' thoughts on Albertville," *Pioneer Press*, February 23, 1992.
12. Ferstle, *Pioneer Press*, February 23, 1992.
13. *Birch Scroll*, Results 1992.
14. Gregg Wong, "Nagl, King glide away with Birkie," *Pioneer Press*, February 28, 1993; Irv Mossberger, "Mad dash goes Nagl's way," "King comes on strong, charges to women's crown," *Duluth News Tribune*, Birkie Extra, February 28, 1993.
15. Donald Griego, "Czech skier wins," "Norway is just a dream," *Milwaukee Journal*, February 27, 1994; *Birch Scroll*, Results 1994.
16. *Birch Scroll,* Results 1994.
17. Tim Norris, "Jungen leaves skiers in wake," "Theurl beats field after beating cold," "A perfect day for a great race," *Milwaukee Journal*, February 26, 1995.
18. Kris Sorensen, "The tradition continues: Birkebeiner XXIII," *Sawyer County Record*, February 22; Boettcher, "Record numbers ski Barnebirkie," *Sawyer County Record*, Birkie Express, February 24, 1995; Norris, *Milwaukee Journal*, February 26, 1995.
19. Frances Wise interview.
20. Frances Wise interview; Berard interview.
21. Frances Wise interview.
22. Doug Grow, "Often broke, but always Wise," *Star Tribune*, April 11, 1995.
23. Peterson interview.
24. Koch interview.
25. Andresen interview; Koch interview; Caldwell interview; Peterson interview; McLean interview; Scott interview.
26. Peter Graves, host, "Tom Kelly's 50-Year Cross-country Legacy," *Cross Country Skier* podcast.
27. Caldwell interview.
28. St. Germaine interview, February 25, 2024; Allison Slavick, "The Legacy of Ernie St. Germaine," *Cross Country Skier*, February 24, 2022, www.crosscountryskier.com/the-legacy-of-ernie-st-germaine-who-has-skied-the-american-birkebeiner-more-than-anyone-else/.
29. Boettcher, "Tony Wise remembered on 100th birthdate anniversary," *Sawyer County Record*, March 10, 2021.
30. Karlson, "World class visionary," *Pioneer Press*, April 16, 1995; "Tony Wise's legacy lives on," *Sawyer County Record*, April 12, 1995; Frances Wise interview.
31. Grow, "Auction recalls a Wisconsin giant," *Star Tribune*, August 14, 1996; Frances Wise interview.
32. Andresen interview.
33. Foundation board minutes, August 21, 1995, Birkebeiner archives; *Birch Scroll*, Pre-race 1996.
34. *Birch Scroll,* Results 1996; Foundation board minutes, Birkebeiner archives.
35. *Birch Scroll*, Results 1992, 1997.

36. Matt Nelson, "Birkie brings the world—and its money—home," *Duluth News Tribune*, February 23, 1997.
37. Foundation board minutes; Hughes interview; Shellie Milford, interview by the author, May 4, 2023.
38. *Birch Scroll*, Results 1998.
39. "Colorado skier makes most of short track," *Milwaukee Journal Sentinel*, February 22, 1998; *Sawyer County Record*, Birkie Results, February 22, 1998.
40. Paul Mitchell, "Laura McCabe takes Birkie women's title," and "Worldloppet leader crushes Birkie field," *Sawyer County Record*, Birkie Results, February 28, 1999.

CHAPTER 9

1. Foundation news releases, "Preparation in Full Swing for Saturday's race," February 22, 2000; "Everything a 'go!' for Saturday's race, February 23, 2000, Birkebeiner archives.
2. Milford interview; *Birch Scroll*, Non-results 2000.
3. *Birch Scroll*, Non-results 2000; Scott Wilson, interview by the author, March 15, 2022; Kevin Brochman, interview by the author, January 5, 2024.
4. Jerrold Schneider, interview by the author, October 19, 2023.
5. Schneider interview.
6. *Birch Scroll*, Non-results 2000; Schneider interview.
7. *Birch Scroll*, Non-results 2000; Boettcher, "Birkie Foundation affirms Kortelopet course changes," *Sawyer County Record*, August 9, 2000.
8. *Birch Scroll*, Fall 2000.
9. Rick Olivo, "Telemark loan re-approved by Bayfield County Block Grant panel," *Ashland Daily Press*, November 11, 2000.
10. "American Birkebeiner legacy lives on with support from Johnson Bank and Johnson Family Foundation," Johnson Financial Group, www.johnsonfinancialgroup.com/about-us/newsroom/american-birkebeiner-legacy-lives-on-with-support-from-johnson-bank-and-johnson-family-foundation.
11. *Birch Scroll*, 2003 to 2005.
12. *Sawyer County Record*, Birkebeiner Preview, February 18, 2015; Ned Zuelsdorff, interview by the author, November 30, 2022.
13. Zuelsdorff interview; *Birch Scroll*, Pre-race 2008, Pre-race 2009.
14. *Birch Scroll*, 2008 Pre-race, 2009 Pre-race.
15. *Birch Scroll*, 2009 Results.
16. Zuelsdorff interview.
17. Zuelsdorff interview.
18. Boettcher, "Birkie Foundation members elect directors, discuss future plans," *Sawyer County Record*, August 13, 2009; Kruse interview by the author.
19. Mitchell, "Birkie founder Tony Wise remembered," *Sawyer County Record*, February 24, 2008.
20. Andresen interview; Johnson, "Why do they do it? Because it's there," *Chicago Tribune*, February 23, 1992.
21. Andresen interview; *Leader-Telegram*, March 3, 1996.

22. Birgitta Wiik Lindgren, interview by the author, June 10, 2022.
23. "Birkie legend signs autographs," and "Birkie '09 is second largest," *Sawyer County Record*, February 26, 2009; Olivo, "Men's Birkie winners have to overcome early leaders for victory," *Sawyer County Record/Ashland Dailly Press*, February 26, 2012.
24. Jerry Poling, "Cancer-free Tenorio finishes Birkie; Norwegian secret," *Leader-Telegram*, March 2, 2012.
25. Anonymous, "Historical primer on the Birkebeiner," undated, Birkebeiner archives; Erik Opsahl, interview by the author, October 28, December 18, 2024.
26. Elizabeth Madsen-Genszler, "Prince Haakon's descendant skis the legend at Birkie 2006," *Sawyer County Record*, Birkebeiner Special, February 8 and 11, 2006.
27. Laurie Landgraf, interview by the author, October 26, 2023; Tom Held and Breann Schossow, "Two cyclists hit by drivers die," *Journal Sentinel*, August 9, 2011.
28. Landgraf interview.
29. "Torch lit at opening ceremony in memory of Birkebeiner founder Dave Landgraf," *Sawyer County Record*, February 26, 2012; St. Germaine interview, February 25, 2024.
30. St. Germaine interview, February 25, 2024.
31. Landgraf interview; St. Germaine interview, February 25, 2024.
32. Sam Cook, "Ignoring warning signs, 85-year-old Duluth skier finishes 54-kilometer Birkebeiner, Superior Telegram, February 28, 2012.
33. Joe Knight, "Eau Claire resident skis his 40th—and last—Birkebeiner," *Leader-Telegram*, February 16, 2013.
34. Crandall interview; Boettcher, "Telemark owners vote to surrender lodge, land to lender," *Sawyer County Record*, September 15, 2010.
35. "Bankrupt Telemark for sale for $4.5 million," *Duluth News Tribune/Associated Press*, December 8, 1998; Held, "Deal reached to keep Telemark open," *Journal Sentinel*, March 9, 2011; Kathy Hanson, "Sold! Telemark Lodge sells for $926,000," *Sawyer County Record*, October 16, 2013; Mike Creger, "Telemark Lodge sold at Bayfield County auction," *Duluth News Tribune/Pioneer Press*, October 16, 2013; Barry Adams, "Telemark Lodge step closer to rebirth," *Wisconsin State Journal*, November 28, 2017; "Telemark Lodge deal reached," *Duluth News Tribune*, November 28, 2017.
36. "Birkie submits proposal to Telemark," *Sawyer County Record,* April 24, 2012.
37. Olivo, "Men's Birkie winners have to overcome early leaders for victory," *Sawyer County Record/Ashland Daily Press*, February 26, 2012.
38. "Birkie Preview," *FasterSkier*, February 22, 2013, https://fasterskier.com/2013/02/birkie-preview/.
39. Boettcher, "Birkie 1973 winner honored at welcome ceremony," *Sawyer County Record*, Birkie Results, February 24, 2013; Ersson interview.

CHAPTER 10

1. Foundation Board of Directors meeting minutes, January 21, 2013, www.birkie.com/uploads/board-minutes/BODJanuary2013.pdf.
2. Ben Popp, interview by the author, November 9, 2023; Hanson, "New leader takes helm at Birkie," *Sawyer County Record*, Birkebeiner Preview, February 12, 2014.

3. Boettcher, "State, local officials meet here to discuss Birkie's future," *Sawyer County Record*, December 9, 2015; Anna Kurth, "County passes Birkie trail fees on split vote," December 26, 2013.
4. Popp interview; Boettcher, "Birkie has 'exciting future,' directors say," *Sawyer County Record*, August 15, 2013; Foundation Board of Directors meeting minutes, March 17, 2014, www.birkie.com/wp-content/uploads/2014/02/Board-Meeting-Minutes-March-2014.pdf.
5. Foundation meeting minutes, March 17, 2014.
6. Wilson interview.
7. Olivo, "Skiers battles slow course, wind," *Sawyer County Record/Ashland Daily Press*, February 23, 2014; *Birch Scroll*, Results 2014.
8. *Birch Scroll*, Pre-race 2014.
9. *Birch Scroll*, Pre-race 2015.
10. Regan Kohler, "Birkie Fever is back and busy," *Sawyer County Record*, Birkebeiner Preview, February 18, 2015; Frank Zufall, "Birkie Bridge will offer 'exhilarating' view to finish," *Sawyer County Record*, Birkebeiner Preview, February 15, 2015; Zufall, "Out-of-town skiers comment on the Birkebeiner, bridge, and more," *Sawyer County Record*, February 22, 2015.
11. Olivo, "Vittoria Italiana! Sergio Bonaldo wins four-way men's Birkie shootout," *Sawyer County Record/Ashland Daily Press*, February 22, 2015.
12. Boettcher, "Milford honored for years of service at Birkie party," *Sawyer County Record*, February 25, 2015; Milford interview.
13. Foundation news release, "Birkie establishes award honoring Shellie Milford," SkinnySki, February 28, 2015, www.skinnyski.com/racing.
14. "Slumberland is new title sponsor of Birkie," *Sawyer County Record*, April 3, 2015.
15. "Minneapolis' Caitlin Gregg makes Birkie history as US sweeps," *Pioneer Press*, February 21, 2016; Alex Kochon, "A tale of two races: Gregg and Norris emerge as 2016 Birkie champs," FasterSkier, February 21, 2016, https://fasterskier.com/2016/02/a-tale-of-two-races-gregg-and-norris-emerge-as-2016-birkie-champs/.
16. "Birkie museum opens," Duluth News Tribune, August 4, 2016.
17. "With snowstorm a miss, Birkie is canceled," *Pioneer Press*, February 24, 2017.
18. Zufall, "Jessie Diggins: 'This is where she learned to love it,'" *Sawyer County Record*, February 28, 2018.
19. *Sawyer County Record*, November 14, 2014; Popp interview.
20. *Birch Scroll*, Pre-race 2015.
21. Alex Kochon, "Caitlin Gregg on her record-setting fifth Birkie title: "I'm trying to set the bar pretty high," FasterSkier, February 25, 2018, https://fasterskier.com/2018/02/caitlin-gregg-nabs-record-setting-fifth-birkie-title-gloersen-outlasts-mens-field/.
22. *Birch Scroll*, Annual 2019–20.
23. Serrano interview.
24. Boettcher, "Birkie directors recap rapid growth and impact of outdoor events, lifestyle," *Sawyer County Record*, August 10, 2018; Zufall, "Birkie trail users to experience improvements," September 29, 2018.

25. Olivo, "First timers sweep the Slumberland American Birkebeiner," *Sawyer County Record/APG News Service*, February 23, 2019.
26. "Bankrupt Telemark for sale for $4.5 million," *Duluth News Tribune*, December 8, 1998; Held, "Telemark resort deal in place," *Journal Sentinel*, March 8, 2011; Adams, "Telemark lodge step closer to rebirth," *Wisconsin State Journal*, November 28, 2017; "Telemark lodge deal reached," *Duluth News Tribune*, November 28, 2017.
27. *Birch Scroll*, 2019–20 Annual.
28. Zufall, "Australian and Norwegian skiers triumph on fast and sun-soaked Birkie Trail," *Sawyer County Record*, February 22, 2020.
29. Mitchell, "Birkie Trail bridge installed across Hwy. 77," *Sawyer County Record*, November 4, 2020.
30. Kohler, "47th American Birkebeiner offers in-person, virtual events," *Sawyer County Record*, February 18, 2021; Zufall, "Nearly 30% of county has received vaccine," *Sawyer County Record*, March 17, 2021.
31. *Birch Scroll*, 2021–22 Annual; Boettcher, "Birkie Foundation continues outdoor recreation mission," *Sawyer County Record*, August 25, 2021.
32. Zufall, "Fabled Telemark lodge to be sold—piece by piece—through online auction," *Sawyer County Record,* January 9, 2020; Boettcher, "Birkie Foundation, developers detail plans for Telemark property; lodge will be razed," *Sawyer County Record*, June 11, 2020; Popp interview.
33. Frances Wise, letter from Mt. Telemark Village project to Birchleggers, December 8, 2023.
34. Mt. Telemark Village, www.birkie.com/mtv/.
35. Chelsey Lewis, "Once a hopping ski resort, Telemark Lodge is nearing its end. But it could be busy again soon," *Journal Sentinel,* May 13, 2021.
36. Lewis, *Journal Sentinel,* May 13, 2021.
37. Lewis, *Journal Sentinel,* May 13, 2021; "Gov. Evers presents tourism grants to Freshwater Fishing Hall of Fame, American Birkebeiner Ski Foundation," *Sawyer County Record*, February 2, 2022; Boettcher, "Governor presents tourism grants to tourism organizations," February 9, 2022; Boettcher, "Birkebeiner provides update on Telemark property plans," November 2, 2022.
38. Zufall, "A dramatic day of Birkie finishes," *Sawyer County Record*, February 26, 2022; Zufall, "Open track skiers give new format 'thumbs up,'" March 2, 2022.
39. Zufall, "David Norris takes men's skate by wide margin; Alayna Sonnesyn wins women's in last 100 meters," *Sawyer County Record*, February 26, 2023.
40. Zufall, "David Norris takes men's skate by wide margin; Alayna Sonnesyn wins women's in last 100 meters," *Sawyer County Record*, February 26, 2023.
41. Dave Kallmann, "A mecca to some and mystery to others, the Birkebeiner has impacted two small towns and a sport. It's time to celebrate No. 50," *Journal Sentinel*, February 19, 2024.
42. St. Germaine interview, May 16, 2024.
43. Malesevich, *Telemark Memories*, 4–5.

44. Zufall, "10K loop of man-made snow ensures at 2024 Birkie," *Sawyer Sawyer County Record*, February 21, 2024.
45. "Changes to Birkie Week 2024: Lapped courses and race distance changes," February 13, 2024, www.birkie.com/2024/02/changes-to-birkie-week-2024/.
46. Peterson interview.
47. Brochman interview.
48. John Teaford, "Victories by Diggins and Schumacher highlight American Birkebeiner," *FasterSkier*, February 25, 2024, https://fasterskier.com/2024/02/victories-by-diggins-and-schumacher-highlight-american-birkebeiner/.
49. "Diggins and Krueger awarded Holmenkollen medal," *FasterSkier*, March 10, 2024, https://fasterskier.com/2024/03/diggins-and-klaebo-awarded-holmenkollen-medal/.
50. 2024 Birkebeiner results, www.birkie.com/2024-results/; post-race news conference and awards ceremony, attended by the author.
51. St. Germaine interview, February 25, 2024.
52. St. Germaine interview, February 25, 2024.
53. "TGB Recognizes St. Germaine for Skiing All Fifty Birkebeiner Races," March 5, 2024, Lac Courte Oreilles, www.lcotribe.com/post/tgb-recognizes-st-germaine-for-skiing-all-50-birkebeiner-races.
54. *Birch Scroll,* Annual, 2023–24; *Silent Sports,* February 2023, 22–25; St. Germaine interview, February 25, 2024.
55. Kotar interview.
56. Madeline Heim, "As Wisconsin's climate gets warmer and wetter, beloved winter activities could be in jeopardy," *Journal Sentinel/USA Today Network*, February 1, 2022; "Northwest Wisconsin Divisional Average Snowfall," Wisconsin State Climatology Office, www.aos.wisc.edu/oldsco/clim-history/division/4701-S.html; "Division Climate Normals," Wisconsin State Climatology Office, https://climatology.nelson.wisc.edu/wisconsin-climate-divisions/climate-normals/; Tatiana Schlossberg, "Can a ski race with 800 year old roots survive 21st century winters?" *Outside,* March 25, 2023.
57. Zufall, "2023 Nov–Dec. snowfall accumulation lowest in 52 years," *Sawyer County Record,* January 3, 2024; Adams and Lucas Robinson, "Lost season may not be the last in Wisconsin; unusual high temps, lack of snow could be new normal in future," *Wisconsin State Journal*, February 27, 2024.
58. Elisa Raffa, "Winter Is Here, But It's Losing Its Cool," CNN, December 1, 2023, www.cnn.com/2023/12/21/weather/us-winter-temperatures-climate-change/index.html.
59. Andrew Freedman, "Earth had warmest February on record, as this year trends hotter than 2023," Axios, March 7, 2024, www.axios.com/2024/03/07/weather-heat-climate-change; Reuters, March 20, 2024; Emma Farge, "UN sounds 'Red Alert' as world smashes heat records in 2023," March 20, 2024, www.reuters.com/business/environment/un-sounds-red-alert-world-smashes-heat-records-2023-2024-03-19/; Dinah Voyles Pulver, Doyle Rice, Elizabeth Weise, and Ramon Padilla, "Earth passes a critical climate change threshold, scientists announce," USA Today, January 10, 2025,

https://www.usatoday.com/story/news/nation/2025/01/10/2024-hottest-year-annoucement/77543576007/.

60. Mackenzie Moran, "Mikaela Shiffrin, Jessie Diggins, and other skiers demand climate action," *Outside,* February 17, 2023, updated March 7, 2023, www.outsideonline.com/outdoor-adventure/snow-sports/mikaela-shiffrin-jessie-diggins-and-other-skiers-demand-climate-action/; John Teaford, "Victories by Diggins and Schumacher highlight American Birkebeiner," *FasterSkier*, February 25, 2024, https://fasterskier.com/2024/02/victories-by-diggins-and-schumacher-highlight-american-birkebeiner/.
61. Birkie Green, www.birkie.com/live/birkie-green/; Ben Popp interview.
62. "What happens to our winter traditions as Wisconsin warms?," *Journal Sentinel*, February 1, 2022.
63. Roger Lohr, "Cross Country Skiing Trends for 2022–23," accessed November 27, 2024, www.xcskiresorts.com/resort-features/2019/11/6/cross-country-skiing-trends-for-2022-23.
64. Lohr, "Cross Country Skiing Trends."

INDEX

Page numbers in **bold** refer to images.